ROMANCING THE SOUL

CW00435124

ROMANCING THE SOUL

True Soul Mate Stories
from around the World and Beyond

EDITED BY

DOROTHY THOMPSON

(Foreword by Kelley Rosano)

Zumaya Publications   Burnaby BC

2004

ROMANCING THE SOUL: True Soul Mate Stories from around the World and Beyond

© 2004 by Dorothy Thompson
ISBN 1-55410-095-X
Cover art by Serik Kulmeshkenov
Cover design by Martine Jardin

Published by Zumaya Publications 2004
Look for us online at http://www.zumayapublications.com

Library and Archives Canada Cataloguing in Publication

Romancing the soul : true soul mate stories from around the world and beyond / Dorothy Thompson, editor.

Also available in electronic format.
ISBN 1-55410-095-X

1. Soul mates. I. Thompson, Dorothy, 1954-

HQ801.R646 2004   306.7   C2004-904347-1

DEDICATION

This book is dedicated to all the soul mates in my life;
but, especially to my twin flame,
for without his guidance from the beyond,
this book would never have been born.

It was he who encouraged me to follow my dreams
no matter where they lead,
to keep my head up,
and to always believe in the power
of everlasting love.

It is through him
that I dedicate this book
as proof of the power of two souls
finding their way into each other's realm again.

TABLE OF CONTENTS

Part II—Karmic Soul Mates

Part III—Companion Soul Mates

FOREWORD

IF YOU ARE SEEKING DEEP MEANINGFUL ANSWERS IN YOUR SOUL MATE QUEST, you will be thrilled with delight and brought to tears of joy when reading *Romancing The Soul*. Dorothy Thompson has hit the target with incredible precision, explaining the mystery behind soul mates. *Romancing The Soul* demonstrates authentic soul mating, soul relating, soul dating and soul merging—when two souls truly become one. This book will empower and strengthen the reader on the path questing for their other half, the divine lover, their one true love.

Moreover, how can one attract the deepest most powerful connection you will ever experience if you have yet to make that connection with Self? "Know Self" and "To thine own Self be true" are the author's battle cries. Ms. Thompson has provided you with the secret keys to empowering Self and preparing for your soul mate. Are you ready to inherit the most powerful, deepest connection in your life: your soul mate?

Meeting one's soul mate can occur at any time and always when we are ready. This noble relationship (your soul mate) will always be sent from above (spiritually sponsored and directed).

Sadly, many people have chosen to stay in bad karmic relationships, living lives of quiet desperation. This book is for those who have the courage to live authentically, boldly stepping out of the negative past and realizing their dreams. Living soul mate success in life, love, and work is why we are here in embodiment.

Many people have chosen to stay in negative relationships and have no passion in their lives. Soul mates give us gusto, support and are our champions, not our competitors. True soul mate love is not for the weak at heart, but for the dreamers who believe true love is more than a myth—it is a reality on Planet Earth. Soul mates together in love, work and life, will bring, in this promised Age of Aquarius, an era of truth, beauty, freedom and, above all else, love.

Be ready to have a box of tissues next to you when reading these true-life soul mate stories—powerful, authentic, deeply moving soul mates in love. Enjoy and feast upon this delicious soul mate banquet in front of you: *Romancing The Soul.*

— Kelley Rosano
Author of
*If You Are My Soul Mate,
Why Am I So Unhappy?*

PREFACE

"Friends will keep you sane, Love could fill your heart, a lover can warm your bed, but lonely is the soul without a mate."

— David Pratt

THE IDEA BEHIND THIS COLLECTION OF TRUE SOUL MATE STORIES EVOLVED from a dream I had when my soul mate passed over on September 13, 2001. That same week terrorists created havoc in America, destroying the lives of thousands of people in just a few minutes of destructive madness. Not only was I mourning for America, I was mourning for my best friend, my spiritual comrade, who would never see America, the home of the free and the brave, again.

One week following the funeral and after a very fitful sleep, I woke up with sweat pouring off my brow. The sheets were soaked. I jumped out of bed in the pre-dawn hour and tried to write everything down I had been told. My soul mate had appeared in a dream and gave me a message. First and foremost, he wanted me to be happy. However, he knew there was only one thing that made me happy, and that was to write.

The dream was vivid, yet surreal. He told me to write down our story. But it was not only our story he wanted to tell. He wanted me to tell the stories of others, too, for the world needed to know the power and the mystique of the soul mate connection. He even told me to call this project *Romancing the Soul—True Stories of Soul Mates from around the World and Beyond.*

When I first embarked on compiling this anthology, I did not know the full scope of the soul mate phenomenon. I knew he and I shared something very special, something that could only come once in a lifetime, if then. It wasn't until I started exploring what the soul mate experience was truly all about that I discovered what a gift I had been given. I asked myself, "Why did it take forty-seven years for this to happen?"

The answer to that question is: many things have to come into play in order for the soul mate experience to work. You might say you have to be in the right place at the right time. Well, that "right place" lies in you. You have to be happy with yourself. You have to get rid of "excess baggage," such as bad relationships, depression and unhappiness. Sure, that's easy for me to say, huh?

It can be done. If I can do it, you can, too! Take one day at a time and get rid of the bad karma and usher in the good karma. Believe me, I'm a walking case history of this. Five years before I met my soul mate, I was in a woman's shelter for victims of domestic violence. For twenty years, I was the victim and never had the controlling hand in my relationships. After I separated from my husband of nineteen years, I looked everywhere for someone to fill the emptiness in my life and my heart. It was not to be. The problem was that I was continuing the path I had traveled all my life. I was never in charge of my destiny. In order to break this pattern of bad karma, I had to reverse things. How did I do it?

Upon leaving the shelter, I found a small house and moved in with my two children and two cats. I vowed I was always going to take care of me, and I would never allow myself to depend on anyone else to take care of me again. I was in total control of my destiny.

It was rough at first; but when I declared my independence, my life made a turn for the better. I rid myself of my need for dependence (bad karma) and brought in a stronger, more confident me, thus producing independence (good karma).

It was at this time I became a children's book author and an editor of four websites. My articles were being accepted by paying markets. It was hard to believe that just one year before I hadn't even known how to use a computer. My writing was finally paying off, and my life took on new meaning.

This was when I met my twin flame.

Good karma infiltrated my life and changed it drastically. I had done something I never dreamed was possible—I had changed my destiny. And so can you.

It's not easy trying to keep bad karma from creeping in, but you have to realize when it does and take steps to not allow it into your life. In an abusive relationship? Dump him! Have no job or the abilities necessary to make it on your own? Go back to school! Feel you are too overweight to attract anyone? Go on a diet, get an exercise bike or take a walk each day! Become the person you want to be. How do people become successful in their relationships? They become successful at becoming the person someone would want to love.

Reading each submission for this book, I learned something new. Tears came to my eyes after each and every tale. Some stories were quite moving and told of unrequited love, while others told of unbridled passion and devotion.

This concept might seem farfetched to those who do not fully understand the soul mate phenomenon, but after you read my story and the stories of the other talented authors who have contributed to these pages, you will understand. You will learn that the soul mate experience is the most beautiful and eternal love there is.

There is an old Chinese proverb that goes "A man is a bird with one wing and he searches for his mate, the other wing. For without his other wing, he cannot fly." This is what the soul mate experience is all about.

To love someone is the most beautiful gift our Creator could bestow upon us, but true love goes beyond ordinary physical attraction. It requires we help each other, not only on the physical level but also the mental and spiritual levels. Sometimes, fate steps in and brings you and your soul mate together.

In doing research for my book, I unearthed a wealth of information about the soul mate phenomenon; but no words could make me fully understand until I experienced it for myself.

My soul mate is dearly missed. I see him in my dreams. I hear his voice. The identity he has taken on now is foreign to me; yet I still search for him. I still hang on to the tiny thread of hope that he is waiting for me to join him when it is my time to leave this earthly plane.

I have been visited by my departed soul mate many times since he passed over. I know that he is with me, just not in physical form. He is with me as I type our story, sitting beside me, smiling his contagious grin. I hear his famous line whispered in my ear: "Hi, there, young lady"—the words that bring a familiar song to my heart.

To help you understand the whole soul mate experience, read these stories with an open mind and heart. They are messages to you. Soul mates do, indeed, exist; and you will find yours.

I was very fortunate and found my soul mate in this life. He is my guardian angel now, watching over me and protecting me. He is nudging me along as I write this, oblivious to the multitude of tasks he is asked to perform in the hereafter. And so, it is in his honor that I carry on with my mission to bring you his message and the message of others.

I hope you enjoy reading this book as much as I have enjoyed compiling, editing and writing it. I do hope you come away with a better understanding of the meaning of the term *soul mate* and hope this book takes you one step closer in your quest to find yours.

Love and Light,
Dorothy Thompson
September 2004

ACKNOWLEDGMENTS

Romancing the Soul has been two years in the making; and through much hard work and many sleepless nights, it has finally become a reality not only for me but for the many wonderful authors who so graciously helped me explain the soul mate phenomenon through their stories and verse.

The many friendships formed along the way make up for all the hard work and time it took to put this project together and have made everything worthwhile. I wish to thank each and every one of them for making this dream come true. Through their stories, they have helped me in my quest to show the world that soul mates do, indeed, exist.

To my authors, I thank you, and those searching for the truth…they thank you, too.

My sincerest gratitude and thanks go to:

My children Melissa, Ryan and Amanda Jane for their understanding, patience and love.

My companion soul mate Ronnie, for putting up with my endless hours on the computer and for showing me that love conquers all.

Cassie, Max and Skylar, for their patience in waiting for bathroom breaks while I sat at the computer ignoring their little brown eyes staring at me.

My wonderful and incredible editor, Elizabeth Burton, who "found" me in a listserv on the Internet and asked me to send the manuscript to her. Without her foresight and belief that this book was worth publishing, it might not be in your hands today.

Martine Jardin, co-founder of Zumaya Publications, for all the hard work she has put into the company and her wonderful cover art.

Robert Egby for his patience, guidance and direction. Also, to Iro, his soul mate who passed over, for without her communication we would never have known if my twin soul had crossed over and was happy. Through many visits from Iro, Robert would report back to me that not only was he happy and that he forgave me for choosing to remain with my companion soul mate, but that he would be by my side whenever I needed him regardless.

Lisa Daily, for her friendship and guidance.

My deepest appreciation goes to my wonderful friends of my online writing group The Writer's Life: Jozette Aaron, Lauretta Ali, Shery Ma Belle Arrieta, Michael Babinski, Hilde Bakering, Cindy Castillo, Terry (Tez) Clark, Maureen Dennis, Tricia Draper, Ellen M. DuBois, Diane Evans, Janice Romney Farnsworth, Timothy Gager, Charlotte (C.C.) Hammond, Ray Van Horn, Jr., Ayn Hunt, Heide Kaminski, Don Kelley, Sandra Kelsay, Kristin Dreyer Kramer, Jessica McCurdy-Crooks, Margaret Marr, Florence Mattersdorfer, Vanessa Mullins, Nina Osier, Helen Kay Polaski, Richelle Putnam, Carlene Reed, Margay Roberge, Irene Smith, Janet Elaine Smith, Sylvia Stoddard, Vicki M. Taylor, Avis Townsend, Christine West, Tamisa Suzanne Whitely, Barbara Williamson-Wood, Darlene Zagata and many, many others.

Special thanks to my editing/rating team, who helped me choose only the best stories that exemplified the soul mate bond: Heather Froeschl, Ayn Hunt, Nancy Jackson, Heide Kaminski, Michael Kmiec, Hydy Paige, Avis Townsend, Linda Rucker and Larry Retzack.

Rusty Fischer, for his patience and goodwill in helping me begin this momentous project.

Lisa Easterling, for her editing and friendship.

Larry James for his help in obtaining endorsements.

My deepest gratitude goes to my departed twin soul, who guided me from "the other side." If not for him, this project would never have been born.

To those people I have left out, please know that I appreciate and love all of you.

—D. T.

INTRODUCTION

"Love is composed of a single soul inhabiting two
bodies."

— Aristotle

Snow White and Prince Charming. Romeo and Juliet. Beauty and the
Beast. Harry and Sally. These are all names that come to mind
when one thinks of the term *soul mate*. The ancient belief can be
found in cultures the world over. But what does the term *soul mate*
actually mean?

In the dictionary, soul mate means "one of two persons
compatible with each other in disposition, point of view or sensitivity;
someone for whom you have a deep affinity." This explains the basic
qualities, but we all know the soul mate theory goes much deeper
than that.

According to Celtic wisdom, our souls begin their journey
together as one being that becomes broken apart. Two souls emerge
and move on into their life journeys. Perhaps we find our twin soul in
this life. Maybe we find it in another life. Throughout time, we seek to
rejoin our *anam cara*, the Celtic word for "soul friend," a soul mate
who was created as our perfect match.

In order for our soul mate to appear we must be ready for them.
You will not meet your soul mate if you are still coming from a place
of fear or jealousy in relationships. You couldn't run before you
could walk, and you won't meet your soul mate before you are ready
to learn what she/he has to teach you. In order to find our soul mate,

we must be emotionally secure and know what we want from life.

THREE KINDS OF SOUL MATES

Did you know there are three main kinds of soul mates?

They are: Karmic, Companion and Twin Flames. Study the different kinds and discover which category your soul mate falls under. This will give you a broader understanding of why he or she has come into your life. To help you, I will explain the differences.

KARMIC SOUL MATE

The karmic soul mate experience is very common. You can have many of these in a lifetime. They enter your life to teach you an important lesson. Karmic soul mates can be co-workers, family members or close friends. One young woman particularly close to me comes to mind. Her name is Amanda Jane, and she is about twenty years my junior. She jokes that I must be her mother from another life. What makes our friendship special is that we touch on a spiritual level.

I often wonder why Amanda was brought into my life. We are very close, but what lesson am I to learn from her? To enjoy life again? Amanda comes from a dysfunctional family. Am I here to teach her a lesson? Am I to show her that she is loved and cherished? It can and does work both ways.

Sometimes karmic soul mate relationships can be romantic in nature; but if so, they won't last long. That is because these relationships are solely meant for learning lessons and for growth rather than for obtaining a life partner.

Another thing we must keep in mind is that not all karmic relationships are human. Sometimes, pets we consider to be special members of our family can display the same karmic characteristics as humans. An example of this is Avis Townsend's story "Back With Eli" in the karmic section of the book. Ms. Townsend's story shows there are special relationships we can have with our pets to the point where the bond between pet and human becomes so deep it's hard to dismiss it as anything other than the true karmic soul mate relationship.

Another point to remember about karmic soul mates, as well as other kinds of soul mates, is that each one, whether human or animal, comes into our lives for a reason and to teach us a lesson about ourselves.

COMPANION SOUL MATE

A companion soul mate relationship can be a relationship that is romantic in nature. It involves your wife/husband or someone you are intimate with. Oftentimes, these soul mates are not destined to be with us forever but, like karmic soul mates, are brought into our lives for a purpose.

It is possible to spend a lifetime with your companion soul mate if you haven't met your twin soul. However, when the twin soul is found, the companion soul mate relationship could suffer. When this happens, the companion soul mate relationship is generally short-lived or, if it continues, a non-satisfying one. However, this is no reason to jump ship when it happens. Remember, there is a reason your companion soul mate is in your life (for example, so you can raise children together).

When your twin soul comes into your life and you are in a companion soul mate relationship, it is important that you take things slowly. It may be that the companion soul mate relationship will come to an end—or it may not. One thing you must keep in mind is that ending an existing relationship solely because one feels one has found one's twin soul is *never* a good idea, because over time you will realize that both associations are meant to be and both have an important role in your life.

An interesting aspect of the companion soul mate relationship is that we put more of our energies into it. The karmic soul mate relationship tends to go at an easy pace, without much effort from either partner, as it does with twin souls. The companion soul mate bond requires more work on our parts to sustain a healthy, loving atmosphere.

TWIN FLAMES

This is the highest form of soul mate connection. Your twin soul is your other half; to find your twin soul is like finding yourself. We go through our life searching and searching, and what we don't realize is that we are looking for someone just like us. Sometimes, we find them in this life and, other times, in other lives.

I believe they are always around, but for some reason it is not apparent. Perhaps we close our eyes to them. We don't listen and observe. We go through life at such a hectic pace we don't stop and take in things that would otherwise be apparent, so the presence of a soul mate could hit us flat in the face and we wouldn't even know it. This is sad, because we have missed that one, rare opportunity for total bliss and happiness.

A POSSIBLE FOURTH KIND OF SOUL MATE?

Another interesting concept of the soul mate experience is what we call a Soul Tribe. This comprises a group of soul mates you have gathered, maybe unknowingly, in your life who are particularly close to you, a group of like-minded souls you feel mysteriously attached to.

Take my particular case, for example. There are millions of people in the world using the Internet. I paused one day and wondered why it was I have a particular group of people I email daily and help whenever they have need and who do the same for me. Out of the millions of Internet users, why just this group of people? Did I know each and every one of them in another life? Do we have the same interests in this life? I believe the answer to both those questions is YES!

IDENTIFYING A SOUL MATE RELATIONSHIP

In order to find your soul mate, you must know what to look for. I have compiled the ten most important traits in recognizing your soul mate. Read them to help you decide who your own soul mate(s) is.

- ACCEPTANCE
Your soul mate must accept you for who you are. He or she must accept your weaknesses as well as your strengths. Your soul mate does not try to change you, nor do you try to change them. He or she

lets you be yourself, for the more you are yourself the stronger your bond with your soul mate has a chance of becoming.

- ENCOURAGEMENT

Your soul mate makes you feel good about yourself. He or she never criticizes, only encourages. If they cannot do this, then they are not your soul mate.

- NURTURING

Your soul mate cares about you and what happens to you. He is the first to be by your side in accomplishment and defeat. She picks you up when others throw you down. He nurtures your spirit so you can roll with the punches, no matter where they fall.

- FRIENDSHIP

Your soul mate is your best friend in the entire world. She or he laughs with you, cries with you, sings with you. They are there for you when life throws you those bad curves; they are there for you when you surpass your highest expectations of yourself. A soul mate will understand you and give you what you want and need without hesitation. She will make you feel at home, comfortable and at ease.

As you would with any friend, take the relationship slow. Savor each milestone of firsts: the first time your eyes meet, the first time his lips brush against yours, the first afternoon spent together walking through the park or along the seashore or even just in your own backyard. You have to remember that if you end up together, these "firsts" will be ingrained in your memory forever. Cherish them.

- GENEROSITY

Your soul mate is generous. He gives freely of his time and his possessions. She will ditch whatever she is doing to be with you. He will give you your heart's desires. She will give you her heart and soul, if need be.

- CONVERSATIONALIST

Soul mates are interested in what each has to say to the other. My soul mate and I would spend hours contemplating the mysteries of the universe. Since we thought alike, we never did stop talking. We talked about our past, our present and our future. As we had so many things in common, each of us was interested in what the other had to say.

- PREMONITIONS

You may have premonitions of your future soul mate in dreams. Whether they are when you are asleep or when you are in meditation, you will picture your soul mate as if he or she were standing in front of you. You will note the color of their hair, the sound of their voice, their way of walking. You will picture your soul mate as you want them to be. If you are fortunate enough to be able to do this—and it can happen anytime, anywhere—remember it. For, in time, your soul mate will appear in front of you just as you envisioned.

- POSITIVE KARMA

One of the main ingredients for a successful soul mate relationship lies in the power of karma. In layman's terms, karma is basically the theory that whatever you do, there will be another event to follow that is directly consequential to your actions. Therefore, the law of karma teaches us that what we do today may come back to haunt us tomorrow. How does this apply to the soul mate phenomenon?

If you are in a bad relationship, and you continue to remain in that relationship, you are setting up a path of bad karma for yourself because of the negative energies that arise. Once you learn to set up a shield against this negativity, good karma will infiltrate your life and open your soul to a promising and healthy soul mate relationship.

Not until this happens will you ever receive a satisfactory soul mate union. Both parties must bring good karma into the relationship. You have to remember that we are all souls, just pure energy "visiting" this planet; and we have been here many times. Neither partner can come from a place where negativity is present, or the soul mate experience just won't occur.

- SPIRITUAL CONNECTION

You will feel a connection with your soul mate, as if you had known him or her before. You will feel an energy radiating between you. You will look into each other's eyes and see each other's soul, for that is where the true soul mate connection lies.

Not enough can be said about the spiritual connection between soul mates. It is the most important quality in a soul mate relationship. You will feel this in the depths of your heart and soul. Without it, the soul mate relationship is doomed.

- UNCONDITIONAL LOVE

Your soul mate will love you more than anything or anyone he has loved in his entire life, although he will give you freedom to be who you are. "You cannot possess a soul mate any more than you can possess a person in your physical world," says Robert Egby, author of *Thank You For The Flowers*. "Soul mates are free and must always be so. Love cannot be possessed or controlled. Soul mates are together because they share an unconditional love, a mutual vibration. There are no exceptions."

- PERFECT TIMING

Other things come into play in seeking your soul mate that you might not count on. One is perfect timing. If it isn't the right time for you and your soul mate to be together, it will likely not happen.

DID YOU KNOW YOUR SOUL MATE IN A PAST LIFE?

It is some people's belief that there is a past life for everyone. While it is not a known fact, there are real-life cases where past life regressions have been performed on people in which they do recall past life experiences. In one such case, there was a woman who recognized a friend in this life who had been with her in a past one. In other cases, people are amazed that sometimes a close friend may have been their mother, father, sister or brother in a past life, but they are there, nevertheless.

I believe this group of souls follows you throughout your lives until it is time to meet your maker, whichever or whomever you believe.

Popular metaphysical author and hypnotherapist Richard Webster has regressed hundreds of clients. He discovered that everyone has a soul mate. In fact, his first researches into soul mates were done during his hypnotherapy practice.

DO YOU ONLY HAVE ONE SOUL MATE?

I have learned in doing research for this book that many people do not believe in soul mates. They say they have searched and searched for the one person who will make them happy, and have given up. They have come to the conclusion they do not believe there is one, and only one, person who is perfect for them.

They are absolutely right. There is no *one* person who is your soul mate because, as I noted earlier, there are at least three types of soul mates. Those who do not believe at all are missing an important part of their life experience, for it is our *search* for our soul mate that makes our spiritual journey complete.

The bottom line is, don't give up. Our soul mates are out there. Perhaps, they are right under our noses and we don't even realize it.

Lisa Daily, author of *Stop Getting Dumped!: All You Need to Know to Make Men Fall Madly in Love with You and Marry "The One" in 3 Years or Less*, totally agrees.

"Can you have too many soul mates?" she asks. "It depends on whether you're talking strictly in the romantic sense or not. In a romantic sense, I think a person has one, maybe two soul mates in a lifetime. On a friendship level, I think you can have several soul mates—people who come into your life with whom you have an instant connection. These soul mates sort of drop into your life at a time when you most need them (or they most need you) and you touch each other's lives in a way that feels almost pre-ordained. Sometimes these soul mates disappear as quickly as they arrive. Sometimes they are with you for the rest of your days."

THE SOUL MATE MYSTIQUE

I have been asked many questions about the soul mate mystique. For instance, I ran into a friend I hadn't seen for thirty years. The instant I saw Sharon, there was a connection. We reminisced about high school days and couldn't stop talking. It was as if that thirty-year span had dissolved into oblivion. We could almost read each other's thoughts.

She emailed me the other day and asked about my soul mate project. She believed her ex-husband was her soul mate yet she despised him for his lies and deceit. I told her perhaps she and her ex-husband were soul mates, but their mortal experiences here on earth clouded their spiritual connection. I told her that her ex-husband could have very possibly been her soul mate if she were to connect with him on a spiritual level.

Perhaps if my soul mate and I had lived together, had kids together, had mortgages together, things wouldn't have turned out quite so rosy. Some soul mates meet in this life for a specific purpose and nothing more. Did I meet my twin soul? I don't know for sure, but I certainly did meet some form of soul mate who made a lasting impression on me.

All this said, the big question is still: "Do soul mates really exist?" You will find the answer by the time you have finished the true stories included in this book, and the answer will be a resounding *yes*.

I have compiled more than sixty true stories and poems from people around the world showing that soul mates do, indeed, exist. The stories are compelling, often heartbreaking. They will touch your heart as well as your mind. You may even recognize some of the names here because they are creative people whose work you may have enjoyed.

I would like to take the time now to personally thank each and every one of my contributors for opening their hearts and sharing their stories. For some, it was very hard to expose their souls to the world, and they only agreed after much coaxing. Later, they wrote and thanked me for allowing them this opportunity to "let it all out."

I have divided the stories into three categories—Twin Flames, Karmic Soul Mates and Companion Soul Mates—for a reason. It is to give you a better understanding of the different kinds of soul mate relationships by using the stories as examples. Perhaps this will help you understand who your soul mate is and why they have come into your life.

Keep in mind that all soul mates are with us for a purpose, and no one type is more important than another; you need all of them to fulfill your spiritual purpose.

So, let us begin our magical journey through the lives of sixty people from all walks of life. Some are well-known authors, some are painters, poets and actors. Some are ordinary people leading ordinary lives just like you and me.

Read their stories. Listen to their words. They are messages to you. Look beyond your mortal existence and find your spiritual self in these stories. Read in between the lines. The soul mate phenomenon is alive and well.

How do I love thee? Let me count the ways.
I love thee to the depth and breadth and height
My soul can reach, when feeling out of sight
For the ends of Being and ideal Grace.
I love thee to the level of every day's
Most quiet need, by sun and candlelight.
I love thee freely, as men strive for Right;
I love thee purely, as they turn from Praise.
I love thee with the passion put to use
In my old griefs, and with my childhood's faith.
I love thee with a love I seemed to lose
With my lost saints,—I love thee with the breath,
Smiles, tears, of all my life!—and, if God choose,
I shall but love thee better after death.

— Elizabeth Barrett Browning

PART ONE
TWIN SOULS

"From every human being there rises a light that reaches straight to heaven. And when two souls that are destined to be together find each other, their streams of light flow together, and a single brighter light goes forth from their united being."
— *Unknown*

YOU ARE...THE ONE

YOU ARE LIKE THE FLAME ON A CANDLE—
burning warm with fire and passion.
I look into your eyes and I feel
a burst of love rush through my body.

The mere thought of you paints a smile on my face
and it reaches into every part of my being.
You are the one I think of when I am with others
and the one I want to be with when I am alone.

My soul is made whole when I'm with you
and feels incomplete when I'm not.
Thoughts of you swirl through my mind
like the ebb and flow of the tides.

Like the first gentle flakes of snow
you blanket my life with pure, sparkling love.
You are the half that makes me whole,
the angel that makes my world.

You are ...The One

— Ellen M. DuBois

TWO DRIFTERS
By Joyce and Jim Lavene

JOYCE

SOUL MATES? I BELIEVED IT. I KNEW THERE WAS SOMEONE OUT THERE FOR me.

It was 1971. I was sixteen years old. I'd only attended school the equivalent of two semesters in the last two years. I was ill with a disease that had no name and no ready cure. Two years of tests—terrible tests—brought me no relief, no answers. My parents' insurance had been cancelled because of the money it took to keep me alive. They mortgaged the house again and again.

I remember lying in the hospital room as my body wasted away. I heard the doctor talking to my parents, telling them the new medications he'd tried hadn't worked. It was only a matter of time. There was nothing they could do.

My skin was gray, and the whites of my eyes were yellow. I was five feet, eight inches tall and weighed one hundred pounds. I was in constant pain, moving restlessly, incessantly, to try to keep from hurting. I only felt relief when they said they were going to take me home and do what they could for me there. They taught my mother to give me injections and sent a home health nurse. I lay in my bed and looked at the ceiling while they checked my vitals and shook their heads.

Because I was confined to bed, I lived in my thoughts and dreams. When I first got sick, I began to dream about a young man. He walked through my thoughts at night. He was tall and thin with reddish-brown hair and blue eyes. He had freckles on the bridge of his nose, and his name was Jim. So many frustrating times, I watched him then someone would call his name, and I'd wake up. I knew the sound of his voice and his laugh. I saw him walking through crowded city streets.

When I first saw him, I was well enough to look through books and catalogues. I knew he was about six feet tall. Clothing catalogues told me men about his size wore a 14-inch collar on their shirt and had a 32-inch waist. He would wear size nine shoes. I put together as much information about him as I could. But mostly, I dreamed and waited to see him.

I wrote it all down because I was afraid to tell anyone. I thought they might think it was the disease. I didn't want to see their sympathetic eyes or hear the pity in their voices. I knew I'd never meet him. I knew I wouldn't live to touch him or look into his eyes. But I knew he was alive somewhere. I knew he was my soul mate.

So many times he turned when I tried to speak to him in my dreams, as if he could faintly hear me but couldn't find me. He'd look around the room then shake his head and go back to what he was doing.

It was warm that year for February, even in the South. The roses near the house were blooming. Their perfume was so sweet in the moonlight it made me cry. My seventeenth birthday was a few months away. I wasn't sure I'd see it. It was hard to breathe, and there was a rattling sound in my chest. I was so scared—not of dying, but of dying before I had ever had a chance to live.

I read later dying people sometimes do strange things. That night, the only thing I could think of was finding the man in my dreams. If I found him I might live. I didn't know where to look for him. I had no idea what his last name was or where he lived. But I knew I had to try.

I had to use both hands to write a note to my parents. I pulled the IV needle from my arm. It took all my strength to get up and get dressed. I rested for a while then walked slowly out of the house and into the moonlight. It was like a dream, being outside with that strong white light shining down on me. I walked down the road to the main highway about two blocks away. I'll never know how I managed to do it. I just kept putting one foot in front of the other with my soul mate's

3

face before me.

When I reached the road, I stood still, trying to catch my breath. A car slowed down and stopped. The man inside asked me if I needed a ride. I said yes and climbed into the car. He said he could only take me as far as Virginia. I told him that was fine.

He was nice enough to be concerned about me. When I told him I wasn't sure where I was going, he told me he was headed to DC for the big May Day peace rally against the war. It sounded like a good place to live out my last few days. Maybe I'd even be lucky enough to find my soul mate.

DC was crowded and full of protesters when we got there. I stayed with the man and his friends in a small apartment while they plotted their anti-war strategy. I was on my way to the grocery store with them when my life changed.

JIM

I remember hearing a voice calling my name. I had the strong feeling of being watched, even when I knew I was totally alone. At night, my dreams were strange and disjointed. There was a girl. She had curly blond hair and big blue eyes. She was crying. I wanted to ask what was wrong, but when I tried to find her she was gone.

I was nineteen years old, home on leave for a few weeks before I had to report back to the army at Fort Meade, Maryland. My parents weren't particularly happy to see me. With five kids still at home, I was a burden on their finances again.

It was weird sleeping in my old bunk bed. Even the army gave me more privacy than I had at home. We lived in a cramped two-bedroom apartment in a building that had seen its best days twenty years before. Every sound any of us made was amplified. My stepfather didn't like noise. He drank heavily when he wasn't driving his truck, and we had no love for each other. I only came back for my mother and my sisters.

The strange girl was there in my dreams that night. She was with another girl. They stood in a park; trees bloomed around them. The ground was covered with pink blossoms. She wasn't crying this time.

She was talking to the other girl. She looked up, and there was a strange smile on her face when she said, "I know you."

I woke up in a cold sweat. The next day, a buddy of mine said he was going to Washington DC for a few days before we had to report back. I packed my stuff and got in the car with him. My mother cried when I left, but she didn't ask me to stay. My stepfather didn't say anything because there was a football game on TV.

We drove down with a few other friends. There was still snow on the ground in Chicago; but as we got farther south, the skies cleared and the weather got warmer. Grass was starting to turn green. We took turns driving and playing the radio too loud. A few guys got stoned in the backseat.

Three of my friends were going back to 'Nam for another tour of duty. Because my birth father was dead and I was his only child, I was allowed to stay in the States when I was drafted. I didn't mind. The stories I'd heard about Vietnam were bad. A lot of guys went because the pay was good. I couldn't imagine any pay being that good. A friend of mine agreed and shot himself in the foot to keep from going over there.

Times were tense. Guys my age had been killed protesting the war at Kent State. I just wanted to have a week of peace and a few parties before I had to report back. I didn't know if the war was right or wrong. I only had a short time left before I was through with the Army. I wasn't sure what I was going to do when I got out. I had dreams of building something. Maybe a house in the woods. When I was a kid, we used to pretend the tall weeds in the vacant lot next to our apartment were trees. I wanted to live where there were real trees.

Was there a girl in the picture? I thought right away about the girl I'd seen in my dreams. She was pretty, but so thin. She looked sick. Her face haunted me. I kept seeing her crying, those big blue eyes watering like they'd never stop. I felt like I knew her.

I crashed with some friends when we got to DC. The city was in upheaval because of the peace rallies and protests. It was early March of 1971. People were living on the streets in tents and burning pictures of Richard Nixon. My buddies and I didn't wear our uniforms because we'd heard reports of guys being beaten by crowds—the anger against the war had come to include the men and women who fought it. We weren't scared, but we weren't stupid.

Besides, it was nice to wear jeans and T-shirts. My hair was too short for me to really blend in, but no one bothered me.

We walked up to the store for a pack of cigarettes and some coffee early one morning. I kept thinking how the cherry blossoms were all over the sidewalks and the streets, just like in my dream. I saw two girls walking towards us and time slowed to a standstill.

JOYCE

I looked up and saw three men walking towards us. They were dressed in jeans and T-shirts. Their hair was short, and they walked like tough guys. The one in the middle was wearing a light-blue shirt. He had blue-green eyes and reddish-brown hair. There was a dusting of freckles across his face.

I stared at him. I couldn't help it. It was him. It was the man from my dreams.

JIM

One of the girls was very thin. She had curly blond hair and blue eyes. She stared at me. She was wearing blue jeans that were too big for her, no shoes and a white T-shirt. My friend next to me nudged me when he saw she was staring at me. He said something, but I didn't understand him.

JOYCE AND JIM

"I know you," she said breathlessly. "I know you!"
  "Who are you? Where did we meet?" he asked.
  "We haven't. But I know you. I know your name."
  "My name is—"
  "Jim. Your name is Jim."
  "My name is Jim. Who are you?"
  "Joyce."

"You won't believe—" he began.

"That you saw me in a dream?"

"You wanna get some coffee?"

"Yes."

"Now?"

"Sure. But there's one thing I have to tell you."

"What?"

"I love you!"

"It sounds crazy, but I understand. I don't know how. Coffee?"

"If you need to do that first."

"I feel—"

"Me, too."

"Let's go."

(JIM AND JOYCE LAVENE are a married writing team published in romance, mystery and nonfiction, currently residing in North Carolina with their family.)

SOULS ENTWINED
By Linda Rucker

OUR SOULS ENTWINED SO MANY YEARS AGO. ALTHOUGH IT WASN'T LOVE AT first sight, at least for me, there was that deep and abiding connection, that bond that formed on first glance.

Over the years, we became even more connected. Always able to tell when the other was sad or happy, frightened or at peace. If I were down, the phone would magically ring, and just the sound of her voice would chase whatever was bugging me right on away.

She was there for me when I started school, holding my hand and whispering that all would be well. I was sure it wouldn't be, but she was with me every step of the way that first day and for all the years after; and she always helped me through.

When I discovered that boys were so much more than just annoying nuisances, she was there to ease the pain of my broken heart. Without her, I don't think I ever would have recovered.

When she was diagnosed with uterine cancer, I held her hand and cried with her; and when we laid her momma to rest, I hugged her and told her she still had me and she always would.

With joy and tears, we shared my first pregnancy; and with the same joy, I watched her grow happy and secure in her own skin.

When I buried my firstborn twenty-four years after her birth, she was there for me. She knew the minute my Wendy took her last breath because she felt my heart break, even though she was two hundred miles away. That time I was sure nothing could ease my pain, but her words of comfort and love did.

Over the years, we were closer than sisters. She was my best friend in this life, and I know she will be in the next. Our hearts and souls are connected in the way that twins' must be. We always felt each other's pain and happiness and shared every secret. Between us, there were no secrets.

You see, we connected on a cold morning in March of 1949. Cradling me in her arms, she looked into my eyes; my face screwed up in righteous indignation at the smack on the bottom the doctor administered to me, and she knew my soul. And although I couldn't see her, as my vision was not yet clear, my heart and soul melded with hers.

For the next fifty-three years, my mother was my very best friend, my twin soul mate. She was always there for me.

But just as she knew when I was in pain or afraid and needed her, I knew that about her; and so it was that I came to be standing by her bed January 21, 2003. A cold wind blew outside and chilled my soul. I watched her struggle for every breath as she fought to stay with me, with us, the people she loved. She knew how much we loved her and how lost we would be without her.

The cancer had spread to her brain; and she was in and out of consciousness, never lucid for more than a fleeting moment. When she heard our voices, she would struggle to clear her mind and open her eyes and look at us; but I knew she was seeing those she loved who had gone before. She called out to her mother, a smile on her face, and my heart broke and my resolve strengthened.

I knelt down by her bed, and I took her hand in mine. It was so tiny and so frail-looking, this hand that had soothed my fevered brow when I was sick, that had smoothed the hair out of my eyes and dried my tears, that had patted my back when I had done well and smacked my bottom when I messed up. I took her hand and I leaned over and kissed her face and whispered in her ear, "It's okay, Momma, you can rest now. We'll be fine, I promise. I love you."

I got to my feet and motioned for my sister and brother, and they told her goodbye. Told her to rest easy. And as we stood together, our arms around each other, she took her last breath.

I felt her go. Felt the passing of her soul as it left her body, felt it because on its way up it grabbed a piece of mine and left a piece of itself in me.

Our souls are forever entwined, Momma's and mine. I will miss her forever, but I will always have a piece of her with me till we are together again.

My mother was my twin soul mate from my first breath and she will be long after my last.

(LINDA L. RUCKER is a published author currently living in eastern Tennessee.)

TWIN FLAMES A-BURNING

By Heide AW Kaminski

S IXTEEN AND A HALF YEARS AGO, A BEAUTIFUL LITTLE GIRL WAS BORN INTO MY life. Right from the start I felt very special towards her. It wasn't like a typical mother/daughter feeling, but I couldn't describe it with words.

In her later years, as I went through a nasty divorce from her father, she took over the mothering role to her little sister that I should have played. In addition to that, she filled the void that my own heartless mother had left years before. She seemed to have a deep understanding of my pain. Whether it was the divorce or just her natural path, this little girl grew up much faster than most of her peers.

When she started puberty, we went through a year of constant fighting. Her favorite threat was "I am going to move in with my dad!"

One day she went as far as packing her suitcase and demonstratively setting it by the door. Even though I broke down on the inside, I remained calm on the outside.

"Do you need a ride?" I asked with all the repose I could muster.

Her suitcase remained by the door, slowly being emptied piece-by-piece over the following weeks, until it disappeared.

"That was the best thing you could have said," my daughter informed me months later. "I never did want to move in with my dad, but I knew I could hurt you with the threat. You took that power away from me with one sentence of the wisest words you ever said to me."

From then on, we didn't fight anymore. Our relationship changed dramatically. She had never really been my little girl, and I was emotionally stable enough to not need her as a mother figure anymore. We became sisters and friends. It reached the point where I even told her that, if anything were to happen to me, she was the only one I trusted to raise my son, her little brother. I know she is young and this would be a tremendous burden to her, but I truly believe she is the only one who can do this. He is an Indigo child, and I know it takes someone like my daughter to help him through this world safely.

Indigo children are those who have allegedly come into this world to steer us in a more productive direction and are sometimes misdiagnosed as having ADHD.

We started having endless discussions about spirituality, values, and dreams; it turned out that neither of us felt as though we belonged on this earth. We had ideals, goals and a sense for justice that was just too far off the standards of current society.

As I began reading about Indigo children, it not only became clear that my daughter was one hundred-percent Indigo but, more and more, I realized that I am one of the early Indigos myself.

Sarah began writing poetry, beautiful but sad. Then one evening, she came to show me her newest creation, and I had to sit down I was so stunned.

I pulled out my collection of poems I had written when I was younger. One stood out in particular. It was very similar to what my daughter had just written!

Several months ago, my daughter, out of the blue, told her dad that this life was one of her last incarnations. She couldn't explain her feelings about this, she said. She just knew.

About a year ago, I began thinking I was making spiritual growth in leaps and bounds, and I figured I was getting pretty darn close to having one of my last lives in human form.

A few weeks ago I told a psychic friend about my relationship with my daughter. My friend suggested that it was very likely my daughter and I are twin flames, and I looked up what I could find on the subject.

Twin flames are not the same as soul mates; rather, according to Arianni Masters, who is one expert in this field, soul mates are people who come together for a very specific purpose. Their human relationships are not necessarily joyful; they can be extremely painful as well.

Twin souls, on the other hand, according to Masters, are two people in two separate bodies who share the same soul. Meeting your twin flame is extremely rare. Generally, they do not meet, unless they are in their very first or their last incarnation. If they meet before they are ready, their relationship can be disastrous.

One sentence stood out as I read Masters' theory: "Twin Flames are almost identical. They truly complement each other."

Just a few weeks prior to reading this, I had told someone that if we hadn't both been alive at the same time I would have said my daughter was a reincarnation of me.

So, what do we do with this information? It is hard to say. We don't say too much about it to the rest of the family. It might be hard for them to swallow.

Her being more a part of me than just my child scares and delights me at the same time. It scares me because she is experiencing right now what I did during the years in which I was at my worst. I am afraid of her making the same, sometimes almost fatal, choices I made back then. On the other hand, it brings me great joy, as I feel I can be there for her to fulfill the potential I could have achieved if I would have had had someone to guide me.

We both know—intuitively just *know*—that we will be great someday. Not just great in each other's eyes but great in the world's eyes as well.

(HEIDE AW KAMINSKI is a freelance writer and published author in southeastern Michigan.)

I WILL NEVER STOP SEARCHING FOR YOU

I will look the distance,
I will travel the length.
I know you are out there somewhere,
And I know I will find you.
I will swim across a lake.
I will swim across the ocean floor.
I will look near and far,
Up and down,
And then I will look some more.
I know you're out there somewhere,
And I know I will find you.
You may be hiding under a tree,
Or you may be running wild and free.
Wherever you go,
I want you to know,
I'll be looking for you.
When it's dark and when it's cold,
When it's rainy and I am bold,
I will never stop my searching,
Until I have found your soul.
I know you're out there somewhere.
And I know,
I will find you

— Sarah Wyse

AND THEN HE KISSED ME
By Wendi Friend

WHY DO ALL FAIRY TALES END IN HAPPILY EVER AFTER? AS A CHILD, I NEVER asked that question—I was simply grateful. Cinderella's story validated my thought processes perfectly. Like mine, hers was a life of difficult roads to travel. She had a wicked stepmother; I had wicked stepfathers. Cinderella had evil stepsisters. My stepsiblings were boys but just as evil; and I had regular brothers and sisters, too. Cinderella and I had in common rags for clothes, we sang to ourselves for comfort and our only friends were liable to come from the animal kingdom. Naturally, my child mind would conclude that I, too, would someday come across a fairy godmother, a glass slipper and a golden prince. Childhood dreams grabbed me and gave me something to believe in when all else failed.

As a child, living within my family, I had the sense that I didn't belong. Of course, my siblings would gather in force to convince me of my adoption, but I knew better—I looked too much like my mother. Nonetheless, I truly felt I *didn't* belong—not at home, not at school, not at play, not anywhere.

I remember being in the backseat of Mom's green station wagon, looking into the windows of passing cars for boys my age. Each boy I'd see would capture a piece of my imagination. Are you my future husband? How naive was I? Still, dreams of a soul mate, a true love, a knight in shining armor offering rescue, were enough to give me hope through many struggles. It'll be worth it if there's true love at the end of the road, I thought.

The image of my prince changed over the years. In my younger days, he had blond hair and blue eyes. As I aged, his hair and eyes darkened. Still, he was there in my dreams, promising me everything would be okay. Someday, when he found me at long last, life wouldn't hurt anymore. The problem was, I wasn't willing to wait for him to find me. I set out to find him instead.

The search lasted through more than twenty years and three marriages, and produced three children. What was I searching for again? I'd forget amidst all the chaos I'd created in trying to find it. Ah, yes, a soul mate. But what does that mean? What did I hope to gain from finding my "other half?"

I hoped to gain acceptance, love, encouragement and a desire to experience life together always. In my mind, soul mates lasted forever. What I really wanted was a prince to rescue me. If only my prince would come, I'd find happiness.

Turning thirty wasn't difficult for me at all. In fact, it was safe refuge from my twenties! But turning thirty-one flipped my world upside-down. At thirty-something, I was not anywhere near where I wanted to be in my life. Twice divorced, single mother of three, working double shifts at a lousy job, trying to make ends meet, I'd all but lost hope in my dreams. Laced with cynicism, I gave up on the dream for a soul mate. My life, I'd decided, was meant to be raising my children.

But where had I gone wrong? How could I be thirty-something and single when I'd tried so hard with all my heart to love the men I was with? Why did I mistake each one of them for a soul mate? I wasn't a little girl anymore; and somehow, I needed to account for my actions—and my unhappiness.

Looking back, I had several relationships I thought were "the one," starting at age fifteen. My first true love sent my heart into palpitations! He didn't look at me but into me. He talked with me about things most people would call crazy. He believed in me, and in us. We communicated without words, which is what soul mates do.

But we were kids! What we knew about love was immature, undeveloped, and what we produced was frightening. At sixteen, we were parents. Our relationship didn't last. Though we talked about reconciling after the baby was born and a year later still dreamed of the day—after we'd finish school and put our lives back on track—

my son's father passed away when our child was two. He was a soul mate, yes, but he wasn't everlasting love.

My search for a soul mate continued. Though I'd not seen anyone in my environment have a successful relationship, I still believed that, somewhere "out there," someone was looking for me as desperately as I was looking for him. My error was in focusing on certain characteristics of my dream man I found in people who were *not* my dream man. For example, I knew my soul mate would have a great sense of humor and be good-looking. So, when I came across a good-looking man with a sense of humor, I just knew it was him! I'd forget about the rest of the qualities I felt my soul mate would inherently have; I got too excited over the qualities a man did have!

Well, I did meet a good-looking man with a sense of humor, and I did love him. I was also still quite young, naive and trusting. For the second time, I found myself with child—and alone. A pattern was emerging, but I'd not yet recognized it.

My second child was more difficult than the first. During my fifth month of pregnancy, my unborn son was diagnosed with a malformation of the lungs. I was told he would most probably die before or at birth. Naturally, my search for soul mates had to be put on hold for love of my child.

My focus was on letting my unborn son know that, if he wanted to, he could choose to live. I'd talk with him each day, promising him that doctors are human and can make mistakes. At the same time, I had to let him know, for my sake as well as his, I'd not begrudge him if he didn't come into my world. Maybe Heaven would provide a better home for him than I could. Maybe since I couldn't provide him with his own father, he'd be blessed with a Heavenly Father.

I made peace with the outcome, regardless. With my eternal gratitude, he lived.

With both my boys in good health and my heart in recovery, I set out in search again for my other half. Why couldn't the universe understand how much I wanted and needed this? My childhood dreams of true and everlasting love were fading. Please, God, give me something to cling to. Loneliness was killing me, literally. Depression was thick, self-esteem was nil and dreams were getting farther and farther away from reality.

That's when I met the next man who would take a piece of my heart, leaving a piece of himself behind. While playing with my boys at a local playground, I met what I thought was the man of my dreams. He was absolutely everything I thought a man should be—on the outside. I never got past the outside.

Never before had I been so taken by a man's physical appearance that I found it difficult to speak or to breathe. In his presence, I was mesmerized. With him, the sex was different. I wasn't trying to "get" love from him nearly as much as I was trying to offer my love to him. He was the opposite of what I'd experienced, so maybe—just maybe—this time I was right. This was, indeed, my soul mate.

But history tends to repeat itself—until we learn from it, that is. I became pregnant, and my "other half" wanted nothing to do with it. There I was, at twenty-one, a single mother of three. I couldn't figure out how I'd gotten there!

Child three was a daughter, and she completed the childbearing portion of my journey. By age twenty-five, cervical cancer led to a hysterectomy. It was, in one sense, validation for some of my life choices—I might have been young and in dire circumstances when I had my children; but if I hadn't had them when I did, I might never have had the chance.

Being a mother kept my heart occupied most of the time. Yet, without my realizing it had happened, I'd become cynical. Before I'd turned thirty, I gave up on my prince. I finally accepted that he wasn't coming, he didn't exist. No one would rescue me. True love is an illusion.

When that realization came, two things happened. First, I rebelled and tried to recapture my lost youth, making painful mistakes in the process. Second, I poured my focus and all my love onto my children, realizing that they were the loves of my life. That combination of unbridled rebellion and obsessive attention drove one of my children away. Due to my own selfish search for true love, I had lost the truest love of all. I had lost my firstborn son.

For months I grieved over my own stupidity. I cursed my heart for loving the wrong men, I cursed my mind for making the wrong choices and I cursed my soul for being needy. Spiraling into an inner

18

hell, I drove myself through memories.

In times past, when I wasn't obsessed with the need to find my match, I had laughed with my children, learning from them, growing with them, experiencing life's pleasures with them. With them, I'd found ultimate acceptance. With them, I found a place to belong. They and they alone had the ability to communicate without words, to make me laugh when I was sad, to give me strength when I thought my reserves are tapped.

My children have been my reason for living for the past sixteen years. They were the soul mates I'd been searching for all along, and I didn't notice the full value of that until I'd lost one of them.

On one hand, I found relief because recognizing my children as my soul mates meant I'd not have to keep searching for the perfect man. But soul mates don't walk away, do they? Aren't soul mates meant to be forever? Truth unfolded.

None of the men I'd loved were mistakes. Each had a purpose in my life, whether that purpose was to teach me something or bring a child into the world. Each, in his own way, was a genuine soul mate. I had been under the notion that only one soul mate exists per person. This isn't true. Throughout our lifetime, we encounter several soul mates in the form of family, friends, lovers and even animals. The objective is not to cling to that soul with all your might, refusing to let go. The objective is to love—that's all, nothing else.

So, I didn't get a glass slipper. No pumpkin popped into a kick-ass coach to carry me away. I never ever did get a fairy godmother. What I did end up with, having added together the pieces and parts of experience, is an understanding that while relationships don't always last forever true love can and does. Bodies may part, but the soul ties are never broken. Never goodbye; always "'Til we meet again."

Having learned that lesson, the battle had been won. No more would I search for a one and only perfect love.

At the time my eldest child left, we were living in Tulsa, Oklahoma. It was my first attempt at living away from Las Vegas, away from family. In Tulsa, I'd be one hundred percent on my own with my kids. What we went there for, we found in a year's time; but by the end of that year, we had all taken a beating. When my son left, it was to return to Vegas to live with his father's brother.

Returning to Vegas wasn't something I felt wonderful about. I was eager to see my family, yes; but at the same time, it was a resignation of sorts. I was resigned to the fact I would spend the rest of my life investing energy in the two children remaining in my care, and in my career, in an environment I didn't care for.

My older sister, though, had other ideas. Her desire was to see me play the dating game, meet a variety of people then find a man who could serve as a stepfather and "take care of" us. At her nudging, I dated a few people but always came home feeling...tainted. I felt like I was going through the motions of letting men buy me meals or take me to movies when I knew in my heart that none of them came even close to the image in my head of Mr. Right.

When I read about Socrates, I had the next epiphany. He was the smartest of men because he admitted he knew nothing at all. That's where I was. I had to admit that I didn't know anything anymore. I didn't have the right answers, the best way or the brightest path. Maybe my vision of Mr. Right was wrong.

You wouldn't really call it a prayer. It didn't start with "Dear Heavenly Father" nor was it directed anywhere in particular—just up and out. Whatever it's called and wherever it went, its time had come. Late at night, more than asleep but less than awake, I said to the universe, "You know what? I don't know what is best for me. I thought I did, but I don't. So, I'm not going to try to tell you that my true love has to have this color hair or that color eyes or an accent. I won't tell you who is right for me. But I will tell you that I know I'm worthy of love, and that I'll wait until it comes, without expectation."

Letting go of expectation was key, I believe. When I stopped trying to force people into my preconceived mold of what Mr. Right would be, I realized he'd been in my life already for years! I'd known him since my daughter was a toddler. We'd worked together in the past; we were working together again.

Don and I met several years ago as co-workers for my sister's catering company. Our friendship solidified instantly and continued to grow, but at the time, we were both in other relationships. The line had been drawn; our friendship would not be one of a romantic nature. We worked together on several occasions, as well as seeing each other at personal events, such as my sister's wedding. In a way, through my sister, Don had already become a loved and respected part of the family.

I wrote an article about Don called "A Friend, a Soldier, and An Every Day Hero." The article told of his experience in the United States Air Force during the time of the attacks against America. And that's what Don was to me in every sense of the word: a hero. He was a hero not only for his role in the armed forces, but for the way he was each day.

Unlike most men I'd met, Don had a genuine tenderness in his soul. He truly meant it when he'd ask someone how their day was. But our paths separated when I left for Tulsa. With the exception of a few emails, we lost touch. When I returned to Las Vegas a year later, we worked together again. Our friendship remained as true as it was before.

But still, how did I know in my heart that Don was a soul mate to me? There's a song that says the truth "is in his kiss." In my case, it was the opposite. Though we'd been flirting with the idea of getting together, no advancements had been made. Being that I'm a straightforward girl in the modern world, I had no problem making the first move.

But as I leaned in for my magical moment, the man turned his head away. Never before had a man rejected my attempts to kiss him! Knowing he had wounded my pride, Don's eyes glassed over with tears as he explained that if it was right it would be worth waiting for. He knew I needed time to put myself back together after the experiences in Tulsa, and he had some matters of his own to resolve.

Though he turned down the kiss, he never walked away. He stayed by me to help as I rebuilt my dreams. Each day he would bring surprises: a flower, a sweet note, a gift placed secretly in my car or on my desk at work. He even danced with me under the full moon in the middle of the street in front of my mother's house.

It was one Friday night, nearing eleven p.m., that I was walking him to the door. He'd come to my mother's to visit with me for a little while after work. Heading for the door, I moved to pass him, but he caught me in mid-step, stopping me where I stood. With his index finger to my chin, Don tilted my face upward so our eyes met. Before

21

my mind could register what was happening, he lowered his lips to mine.

What I've heard is true. It *is* in his kiss! Six months later, we were married.

Just like in my childhood dreams, the Knight in Shining Armor emerged from the sunset, asking for my hand in marriage. With a romantic love like I've never known, he's swept me off my feet and away into the fairy tale world I've always imagined, and that's where we'll live—happily ever after.

(WENDI FRIEND is a freelance writer currently residing in Brownsville, Kentucky.)

MY ANGEL AND ME
By Peter Fox

THERE WAS A TIME WHEN I BELIEVED IN ANGELS. AND THERE WAS A TIME WHEN I knew one intimately. I'm not a preacher or a Baptist's son, but only a regular guy who, nearly six years ago, caught a glimpse of Heaven.

Her name was Cyan.

I knew her my whole life—in my heart, in my mind. I never actually met her, though, until I was in high school. Here's how it began and ...how it ended.

In May 1998, I was lying in bed, feeling incredibly lonely and aching to have somebody near. As I lay there in the darkness, I prayed to God that I would meet someone, anyone, just...someone. I told Him all that I wished for my angel to be, everything from the tenderness of her heart to the superficial stuff on the outside. I was specific. I must have listed at least thirty things, if not more.

And not generic things, mind you, like "I want her to be nice" or "I want her to be funny." No. It was stuff like "I want her to smile because it's raining outside" and "I want her to understand how life isn't about what we do, but about who we are when no one's looking, that secret part of ourselves that no one knows."

A week or so later, I met Cyan, the embodiment of what I prayed for, right down to her favorite number—seven—and favorite color—blue. And not just any blue. Superman blue.

When I first laid eyes on her as I walked the school halls, I remember feeling the strength run from my body, my legs feeling like wet noodles and, as comedic as it was, my jaw hanging open as she neared. Something about this girl...hit me. Time stilled and I was no longer me but just a little boy, yearning to be held by her, someone distant from what could be called the "conscious realm."

Then the world picked up again; and I walked by her, trying to catch my breath, too shy to say anything or even nod in her direction.

I saw Cyan now and then in the halls, and each time—I was hers. Once, she waved to me and that smile of hers—man, you had to be there—it would make you think the greatest joy you had ever known was nothing more than a bad memory in comparison. That moment would play in my mind throughout the entire day.

The following month a friend of mine, David, had a graduation party at his house just outside the city. What I didn't know was that David was friends with Cyan, so you can imagine my reaction when I came down the stairs into his basement and there she was, sitting on the couch, talking to another girl.

Cyan and I talked a lot that night; all the while my heart was racing, my mind trying to wrap itself around...her. Those "items" I asked the good Lord for? She had all of them. I'm not kidding—she had every single one. And, man, she was beautiful, all I had pictured my forever sweetheart to be. The same girl I saw in my mind when I started to like girls. The girl I was going to spend the rest of my life with.

She was small, only sixteen at the time, with smooth cheeks and long, wavy brown hair, smelling of something that reminded me of strawberries and vanilla. We went for a walk that evening a far ways down my friend's street. I don't remember what we talked about but I'm sure it was more getting-to-know-you stuff, and when the night was over, she gave me her phone number and email address.

A week later, I finally mustered up the courage to email her. She later told me that she had hoped I'd contact her right away; but after a few days went by, she was sad because I hadn't called or emailed. I apologized and told her I was scared. And before you knew it, we had our first date and...our first kiss.

I remember sitting in my car in her driveway, dropping her off after our first outing. We went to the comic shop, Kildonan Park, the Forks and yet another park, just walking and talking and climbing trees. Just getting to know each other, know the stuff—the little things—that make us who we are. Our quirks, the inflections we place on certain words, how we move, how our eyes light up just before we're about to say something exciting.

Then, in the driveway, she asked if she could give me a kiss. I said yes and the rest, as they say, is history.

We celebrated Thanksgiving together, my birthday, Christmas, New Year's. I loved her so much, and she felt the same. There was this one time in December—on the first, actually—when I got up before six a.m. to deliver the morning paper (I had a paper route at the time), and there on the front step was a package for me. A decorated shoebox. I recognized her handwriting immediately and the drawings she had done on the box's lid.

I went back inside and took the box to my room. Upon opening it, I was greeted by the sweet smell of strawberries and vanilla wafting up from the light-blue fabric within. Cyan had put some of her perfume on it. I took the fabric out and, it having turned out to be a pillowcase, opened it to see what was inside.

It was a tape recorder, and on the PLAY button was a little piece of paper that read, "Play me."

And I did.

On that tape, my Cyan poured out her love for me, told me how much our being together meant to her, how it had changed her life. To this day, I can still hear—and feel—her words. Especially when she said, "I promise to love you from now until the end of eternity."

Once the tape was finished, a song came on. It was about Jesus' love for humanity and how He would do anything to be with us. Cyan later revealed that the song stood for how she felt about me, how she would do anything to ensure we'd always be together.

She was my angel.

At the beginning of January following our first, and only, New Year's, she and I became intimate with one another. She was the first girl I ever made love to; and even now I do not regret giving myself to her.

Then, as much as our expressions of love meant to each other, as much as how pure our uniting was...something happened. Something neither of us expected.

We broke up.

We had to. Her parents (and mine) found out we were sleeping together. This soon led to late-night talks with my folks, arguments, me trying to fathom how they couldn't understand that I loved Cyan. My angel had it rough at home, too. Because she was with me, it was making her home life difficult. Her parents wanted us apart.

We had a long talk one night, she and I, roughly two weeks after losing ourselves to—and in—each other; and the next morning, she and I broke up. We parted in tears, completely broken down inside.

It was a relief when, shortly after—a few days, maybe, I can't remember—she and I decided to fight for us. We did it by getting back together. Our parents fought back—four against two. We were young. We had no place to go and no one to turn to other than each other. In the end, after a period of breaking up and getting back together, trying so, so hard to make it work—we said goodbye for the final time.

These days, when I'm not writing, I think about her. Most of my poetry is about her. Nearly every night I dream about her, and when we're together in my dreams I am so happy. *Happy* actually isn't even a big enough word to describe it. When I'm with Cyan in my dreams, I'm at peace; my heart, still aching from losing her those many years ago, is finally at rest.

Then I wake up and want to die because my angel isn't with me. I've tried to kill myself, the pain of our separation being too much for me. Something broke inside when we parted. A nervous breakdown, some might say. I was admitted to the hospital and put on medication. I still take the pills today. My body's chemistry isn't right anymore. I also found out it was never right to begin with—I've always been predisposed to sadness and fear of loss. My psychiatrist calls this depression. And he's right—I am depressed. I still think of death more often than I should. More often than anyone should, for that matter.

But I'll stick around, because you never know. My prayer, the one I've prayed continuously for years, the one begging God to bring her back, to send her down to me again—might still be answered.

(PETER FOX is an author currently residing in Winnipeg, Manitoba.)

THE MIRACLE ROCK
By Dorothy Thompson

THEY BURIED MY BEST FRIEND ON SEPTEMBER 16, 2001, A DAY I'LL ALWAYS remember the rest of my life. This personal tragedy fell into my lap the same week the terrorists destroyed the lives of many Americans on Tuesday, September 11, 2001. Not only was I going through turmoil for my country, but I was grieving also for my friend, who will never see America, the land of the free and the brave, again.

The funeral was painful, as funerals often are; but the real pain lay in the story of my miracle rock, which I kept pressed against my bosom in the late-afternoon sun. I stood, clutching it in my sweaty palm, tears dripping from my swollen eyes. It was my savior that day, as security blankets often are.

I am a writer; and I write to get published, as any author wannabe will tell you. Writing is my forte, my dream, my conquest. No one in the world knew how strong my drive was more than a beautiful man named Mark. With encouragement and foresight, he prodded me along with a vengeance, believing in me all the while.

He was a quiet man, full of beauty and wisdom. An angel in disguise, he was.

I was waiting on tables, as my writing was at a standstill and bills were piling up. I understood the phrase "starving writer" first-hand. The restaurant was unusually quiet that night, and patrons coming through the door were greatly appreciated and welcomed warmly.

I seated a man accompanied by his son. I took their order and noticed what a warm smile he wore on his weathered face. Having a boyfriend at the time, I did not talk much. As I took his order, I noticed the camaraderie he and his son shared as they played

Hangman on bits of torn napkins. I took drinks to them, he cordially thanked me and I carried on my business as usual.

I went home to my boyfriend, never giving the stranger with the kind smile another thought. A few nights later, he came into the restaurant alone and gazed at me a little differently than he had before. Remembering the generous tip he had left me the last time, I gave him the best service I could.

We struck up a conversation, exchanging tales of our sons, the loves of our lives. As it turned out, he had been through some rough times, with his ex-wife trying to keep his son away from him. As he talked, I saw pain behind his sea-blue eyes. However, he had seen the pain in mine first.

I felt an urge to talk to this man, never quite understanding the source of this impulse. I felt comfortable opening up to him and told him about my problems with my boyfriend. I told him I was trying to work things out, but I guess my sagging enthusiasm showed.

He offered me his guidance. I savored his words as if it were my soul talking to me. There was a strange bond between this stranger and I, a bond that crossed barriers of time. It was a connection of kindred spirits in a time of despair. I felt like a weight had been lifted off me.

My boyfriend had no idea I was conversing with this stranger. It was hard for me not to acknowledge the strong pull I had with this man, and I found myself confused about the feelings that were raging inside of me.

I saw the stranger again a week later. It seemed he could not resist the strong pull himself. I started telling him about my aspirations to become a professional writer. He read my articles and was deeply impressed.

"These need to be published," he would say.

I saw him a few times after that, pushing manuscripts in front of his nose for his careful scrutiny. We laughed, we talked, we cried together. I found I could tell him anything, and he could do likewise.

I had written children's stories when I was a young mother, and I told him to read them for me. I remember him sitting at table 13 concentrating on every word. He looked up at me proudly. I knew without him saying a word that my time had come.

I sent off *No More Gooseberry Pie!* to a publisher, and a month later there was a contract in the mail.

We celebrated spiritually. As we were just friends, albeit very close friends by that time, I felt comfortable in accepting his invitation to his house tucked in the pines. I knew this was wrong, but my inner voice was telling me otherwise.

He cooked dinner for me, and we shared deep conversations under the glow of the candlelight. We talked about goals in life, our children and our respective futures. We talked about journeys we had traveled and journeys yet to take. We talked about dreams we had lost and dreams we had yet to find.

We continued our conversations for a year, until our friendship was interrupted. My boyfriend found our relationship to be too close, and he forbade me to ever see Mark again. I understood the reason for his demands and questioned if I were doing the right thing by continuing to see this man, even though in my heart I knew it was right.

Because I felt the situation wasn't fair to either of them, I decided I had to make a decision. That decision was to do what was proper by society's standards and tell my twin soul I couldn't see him anymore. It broke my heart; but little did I know, it would break his permanently.

I made one last visit to him. The look on my face told him what he dreaded to hear. He did not cry and tried to act brave, but he knew this would be the last visit I would ever make to him. His face suddenly seemed much older, and I knew my bad news took every bit of life from him.

This was the hardest thing I had ever done in my life, but I felt that it was best for all involved. I did not want to hurt him anymore, even thought the pain in my own heart was unbearable.

Before I turned to leave, he pressed an object into my hand. I opened my palm and saw that it was a blue rock with the inscription "Miracles." I looked at him, at the tears in his eyes, and knew the hidden meaning in this gift. It would take nothing short of a miracle for us to be together. I was unable to speak. I put the rock in my purse and went home.

The days passed, and I couldn't get my mind off my friend, my mentor. I couldn't understand the concept of loving only one person to the exclusion of all others. They say a soul mate doesn't have to be your boyfriend or your husband. A soul mate is one who connects with you on an astral plane. Perhaps it is someone you knew from another life. Perhaps it is your life partner, transcending the ages.

Knowing that, I also knew that the present man in my life was meant to be. He was my companion soul mate and had come into my life for a reason. He was part of my life's journey, and I knew that I would come to understand the meaning of his presence as I explored my past, present and future with him. I decided to work things out and continue my relationship with him, thinking that this was for the best.

A couple weeks later, I learned my twin soul had died.

They found him on September 14, lying in his son's room. Perhaps this is where he wanted to be when he took his last breath. The coroner's report stated that he had an enlarged heart. I could have told them he had a heart the size of Manhattan.

I stood at the funeral with tears on my face as I watched his brave son sitting next to his mother and grandparents beside the coffin of my best friend. He wore tears of pain, as did most on that tearful day. I leaned over and told him to give me a hug. I whispered in his ear, "Your father loved you, don't ever forget that." He nodded like he understood.

I leaned down to Mark's stepmother, whom he often talked about fondly. I introduced myself. I told her I was a writer, and that her stepson was my best friend. She smiled at me and said that he had said good things about me. I will never forget it. Feeling at first like an outsider, I started to sense a common bond, as if I were one of them. We were all there together, grieving for my friend who would never experience the love of his family and friends again.

That rock that says "Miracles" took on a new meaning that day. As I stood by Mark's casket with tears streaming down my face, I knew. Mark was in Heaven playing with the angels now, but he would always be there for me. He was my miracle, and I knew he would guide me the rest of my earthbound days.

My Miracle rock sits beside me every day, wrapped in the tearstained tissue I used at the funeral. Whenever I get upset, all I have to do is hold it in my palm; and suddenly, I am calm. Mark had that effect on me—then and now.

I know I will see my friend one day. The miracle then will be the everlasting love of our Savior, who put him in my life for eternity.

(DOROTHY THOMPSON is an author, editor, journalist and professional reviewer currently living on the Eastern Shore of Virginia.)

MY SPIRIT'S BELOVED
By Janice Romney Farnsworth

AUTUMN FINALLY ARRIVED AFTER MONTHS OF UNRELENTING, SULTRY summer nights. The air was crisp, with bright orange leaves dancing in cool breezes, and I welcomed the change. After many years of sorrow, I felt liberated from the past's formidable chains of violence in my marriage and problems with my children—my life had new meaning, and I was healing.

The last thing I was looking for was romance. I wasn't ready. I certainly didn't trust in my ability to choose wisely after a frightening fifteen-year marriage to an abusive man. That marriage was finally over, but much had been destroyed, and I needed healing time.

My children and I had moved to a small town in old Mexico. They were thriving in a safe environment but still struggled with the effects of their traumatic childhoods. More than anything else, I just wanted to feel whole again and enjoy nurturing and caring for them.

But time seemed to fly! Eight months after I filed for divorce, I received my decree, which gave me tremendous relief for the chance to start over.

And then I started dreaming of a man without a face.

It all started with a desire for deep spiritual inner healing and a longing to know my soul's destiny. Somewhere within the deepest portion of my being a voice called out to me, and I knew there was something grand in store—a bright future with a soul mission.

I couldn't stop searching for answers that would shed light on my deepest feelings. Each day brought an array of new challenges. I was healing yet I still struggled with physical debilities and depression. I sensed angels watching over me—I could feel their presence—and each day I felt drawn closer to their love, wisdom and power. Learning from my inner wisdom, I felt divinely guided. But each time I strengthened in my intuitiveness, I was challenged to trust even more in an unseen power.

Late one night, feelings of unrest made it difficult for me to sleep and so I got out of bed and went into my living room. I lit several candles and played soft music. I gathered my scattered thoughts inside a bubble of light I visualized surrounding me and let go of fear and silenced my inner turmoil.

Feeling safe and protected, my thoughts and feelings seemed to leave this earth plane and enter a different realm where nothing seemed impossible. Much later, I went back to bed and drifted off to sleep.

That night, a vivid dream caused me to feel wide-awake. A tender feeling of love captivated me as I felt myself crossing the threshold of a sacred chamber where the angels of love untie heart and soul; I felt the fire of my heart beat with a love so rare. Mesmerized by dancing candlelight, I was in a garden of dreams, where the sounds of music played in a higher octave, and I felt the presence of my beloved. Not once did I see his face, and yet the love we shared in silence was mesmerizing.

Without a doubt, I knew this man and yet we had never met. I didn't know his name or see his face, but he was real to me—and so was the love I felt flowing between us.

Several nights later, he was once again with me. Not a word was spoken, just two hearts beating in the silence. Then soothing waves of love flowed through me, and I felt healing rays of light comforting my soul.

In awe, I awoke. In disbelief, I made my way through the day, longing to return to that other place, to feel that love so tender and so rare. Yet I wondered. *What is happening to me?*

The world around me no longer seemed real. I felt separated, as though a part of me were transcended into another dimension. With each passing day, my longing grew deeper. Each night I wanted to dance the night away in rhythm with the stars and feel his hand in mine. My soul yearned to wake in that same bed of sacred fire, the fusion of eternal love. I was in love with a faceless man, a man who did not exist except in my dreams.

Several more nights passed. I had the same dream again, but this time I awoke before morning; and I felt the presence of spiritual beings. A voice whispered from my bedside, infusing my heart with knowledge of another time. Dimmed by years of separation, this sacred love had reunited my soul, and I could not deny it.

"You have known him for all time," she whispered, so low I wasn't sure she had spoken at all.

For weeks I lived in a world where poets find the visions that touch the hearts of those who listen and paint the world with breathless moments of ecstasy. I felt powerless to change this mysterious course. I was a ship lost at sea, guided fearlessly through dense fog and raging waters to where two hearts were one, drawing nearer to their eternal source of life.

When I alone could not understand, God made sure someone else would enter my life to provide the answers. In this I believe Spirit does work in mysterious ways.

During this time I went to visit a wise and spiritually gifted teacher who had a message for me. She said, "Janice, soon you will be reunited with a man who has always loved you."

My first thought was to ask her, "How did you know about my dreams?" But I didn't say anything other than to respond with "You mean someone like my soul mate?"

She answered me, "Oh, no, my dear, this one goes much deeper than that. He is your twin flame."

She went on to explain that he had promised before God and the angels that he would be here on earth with me. Patiently, he would wait until my soul had reached a certain level of understanding and awareness; and when the time came, he would enter my life.

Where was he? Did he live close by? How would we ever find one another? Did he know about me? I was reassured that the moment we met he would know—his soul would tell him. Still, it seemed impossible.

I wept oceans of tears that day, and tears continued to blur my vision as I drove three hundred miles home; but they were tears of joy and thanksgiving. I felt my soul's rejoicing, knowing that my spiritual journey was now taking flight. In solemn humility, I gave thanks to God and to His endearing and loving angels who had stayed with me, who had rescued my soul from the earth's cold grave so it might complete its most sacred mission. I so much wanted to shout to the world. I wanted to share my heart's deepest feelings, but they were sacred messages from Heaven and not everyone would understand.

Once again I was to learn patience. But what is patience? Patience was something I had yet to experience, or at least to master. Besides, patience always seemed to be a fool's word to me. Those who are patient miss out in life; and if I didn't do something, my beloved and I would simply be two ships passing silently in the night.

I had no idea where to start looking. Where I lived was so remote and distant from any possible romantic encounter that I almost lost faith in divine intervention or in Cupid's magic.

Several months later, my mother asked me to join her and my sisters for a Christmas holiday in Utah. My children had plans to stay with their father, so I would be alone in my small red-brick home on Christmas Eve. My answer was no. A strong intuitive feeling let me know I wouldn't be alone.

A loving messenger came to me one night in early December, just weeks before my children would be leaving for Arizona, and told me that the time was drawing closer, but that I was to be patient.

"Don't interfere once you know his name," she said. "The time must be right."

Then, one afternoon, I was styling Aunt Marene's hair. She really wasn't my aunt, but I felt close to her. I rode horses with her sons and often had dinner with them in the evenings. Casually, she mentioned her nephew, who happened to be single. She said, "I would love to introduce you to him, but I know he's not interested in raising six children."

I thought, that's fine. I always knew a divorced mother with six children might not appeal to most men.

"Besides," she said, "Richard is flying to California in a few weeks to meet some woman who knows his sister."

My heart stopped beating. I literally froze. The name sent an electrical charge through me that left me weak in the knees. I was breathless. That same feeling came over me, the one I felt in my dreams. Then I panicked.

"What do you mean, he's flying off to California to meet some strange woman?" And I really was demanding an answer from her.

Aunt Marene didn't bat an eyelash. "Why shouldn't he?" she asked.

"Because he belongs to me!" I shouted.

I put down the comb, told her I had to leave and rushed out of the room. In a panic, I thought, what am I do to? What if he falls head-over-heels in love with this woman and marries her? I was completely beside myself, and yet I felt helpless.

Then I had an idea. I threw caution to the wind, completely turned a deaf ear to the angel's warnings and took matters in my own hands. I just couldn't leave something this important in the hands of someone I couldn't see...

Later that night I called Jay, Aunt Marene's son, who also happens to be Richard's cousin. I wasn't helpless after all. Innocently, without trying to sound desperate, I asked Jay to set me up with his cousin. I silenced the little annoying warnings that crept into my heart, and kindly told the angels to mind their own business—I wasn't about to take any chances. Richard could marry this other woman before we ever met. It was up to me—at least, that's what I said to myself.

Jay didn't hesitate. He told me he would get in touch with Richard that night. Sitting on pins and needles, I had to wait several hours for Jay to call me back. I didn't want him to know how frantic I was, so I remained inside my home, acting calm and patient (I can do that, although sometimes it isn't easy).

Finally, Jay called me back. He had reached Richard, who was living in Tucson, that night; and he was quite proud of himself. He said he did a real good job selling the idea of meeting me (due to that fact I was a mother of six children) to his cousin. In fact, he said, he did such a good job that Richard actually sounded really interested. Little did he know he was bringing together a match made in heaven and his skills didn't have anything to do with it.

Jay said something a little strange, though. He told Richard he would have to wait until Sunday to call me. That was seven days, approximately 336 hours away. For a moment I was furious with him. I thought that was such a dumb thing for him to say, and now I was still going to have to wait.

I counted the days and the hours and the minutes until the hour he was to call me. Finally, the moment arrived. The clock on my mantle said it was four p.m. I sat calmly by the telephone waiting. I waited and I waited, but it didn't ring. Then it dawned on me—there was an hour difference between my hometown and Richard's. I still had one more hour to go.

Normally, Sunday afternoons were peaceful at my home. The kids were usually tired and either watched TV or took a nap. Today was different. I just know Justin could feel it in the air—his mom was waiting for another man to call her. That didn't go over too well, so he started complaining. Then he started fighting with anyone who would fight back. He had everyone in an uproar; that's when he really started irritating me. I was waiting for the most important phone call of my life, and my son was acting like a spoiled two-year-old.

The phone rang. Justin grabbed it, and I knew he wasn't going to let me talk to Richard. I threatened him with his life if he didn't hand over that receiver. First, he played a little game. He said he was going to hang up, and I was praying that Richard couldn't hear us on the other end. Finally, Justin gave me the phone, but he wasn't ready to give up that easily. I had to ask Richard to hold on while I went to find Rob.

Rob is bigger than Justin, and I knew that if anyone could drag Justin outside and sit on him until I was finished, he could. He was only too happy to oblige. But, acting like a bully, he only made things worse as he grabbed Justin by the ankles, dragging him outside. I was dying of sheer embarrassment as I tried to cover the receiver with my hand so Richard couldn't hear what was going on.

Then, while Justin was outside in the yard screaming at Robby to get off him, I was huddled in the bathroom, sitting on the toilet seat with the water running and the door closed, trying to calm my nerves while softly speaking to Richard as if nothing was happening outside. I knew he heard the chaos, but he didn't let on. His voice was soothing, loving, kind and gentle with a wonderful sense of humor. I melted into a puddle of emotions sitting on that toilet seat.

We made our plans that afternoon. I was to take my children to Mesa on December twenty-first to drop them off at their dad's. Then I was to spend the night at a friend's house and return to Tucson by noon the following day.

Early the morning of the twenty-first I woke to heaven's melody, my soul's love song, feeling happier than I had ever felt before. I dressed with care. There was an inner glow about me. At that moment, I was a winter's bride in glistening snow waiting to take the hand of her beloved, to stand before God and the angels to reconfirm sacred vows made long ago. Of course, there wasn't any snow, since we were in Arizona, and I wasn't betrothed to anyone; yet in silence I listened to the whisperings of my soul, and I knew where my journey would soon take me.

Just off the freeway as you first enter Tucson's city limits is a MacDonald's. Richard had said to stop there and call him. He lived just minutes away and said he would meet me there. Nervous, I pulled into the parking lot wondering if he had already arrived. Of course, if he were, would we recognize each other? I didn't have a clue, I just remember shaking like a leaf.

The telephone was inside by the restrooms. Timidly I walked to them, knowing I had to call him, and I couldn't chicken out; but I was so nervous. I went into the bathroom, stared at the face in the mirror and couldn't help but wonder: am I still pretty enough?

I left the bathroom and stood by the pay phone—hours could have passed or just minutes, but I know I stood there for a long time. I didn't dare dial his number.

A stranger walked up to me, looking right at me; and he spoke. For a moment my heart stopped. If this is him, I thought, I'm running.

I wasn't the least bit interested in the looks of this quaint little stranger. With a blank look on my face I asked him if he was there waiting to meet someone and he said, "No, but I would like to use the phone, so if you're not going to call anyone, would you please move out of the way?"

Relief washed over me as I nervously laughed and said, "Thank God, you're not Richard."

That's when I found the courage to call him. He couldn't look any worse than that quaint little stranger.

His voice—and I still love to hear his voice today—was quick to answer. I told him I would be waiting outside the front door of MacDonald's. I thought I would die a thousand deaths before he got there; then all of a sudden there he was. Instantly, he recognized me. He knew my mother, and he said I looked just like her.

I don't know that I saw his face. I was still so nervous that I hardly said a word, but I do remember following behind him in my car. Over a dusty, unpaved road, I sped to keep up with him. From a distance, I saw a shadow of a spirit embodied in a man I had never met before; but my heart was in love with his soul, and for a moment I felt suffocated in my body. I wanted to soar through the air, above the blue yonder and return home again with my beloved. Two stars created from a flame of light fell to the earth years ago, each vowing to find each other; and this was that day, and my heart rejoiced.

Still, life had given me many hard lessons; and my body felt it, and I was still trying to grasp the strangeness of this whole situation. His face wasn't familiar at all, and yet I loved him long before we met and a part of me was frightened. I wanted to turn my car around and drive across the desert and disappear into the fading sunset. Then I thought, No, I'll stop and sit in the hot, scorching sun until reason returns. That shouldn't take long—even in December the desert is hot in mid-afternoon.

I was willing to ask anyone who would listen, even if my only audience was a prairie dog, if they thought I was a fool to allow my heart to feel again, to love and to trust again?

The moment I walked through his door, I knew I had been there before. What I saw was a little different from my dream, but the feeling was one of familiarity, one of being home. We talked for hours, not as strangers but as one in heart and spirit separated not by choice but by what had to be. When I looked into his eyes, the windows to his soul, I knew I had no secrets from him. He knew me, he really knew me!

Years of pain dimmed in my memory; a heart scorched and withered felt renewed, alive and so filled with joy. I felt myself wanting to reach out, grab him, love him or curse him for making me go through life without him. *Where have you been?* my heart screamed over and over. Part of me was angry with him, but I loved him. I had no doubt.

Then my head would begin to reason, and I couldn't believe my own feelings.

Soon, darkness covered the earth like a thick blanket; yet even in the shadows, I felt his light. My eyes drank in each line on his face, mesmerized by his smile and captivated by the way his eyes warmed my soul. I didn't want to move from where we were sitting, as if that would awaken me from my dream. In his presence, I felt at home. Curled up on his couch, I was where I belonged. I had finally come home, and sharing my heart with him reminded me of a burning fire warming me from the chilling winter's wind. Dear God, I silently prayed, please be with me.

No one remarries after a year and a half of being single. No one remarries after they have six children by another man and expects someone else to help raise them. No one says "I do" before they are even asked. No one agrees to say "I do" even if they are asked hours after they first meet. No one remarries when they carry wounds from the past inside their hearts and if they do, do they make it? Thousands of questions raced through my mind. But my greatest fear was this: can a new marriage survive my children and me?

For a moment, I prayed that he would just love me, if only for a night.

We dressed for dinner. He said he was taking me out, even though I don't know why. My heart was dancing the tango, my stomach was filled with butterflies and my head was spinning with too many questions, but I was lost in love. We drove to Red Lobster and went inside. He couldn't stop touching me—my hand, my back. But it was the gentleness with which he spoke that endeared him closest to my heart. I did have to silence my laughter—he seemed as giddy as I. We weren't young teenagers on our first date. We were both older, divorced and experienced; yet we seemed even more vulnerable than young lovers blinded by romance and lust.

I hardly touched my food. It's just that way for me when I'm nervous. I simply shift my food from one side of my plate to the other.

The waitresses were getting ready to close the restaurant. Not once, from the moment we met, did his eyes lose sight of mine; and not once did the feeling go away that he knew what I knew. I had no doubt.

Finally, after talking straight through dinner, I was hungry; but by then my food was cold, and the waitress had cleared our table. It was time to go home—and that's when the little heart flutterings started all over again. We were going home...where we would be alone.

Richard wanted to know everything about me and my past. I told him about my children. I know what I said affected him, but he didn't run. I couldn't tell him enough. It was the sharing that I longed for; just to talk to him was healing, and, somehow, he was part of my past. He felt my pain, and I was in awe with his compassion.

Our journeys in life had been as different as night and day, and yet similar. Once I was a battered wife; his ex had many faces, and sometimes she was violent. There was a parallel of different experiences that bonded us, and yet he was not wounded. His soul remained untouched. What he had experienced gave him understanding and compassion while he remained strong and resilient. I knew that he would have to be if he were to live with me.

When the hour approached early morning, it was time to go to sleep. I stayed in his guest room upstairs and yet felt close to him despite floors and closed doors. The next morning we were to make plans.

It felt wonderful to wake knowing I was there with him. As I look back over those first few days with Richard, they remain as the most precious and sacred memories of my life with him. It is difficult to recreate those memories through my writing—they simply escape their capture on paper—but they are here in my heart; and tears easily flow as I remember how dearly and how deeply he loved me. I knew it long before he said the words.

We were ready to go out again when I gently touched his hand. Instantly, he responded. He turned to me and held me close as though he would never let me go. With tears streaming down his face he whispered, "I love you."

At that very moment, without a doubt, we both knew we would marry and be husband and wife. Even without the ceremony and that piece of paper that verifies it, we were, from that moment on, inseparably one.

The night before, when I had left him and gone upstairs to bed, he closed his door behind him. From the moment we met, he had felt a rush of emotions swelling into a river of love. Separated from me after our being together for the first time, his spirit mourned. Wanting to feel me close again, he finally drifted into a restless sleep, only to awaken.

"I'm in love with her," he said over and over, "but I can't take on six children, seven with my own."

And yet, without a doubt, this love he felt went beyond physical desire and left him weak and willing to surrender. Richard was torn between his love and reality.

That night, in his dreams, a messenger appeared to him, vivid and so real; and he felt more alive and in tune with each word that was said to him. *Your love is not a love of this world, and this love will carry you through difficult times. You need only trust in your feelings and always keep your heart open, for this is where we will guide you.*

I had been honest with Richard from the very beginning. He knew that my little family was shattered by the violence we had lived through. I was recovering, but I still had a long way to go. For years I had battled against debilitating depression, and it wasn't that long ago that a breakdown had left me unable to cope with tying my shoes, taking a bath or combing my hair. Worst of all, depression had robbed me of time with my children.

Now, listening to him speak of his experience, my heart stood still. I didn't dare let go and just breathe. Instead, I found refuge in his warm embrace. As the wings of a bird open as it takes flight, my soul drifted into another realm; and I felt the heavens open and rejoice at the reunion of twin flames. I felt his heart beating, his breath upon my hair and his hands gently wiping away my tears; and my soul wept within the depths of my heart. I softly whispered to it, He knew, just like my spirit teacher said he would. Without a doubt, his soul remembered; and soon I will be his winter bride.

The sounds of Christmas played throughout his house as Richard prepared dinner for his mom and dad and his siblings. If they were positively shocked at our engagement—they didn't say a word. But they were happy for us. Later that evening I silently gave thanks for that intuitive feeling. A message from heaven had reassured me I wouldn't be alone on Christmas Eve, and this was my gift: sharing sacred moments with my spirit's beloved.

Monday morning we drove to the county jail. Richard had remembered that they offered marriage licenses to the public; and since we were in such a hurry, it didn't seem all that unromantic to fill one out in such a place. Later, with papers in hand, he took me to buy a wedding ring. Excitement filled the air as we walked into a jewelry store in the mall. I was to choose my favorite wedding band, he said, one that symbolized a circle of eternal love. One ring caught my eye, Victorian in design and majestic in simplicity. I said, "This is the one."

Once he purchased the ring, he asked for my hand, right there in front of the sales clerk. For the first time, I protested. I whispered in his ear, "Now this isn't exactly what I would call romantic. Can't you find somewhere away from gazing eyes to slide that ring on my finger?"

Without hesitating, he swept me out of the store; and dancing through flocks of Christmas shoppers, he guided me to a more romantic place—in between racks of clothing in Dillards Department Store. Bedazzled by his overture of rapture and romance, I looked around me.

"How appropriate," I said. "Now we're alone, hidden behind women's intimate apparel—how could any other place be more romantic?" I giggled with girlish laughter as Richard took my hand in his, placed the ring on my finger and gently kissed my lips.

We must have been in a world of our own that day. It just didn't enter our minds that someone else might think we were a little too hasty in our decision to marry, but the bishop did.

This is something I know I cannot explain—you would just have to have been there. As soon as we arrived home, Richard called his bishop to ask him if he would marry us that evening. Without knowing all the little details, the bishop gave us the hour to be at his home. The only suitable dress I had with me was one of black lace. Knowing that black isn't exactly what one should wear to her own wedding. I hastily gave the dress a blessing. Besides, what else was I to do?

At eight o'clock that night we arrived on the bishop's doorstep. The moment he heard how we met he said, "What do you mean, you've only known each other for three days?" His eyes were wide as saucers. In shock, he asked, "Are you sure you want me to marry you?"

At first he just couldn't do it. No one gets married after knowing each other for three days, unless they are insane. I know that's exactly what he was thinking; but you must remember, this happened eight years ago and today we're still married. Of course, the bishop was wise enough to know what generally happens when people fall in love overnight and get married the next morning.

Finally, he consented, but before the ceremony he sat us both down to give us a Bishop's Counsel. He sat behind his desk, and we sat across from him. He opened his book with great care, as if to stall for a few more precious moments; as he spoke he would roll his eyes around in complete circles and raise his eyebrows until they reached the tip of his hair on his head.

Once again he read from his book. He talked about simple things, such as the importance of holy matrimony, but he just couldn't continue it. It must have seemed so absurd to him—two people sitting across from him asking to be married three days after meeting.

Exasperated, he closed his book, exclaiming, "Are you guys sure about this?" Then he waved his arms, saying, "Of course, you must know what you're doing, but are you sure you know what you're doing?"

Richard was fifty-three, and I was thirty-nine. I'm sure he was thinking age doesn't have anything to do with how foolish people can be.

Knowing that we weren't about to change our minds, we followed him into his living room. where he performed our wedding ceremony. We exchanged our vows, and Richard placed the wedding ring on my finger. The bishop and his wife gave us both hugs and said they were happy for us, but I would have loved to remain behind as a fly on the wall just to hear their conversation once we closed their front door.

Without any fanfare, we simply drove away. Now I had to go home and call my mother.

To be honest, I didn't dare call my mother for several days. I had a ring on my finger, and I was lawfully married; but when I last saw my mother, I didn't even have a guy in my life. I knew she would fly through the ceiling when I broke the news to her.

Soon, the word was out. Richard had called his Aunt Marene, which was like putting an ad on the front page of the town's only newspaper. Phones were ringing off the hook, and everyone called Aunt Marene to hear it straight from her. You'd think no one had ever been married in this small town before, or just maybe no one expected me to get married.

Finally, I called my mother. She was still visiting with my sisters in Salt Lake City. When I first told her she said, "You're just kidding me, aren't you?" When I told her no, she handed the phone over to my sister. I could hear her say, "Janice is just playing a game with me. Tell her it isn't funny."

My sister Marsha immediately grabbed the phone and said, "Janice, you're really not serious, are you?" When I said yes, she laughed and said, "I don't believe you." Over and over I tried to convince her that I really was married. She just couldn't stop screaming, "No, you're not, you couldn't be."

I eventually realized how crazy I really did sound. I finally said, "Don't sound so panicked, Marsha. Of course, I'm just kidding."

We said goodbye, and I hung up. Richard walked into the room and asked, "How did it go?"

I told him they wouldn't believe me so I had just agreed with them and said we really weren't married. A few hours later, I called my sister back and told her not to say a word, but just listen. I explained to her how I felt and what had happened between Richard and I; and that, yes, we were married.

There was a long silence at the other end of the phone. This time Marsha believed me. Stunned, she didn't say a word until I said, "It's okay. I know how you must feel, but just tell Mom for me."

A few days later, Richard and I flew to Salt Lake and talked with my mother and sisters in person. It took my mom a while before she

45

could talk without crying. She had witnessed many years of her daughter's unhappiness. I never told them how violent my ex-husband was during our marriage, but the signs were impossible to deny; and once I left him, my secret wasn't a secret anymore. After my divorce, my mother experienced the devastation of that violent marriage with me and my children. I worried her day and night because I was so physically and emotionally ill.

She was gravely concerned for me now that I had jumped so quickly into a new marriage, until she had spent some time with us. It was evident to everyone that this marriage was meant to be, and she gave me her blessings.

Richard and I had awakened in spirit to remember what had dimmed long ago, and we were blissfully happy. A lover's glow emanated from our hearts, reaching into those of others; and our soul love was felt at the deepest level. Our marriage is a marriage of our souls; this love is incomparable—it is the essence of this pure love that reminds and inspires others with its power.

Christ taught that unless marriage is transformed by the Holy Spirit it will only be an outer experience, that there is a sealing of this interchange of souls in the purity of God's love. It is the most sacred of ceremonies ever performed and a reunion of spirits created as one, embodied in mortality as two.

The following years were difficult ones. Even though his love was healing and I was happier than I had ever been, my little family completely unraveled and fell apart. Over the next four years, I struggled to survive. Deep in depression and addicted to a variety of prescription drugs, I was unable to cope. Knowing our soul's commitment, and the purpose of my incarnation, he never gave up. When it was necessary, he uprooted my youngest three children and me and moved us to a better place. He made difficult choices in which he was required to sacrifice many things, but his choice was always to follow his heart.

At first I was angry with him; I didn't understand why he was taking me away from a home we had built together, the only home in which I felt safe—and yet I wasn't.

Over the following years, healing angels stayed with me, mending

46

a heart and body that had been severely ravaged by emotional pain. I felt that I had entered the threshold of purifying fire and crossed the bridge of pain in order to be with my twin flame and begin our spiritual journey hand-in-hand. Even though our life together has not been easy, not once have we lost our soul's love. With his undying love, his unabated devotion and his soul's memory, not once has Richard missed a beat in romancing my heart and keeping alive this seed of dreams. Not once did he give up on me.

Angels have always journeyed with us. They have always been by our sides, even when I doubted and floundered in this world of mine that doesn't allow me to believe in myself. Not once did they give up on me. Together, Richard and I have nurtured and nourished with the light of love a tiny seed that we planted—the seed of dreams, the seed of spiritual healing for other women: a book entitled *Beneath Wings of An Angel*. With the angels' faith and Richard's unwavering belief in me, I never gave up.

Today many things have changed in our family. The worst is over. I have healed, and my children are learning. My book has been completed, and our spiritual mission is just beginning. The power and the glory to my life with Richard is that through valleys of tears and rivers of pain he never once lost sight of his promise to be my guiding star, my anchor in a storm, my friend and my lover. The light of his divine love has been my magnet, pulling me from a world of darkness filled with burden and turmoil into a world of peace. His love vibrates at the frequency that breaks away the hardness of my outer shell, and his sacred love opened my heart so that the light of my soul shines forth. He is my spirit's beloved.

(JANICE ROMNEY FARNSWORTH is an author currently residing in Arizona.)

TIME WILL TELL
By Ellen Godwin

SHE LOVES HER HUSBAND. SHE LOVES HER CHILDREN WITH A FEROCITY THAT would shock one who hasn't any. And she loves another who cannot be in her life right now. Fate has plans for them - she feels it, but now is not the time. It is as if she is the alpha female wolf and her husband is the alpha male; but on a distant hilltop there sits another, howling to let his presence be known, awaiting his turn to be her mate. There is little that she can do for she is where she belongs at the moment, raising her cubs with protectiveness and pride; but she lives with the knowledge that she is destined for something else as well.

We've many soul mates in the life of a soul. In some lives we may encounter only one, but in other lives there may be many more. It is the intricate web of the spiritual world that weaves us together. Our souls enter into life again and again, on paths of lessons that need to be learned. Into each life we bring our lesson plans, and for each of these there is a teacher. Over the span of many lifetimes, we develop relationships and find soul mates. Some are found within the family, such as a grandparent connection - one who will teach you unconditional love. Some are deep friendships, where we may learn the value of support and companionship. And some are the romantic version found in books; these give us joy and, most important, love of self and the gift of giving abundant love in return.

She met him in junior high school. They sat together in science class for three years, where their knees touched under the table and their arms brushed as they took notes. She was intensely shy, and he was immature. They were friends, but she was secretly in love.

Perhaps he was, too. At school dances they would always make it a point to share one slow dance together. It was as if they knew, even then, that there was something there to be kept alive.

Years passed, and in the months prior to graduation she met her husband-to-be. She flaunted his attention in front of the other boy, wanting to make him jealous enough to take action. She desperately wanted him to take a stand and be honest with her. He took it as a sign that she had moved on.

Four more years passed, and she'd been married for over a year when she got a letter from him. He said he was ready to settle down. He seemed to be feeling her out. She called him and heard in his voice that which she'd longed to hear all through school. He wanted her and was no longer afraid to let her know. But she was married, and she loved her husband. She let him know, and she didn't hear from him for many years.

Every so often she would hear of him, though. Old school friends took note of him and let her know what he was up to. Every now and then she longed to go to him. Her children kept her mind off of him for the most part - babies need so much love and care.

Time ticked away and she started dieting to prepare for her high school reunion. A school dance. She wrote to him and asked him to save her a dance for old times.

The reunion night came; and she was as nervous as she had been back in school, waiting for him to pass her a note. Her husband at her side, she enjoyed meeting her old friends. She watched the door with anticipation and was disappointed when he didn't arrive. After a few drinks, she made her way to a payphone in the lobby and called his childhood home.

He wouldn't be coming.

She decided to stay in town for a few days while her husband returned home. Feeling a need to take action, she called again; and this time he answered. With more bravery than she actually felt she told him about the reunion, chided him for missing their traditional dance and asked him to meet her at a restaurant that night - chaperoned, of course, by her closest girlfriend.

They met and fell into their seats like they had never been apart. Hours flew by as they talked of life and she learned he had never married. They wondered aloud why they had never gotten together, and each stated that the other had always had someone else in their life. When her chaperone had to take a bathroom break for all of the beer they were drinking, she was not surprised and very pleased when he looked at her directly.

"Are you happy?" he asked.

The moment is frozen in her mind. She lied. "Yes."

Just a week later she wrote to him from her home some four hundred miles away and told him that she'd lied. She wasn't happy but couldn't do anything about it, for she couldn't bear to hurt her children. He didn't write back.

Three years later she found herself back in the same restaurant. She'd dropped him a note letting him know she'd be there with the same girlfriend. The women talked for quite awhile, and she shared her feelings with her friend. Her marriage felt like a brother/sister relationship. She loved her husband and believed she was supposed to stay with him, but she felt there should be more in life. She wondered if she could ever do anything about it.

As she looked up from their serious conversation, there he was, walking toward them. They kissed hello, and he sat down next to her. A feeling of completeness came over her. She was comfortable and wonderfully anxious at the same time.

Then he asked her, "Still married?"

She answered, yes, eleven years next month.

He said, "You're an example for us all. Congratulations."

And she thought, yeah, an example of what not to do.

So, are we destined to be with every soul mate that enters into our lives? Time will tell. Perhaps these two are meant to be together later in this life. Or perhaps they will have to wait until the next.

(ELLEN GODWIN is the pseudonym of a real live person who is an author and editor under her own name, which will remain anonymous.)

HEARTS BEATING TO THE SAME DRUM
By Athena Sydney

MY WORLD TURNED UPSIDE DOWN WHEN I MET HIM.
It took just one look; our eyes locked and our souls recognized each other. Soul twins -that is what we are, that is what we will remain always. Even though our paths have taken opposite directions, the bond between us will stand the test of time, and our hearts will continue to beat to the same drum.

I was nineteen years old when I met him in London. His Australian accent brought goose bumps to my skin; it was so exotic, yet so familiar. Our eyes met, and it was as if the world stood still for several minutes. My heart skipped a few beats, and I got lost in the depths of his eyes.

At first, I was sure it was just a physical attraction, but it proved to be so much more. His fiancée threw angry looks my way, for she must have felt the instant attraction of our souls - she soon disappeared from his life.

Our relationship started off as a friendship because he was engaged and I was also involved with someone—the time just wasn't right. As a matter of fact, until now, the time has never been right for us. But I am getting ahead of my story.

I remember the day a bomb exploded in the area where we both worked. I was standing opposite the hotel when the roof blew off and flames shot from the window into a tree that stood right across from it. After the initial shock, I wondered how he was doing yet at the same time I knew he was okay. However, I didn't see him until late that evening, and as I sipped my Tia Maria and Coke, I was relieved to see him.

Then I got fired from the hotel where I worked, and I applied for a job at the London Hilton, which I got. I moved to the other side of town and didn't see him for a few weeks. When we did hook up, both available this time, we kissed for the first time.

We had a steamy fling until something else got in the way , and we broke up. I can't remember the exact reason. I can remember being all broken up about it. Soon after, my knee started playing up from being on my feet all day. I had to return home; but before I did, I walked - or should I say skipped - to the hospital, and I bumped into him on the streets of London.

He carefully touched my face as he asked what had happened. He grinned as I told him I had torn the ligaments in my knee a few months earlier when I went skiing for the first—and the last—time. I had wanted it to heal fast; and when I took on the job at the Hilton as a restaurant hostess, I hadn't thought about my knee at all.

He smiled when he told me he'd never seen snow in his life, and that he was about to embark on a trip across all of Europe. He couldn't wait to see the snow fall and to just play around in it. The expression on his face was like that of a child seeing snow for the very first time in his life - it was truly endearing!

As we said our goodbyes, he brushed away my bangs and carefully kissed my forehead, leaving me with butterflies in my stomach and Jell-o knees. The tears gathered in my eyes when I watched him walk away. I wanted to run after him, grab hold of him and never let go…

For years, I didn't hear from him. I tried sending him letters; and although they never came back, they didn't get answered, either. Then I moved to the U.S. I didn't write him about it, nor did I hear from him while I was there. I got pregnant; and when I was about seven months along, I came back home. Two days after I landed in Amsterdam, I went into premature labor - my body was rejecting the child inside me.

I was admitted to the hospital immediately. My son was stillborn, and the day I came back from the hospital, the phone rang. My mother answered, and all she could say was "She's fine, but the baby is dead." Then the person on the other end hung up. She stared at the receiver as if it had bitten her, then she said his name—it had been him, or so I thought.

After this phone call, I wrote him a letter, although I couldn't find his address anywhere. Then the wind blew a scrap of paper from my diary, and, yes, it was his address. Although the reason for writing him was sad, this brought a watery smile to my face.

A few months later, he called. My heart skipped a few beats when I heard his voice, and the butterflies started to stir again in my stomach. Then my heart started to pound so loudly I could hardly hear him. We spoke for about thirty minutes, and then it went quiet again. He told me he was now married and had a daughter, but I was welcome to stop by anytime. He gave me his address and telephone number, but I was too afraid to call.

About six months ago, he called again. As I answered the phone, I heard his voice—just hearing him say the word "Hi" caught my attention and sent me into love mode again. He told me his wife hadn't been too happy about him giving me his address and telling me to stop by, and that he was now moving back to Australia. Of course, I was welcome to stay whenever I wanted, as if a twenty-four-hour plane ride would be as easy as jumping on the bus to the next town over. But still, it's the thought that counts.

Whenever I'm down, I will find something that reminds me of him, even if it is just the scrap of paper on which he wrote down his address. Or an email from him—this, too, happens occasionally. Whether he likes it or not, we are connected forever, and one day he may just realize it, and maybe one day I will take him up on his offer to visit him in Australia.

(ATHENA SYDNEY is the author of the forthcoming fantasy novels *Heiress to Evil* and *Bracelets: Star's Quest for Avalon.*)

THE DANCE OF THE SOULS

*In the days before we held each other up to
impossibilities,
before blushing skin and nervous gestures
like stroking a tie or
tucking hair behind an ear
were dripping like honey over bravado,
yet sweetening our fear
until our tongues yearned to taste the thrill…
In the days before we knew that promises
were for children yet still
were rarely kept,
before midnights soaked us in moonlight and stars
filled
our vision and taught us how to shine,
before mornings meant half-forgotten dreams
that wet our thighs and woke us to remember…
In the days before words bled us until we became
transparent and crippled,
before voices were music and touches were healing
and love meant forever, I believe
our souls danced in the palm of God's hand
and he laughed with delight!
The Seraphim chanted their song while*

the Cherubim circled us in prayer
and we danced
joyously, in heavenly splendor,
basking in love's holy light.
We danced without fear,
without guilt, without choice,
your soul and mine.
And we were happy!
Nothing can ever be as beautiful as before. For now
we live.
We feel and think and choose, and God does not
hold us then,
for we are flawed and hurt one another.
If it takes an eternity for our souls to be free,
I shall wait.
I want to dance again!

— Lori Williams

A TWIN SOUL TRIBUTE

By Maurie D. Pressman, M.D.

IN 1995, *TWIN SOULS: A STORY OF THE ETERNAL MASCULINE AND THE Eternal Feminine*, was published by Crown Publishers of Random House. This was a story conceived and written by Patricia Joudry, with me as the co-author. I would like to tell you about Pat Joudry and this twin soul story now, because Pat has just passed over to the Other Side, the Lighter side.

Pat and I met in 1989 at a conference, where she had presented some of her pioneer work on sound therapy with the Walkman. In the audience was a young doc who ridiculed her because she was not a professional. Something within me was aroused, and I fairly shouted counter-criticism, saying that I, too, was a doctor. It went back and forth. That made me Pat's hero.

But it was all pre-ordained, for the Powers That Be brought us together in order to write the twin soul story, I and this unique Pat Joudry. It was a meeting of Levity (light and inspiration) and Gravity (seriousness and weightiness)—Joudry and Pressman.

She had tried to write this story for thirty years, but couldn't because she was too full of Levity. Her ideas and insights into the higher planes were all too lofty. I was able to ground them, to connect them, so to speak, from the super-planes onto this earthly plane, for I was able to see the story she had envisioned with her inspiration—the ways that we live it, prepare for it, struggle for it, enjoy it and are buoyed up by it.

Pat had always been an artist—in her childhood, in her aspirations, in her dress, and in the magnificence of her insights and courage. She was one who had flaunted the customs of society, not as a criminal or psychopath or a selfish someone but rather as an explorer who would not be bound by the myths of the time. As long as forty years ago, she home-schooled her children in order to give them a better education. She sat at the feet of the Maharishi Mahesh Yogi at the time of his earliest adventures in the Western Hemisphere. She knew and admired and learned from Roberto Assagioli, who founded Psychosynthesis. She was a friend of Jehudi Menuhin, who paid tribute to her in his book, *Sound Therapy with the Walk Man.*

When I first met Pat, I was somewhat in awe of her knowledge of the spiritual realms. She told me the twin soul story, and I was both attracted and put off by it. It seemed so high and mighty, and she seemed so romantically lofty. I was, after all, a rather heavy academician. But there was something about it that wouldn't leave me alone, an inner intuitive thrill that said, "Yes, this must be true."

And so, we set up a correspondence, in the days before the Internet, and went back and forth. Her ideas enthralled me. She told me how she had been fully immersed in the work-a-day world of business. She had, in fact, authored a number of books in Canada and was well known there as an author. She had also written a very popular radio program, *The Aldrich Family,* which entertained me as a child and youth.

In the midst of all this work-a-day business activity, she had a desire, and she expressed it, for a better life. Then she had this vision, this sudden illuminating apparition, and the story unfolded in its full aspect—the twin soul story that has become famous across several continents.

The story is that God created the world, and souls, in large packets—families. As time went through its eons of descent, these families separated into smaller and smaller groups, each group of souls getting to know its members more and more intimately. Finally, the smaller packet became very intimate until there emerged a single soul, which divided into two—the twin soul origin. In life, the one half looks for the other, each half having not only its own gender but a portion of the contra-gender.

Pat cleaved to this story, tried hard to write it, but couldn't till we met—for, as mentioned, it needed to be grounded. Translated, so to speak. And I needed to be raised in my knowledge of spiritual super-planes.

So, we exchanged, and we created; and as we did so, Pat's poetry became ever more lofty, ever more beautiful, ever more exquisite in its expression. Pat emerged from a prickly-pear anti-socialite into a rather bountiful friend, not only to me but also to her very, very select group of disciples and close friends.

The loftiness of her spirit was never more evident than when she suffered the thing she dreaded the most: a stroke. In fact, several small strokes. These affected her in such a way in that she had to give up one of her favorite activities—walking, for as she walked, she thought. She walked as she composed her stories and literature. Worse than that, another stroke impaired her vision; and so she had to give up, or partially give up, her most favorite activity—reading. Even at that, she read the words of her guru, Sri Aurobindo. She memorized his words, repeated them; and under his instruction and auspices, she raised her mind, lifting it to higher and higher planes of consciousness.

She knew she had an abdominal aortic aneurysm (a ballooning in the wall of the largest artery in the body). She knew the pain in her back was a harbinger of death; and she rejoiced every time the pain became worse, not only because she was tired of the travail of this body but, even more, because she so looked forward to release and the ascension.

She told me she would be visiting, and gave me a sign I would recognize. The sign was and is a breeze, a breeze upon my lips. How appropriate, the breeze and the feeling of the breeze, for the breeze is the touch of the soul.

On October 28th, 2000, at three-thirty p.m. Pacific Time, her dear friend Sylvia called me, told me she had gone into the hospital and had passed, very peacefully. The aortic aneurysm had given its blessing. When I heard this, I immediately saw Pat with a great and beatific smile upon her face, in utter joy as she arose even while visiting me. I felt her presence so very, very strongly. And I have no doubt she was with me and all around me.

I was puzzled by the degree and depth of the sadness that I felt, for I had long expected this. I also knew that it was a beautiful and wonderful release for her. But there is something about the need we humans have for physical contact that makes its claim, and it made its claim on me, for I do feel the grief of longing and missing and wanting.

But I also feel the inspiration of the contact and the adventures and the creations that have come through the evolution of the twin soul story. And, as it is written in the twin soul story, after the meeting and the production, there is a jet propulsion upward in service to people and in personal ascension.

And so, to you, Patricia Joudry, a twin soul greeting, and a twin soul expression of gratitude from the world at large.

(Maurie D. Pressman, M.D., is the medical director and founder of the Pressman Center for Mind/Body Wellness.)

AN ODYSSEY OF TWO SOUL MATES
By W. Paul Smith

D ATING AND COURTSHIP HAVE CHANGED A LOT IN AMERICA IN THE PAST FIFTY years. If I were doing it all over again in the 21st Century, I would court Dorothy Haley aggressively from the beginning instead of holding back as I did. Because I mistakenly assumed that her thinking would go a certain way, I almost let her get away from me.

It was the fall of 1949. I had been studying Spanish in Mexico City that summer. We were both new members of Wycliffe Bible Translators, attending a biennial Wycliffe conference in northeast Arkansas that would last nearly a month.

I didn't make a good impression on Dorothy the first time she saw me in one of the early sessions of the conference. My close-cropped crew cut and black-rimmed glasses made me look more like a high school nerd than an aspiring missionary linguist. Although I was not conscious of it, my woven Mexican huarache sandals squeaked loudly with my every step; and, not being one to sit still for very long in meetings, I frequently paced around the back of the room, punctuating the discussion leader's comments with sounds of strips of leather rubbing raucously against leather.

Why can't that weirdo just sit still and listen to what is going on, Dorothy asked herself.

About six single males attended the conference, and about thirty single women. Dorothy, a tall, slender brunette whose hair always looked as if she had just stepped out of a beauty shop, was the only one who caught my eye.

My roommate said, "Paul, Dorothy Haley is the girl for you."

I replied, "She probably thinks I am too young for her." Fifty years ago we took for granted that a man would marry a woman his own age or younger.

I had it all figured out. I knew she had enlisted in the Women's Army Corps (WAC) about the time I was signing up for Navy duty, that we had both been discharged after a couple of years of military service and that both of us had taken three-year Bible Institute courses after returning to civilian life. She had to have been at least twenty to join the WAC. On the other hand, I was able to join the U.S. Navy just before my eighteenth birthday. So, I figured she was two or more years my senior.

My calculations were correct. As I later discovered, she was twenty-five and I was twenty-three. But I shouldn't have worried about that—soul mates have a way of linking up with each other, even if social mores get cast aside.

With the conference going on for over three weeks, our paths had to cross eventually. One night, one of the older single women baked a batch of her famous cinnamon coffee cake for everybody at the conference; and as I stood in the line leading up to the serving table, Dorothy stepped in just behind me. After a mutual friend introduced us, we sat down at a table and got better acquainted. Later, she told me that after that night she didn't think I was so weird.

We never dated, and seldom were together for more than a few minutes at a time; but as the end of the conference approached, I felt sad that I might not be able to see her again, because she had been assigned to work in Peru and I was heading back to Mexico.

On the last Sunday of the conference, she had already moved back into her home in nearby Gravette, Arkansas. I would be leaving the next morning for my parents' home in Texas. At that crucial moment, Divine Providence stepped in.

Several veteran Wycliffe members had been asked to give a missionary presentation at Dorothy's church that night. When Lulu Reber, one of the invitees, started feeling ill on Sunday afternoon, she asked me if I would take her place.

"Of course!" I said. I wasn't glad that Lulu was ill, but, still, I was glad she couldn't go to that church service! I hoped this would be an opportunity for me to spend a little time with the lovely Miss Haley before our ways parted—possibly forever, but I never dreamed how much that evening would change both of our lives!

The church was full of people. I looked around and saw Dorothy sitting with her mother. I sat with the group that had come up from Siloam Springs, hoping I could at least have a chance to say goodbye to Dorothy after church. After we had sung a couple of choruses in Spanish, I was surprised to see her making her way up to the pulpit. She had been asked to talk about her missionary calling and her plans for the future.

I was surprised again when I heard her say, "I am not sure the Lord wants me to go to Peru."

Until then, I had thought her Peru assignment was a sure thing. Wycliffe worked in only one other country at that time, and that was Mexico. Maybe we would end up in the same country, after all!

I had felt a strong attraction toward this young lady before that evening, but as I listened to her Christian testimony, I fell totally in love with her, and I said to myself, If I can get her to say "yes," that's the girl I am going to marry!

I was unable to talk with her privately; so when I got back to the hotel where the conference had been held, I sat down and wrote a carefully worded letter that was nearly, but not quite, an unmistakable proposal of marriage. I left for my home in Texas early the next morning; and as I was passing through Dallas, I mailed the letter.

I waited an agonizing two weeks before I received an answer from her. Later, she told me she was "flabbergasted" when she read my letter.

She was not too flabbergasted to invite me to come and visit her.

"We've got to talk," her letter said, and so I immediately jumped on a bus and headed back to Gravette. I practically invited myself to stay in her home. Her mother didn't know what was going on, but she graciously led me to a spare bedroom and showed me where I could hang up my suit.

Dorothy's twin sister and her husband were visiting the first two days I was there, and Dorothy and I couldn't find a way to talk in private until they left. As soon as they were gone, she led me down a country lane "to pick up chinquapin nuts," which I had never heard of. Under that memorable chinquapin tree I made my intentions perfectly clear. I asked this Arkansas diamond to marry me and go to Mexico with me.

She said, "I have to pray some more about this."

The next morning I was thrilled to hear her say, "I believe the Lord brought us together."

On November 11, 1949, a cold, snowy night in Gravette, Arkansas, we said our wedding vows and promised to be true to each other until separated by death. Today people are saying that marriage doesn't have to be forever, but the Bible makes it clear that marriage vows are sacred contracts and ought not to be broken. I think everybody would be happier if they paid attention to what the Bible says on this. And if you disagree with us, we don't mind being called old-fashioned!

On the way down to my parents' home in Cross Plains, Texas, we stopped off in Norman, Oklahoma, to confer with the Mexico Director of Wycliffe Bible Translators about our future work with the group. Someone had already told the director we had married.

"Didn't you know you were supposed to consult with me before getting married?" he asked, feigning displeasure. We really hadn't known that requirement. Of course, he would have given us permission to marry if we had asked him, and he wished us the best.

When we arrived in Mexico City in December 1949, the directors told us we had to spend some time in the city getting adjusted to married life before we could move into an Indian village to begin linguistic study. So, we enrolled in Mexico City College to study Spanish for a few months.

We were not very well acquainted when we got married. For example, Dorothy didn't know that I was a photographer who would frequently be sent on assignments throughout Mexico and Central and South America. About all I knew about her was that she was a committed Christian who didn't seem afraid of venturing out into remote places where she might have to endure harsh living conditions and exposure to tropical diseases.

Before choosing a Chinantec village, where we would begin language study and, eventually, Bible translation work, I visited a number of them. Another missionary linguist and I climbed the arid western slopes of the Eastern Sierra Madre Mountains. At the crest, we entered the otherworldly Chinantec cloud forest, populated with fern trees and other exotic flora and perpetually covered with fog and clouds from the Gulf of Mexico. As we made our way down into the Chinantla rain forest, where most Chinantec villages are found, we slipped and slid along rocky trails covered with thick green moss dripping with water, walking sometimes in cool rain and sometimes in hot sunshine that combined with high humidity to sap our strength.

When the survey was over, we had walked 125 miles. Dorothy and I decided to move to Ojitlan, Oaxaca, on the edge of the Chinantla, about seventy-five miles inland from the city of Veracruz. The Ojitlan dialect had the most Chinantec speakers, estimated at ten thousand.

We moved into a 12x24-foot thatched hut with balsa pole walls, a dirt floor, a raised dirt-filled fire table where Dorothy would cook our meals over a wood fire, a carved wooden trough for storing water and a door comprised of a few poles tied together with string. There was no bathroom. Dorothy never uttered one word of complaint about having to live under such primitive conditions.

Later, in 1951, after our twins were born, I built a better house for our family, but that 11x39-foot dwelling at the end of a long muddy trail was still nothing to brag about.

The Chinantec language was extremely difficult for us to analyze and learn. We discovered that the Chinantec dialect of Ojitlan featured four levels of pitch or tone, glottal stops and nasalized vowels. After several months of intensive study, we came up with a tentative alphabet and started translating the Gospel of Mark, with a view of eventually translating the entire New Testament.

My mate seemed fearless, even in the face of imminent danger. When a religious fanatic threatened to chop my head off with a machete because I was translating the New Testament, which he considered religious propaganda, Dorothy comforted me.

"The Lord will take care of you," she said. And then she baked a loaf of banana bread and sent it to the man who wanted to kill me, following the biblical injunction that says if your enemy is hungry, feed him. Her loving gesture may have saved my life—the man never threatened me again.

We learned through that experience that angry people can often be disarmed by a Christian who shows love in response to threats. We treated all our "enemies" with respect, and gradually they came to accept our presence in the village. Having my soul mate beside me made our trials much easier to endure!

We don't believe in trying to force anybody to accept our faith; but as we began translating, some of the people who heard or read the scriptures in their own language decided they wanted to become followers of Jesus. One of these was a remarkable young man named Antonio.

Antonio was a drunkard from a family of drunkards. Every weekend, he, his father and his three brothers would get drunk on the raw white rum the Chinantecs call "water that burns;" and when they got drunk, they sometimes started fighting each other. Chinantec men carry very sharp machetes that are often drawn when they are in an alcoholic daze. If something didn't change, somebody in Antonio's family was going to get killed.

(A Mexican doctor who operated a trauma clinic in Ojitlan told me that the village was "the murder capitol of Mexico," with the highest per capita homicide rate in the country.)

The first couple of times I saw Antonio, he was too drunk to walk straight; but one day when he was sober, he came to our house and asked me take his picture. He had heard about our translation work; and after I had photographed him, he wanted to see the book we had recently published in Chinantec. I brought out a copy of the Gospel of Mark and read a few verses to him. He wanted to keep the book, so I sold it to him for the equivalent of a few cents in American money.

Our family left the village a few days after that and was gone for eleven weeks. As soon as we arrived in Ojitlan from our trip, Antonio heard we were back and came immediately to visit. I asked him if he could read the Gospel I had sold him, and he said, "Yes, I have already read the whole book!"

I was skeptical, as I knew he had attended a Spanish-speaking school for only two years as a child, and I had not given him any reading instructions. So, I brought out a Gospel and put it in his hands.

"Here," I said, "let me hear how well you can read this!"

I was amazed! He read every word smoothly and without hesitation. At that point, I brought out the first draft of the first eleven chapters of the Gospel of Matthew and started reading it to him. He wouldn't let me stop until I had finished reading all eleven chapters to him. Seeing his deep interest in the translations, I asked him if he would be willing to leave his home and live with us in the city of Puebla to help me translate the rest of the New Testament.

Without hesitation, he said, "Yes, I'll go with you."

Dorothy and I had been feeling a lot of discouragement because the translation work was proceeding so slowly. We didn't have a full-time translation helper; and even if we had, we still couldn't work very fast. Just existing in the village took almost all of our time and energy. Our days in Ojitlan were occupied with hauling water, washing diapers, shopping for food and preparing meals. (Since we didn't have a refrigerator, we had to go out and buy food every day.) We could not find reliable servant help for Dorothy, either; it was not in the Chinantec culture for people to hire themselves out as servants.

Besides these things, we spent a lot of time entertaining Indians who dropped by to visit at all hours. So, Antonio's willingness to leave Ojitlan with us really lifted our spirits.

I told Antonio that, if he went with us to Puebla, he could not drink any more rum.

"That's all right," he said, "I have already gotten rid of that habit."

It turned out that, in reading Mark's Gospel, he had become a believer, and his old style of life had to go. Later, his father and mother, sister and three brothers followed his example and became believers. That was the end of the drinking and fighting that had threatened to destroy his family.

Translation proceeded much faster in Puebla, slowed only by the photographic assignments that from time to time took me away from home.

Dorothy and I usually talked over important things and made decisions together; but one of the biggest decisions of our life fell to me, with no opportunity to confer with her first. Again, her response was an example of her love for people and for her Lord, who sent us to minister to the Chinantecs. The decision that I made, and which she later approved, was a huge test of faith for both us.

I had gone to Ojitlan to let our Chinantec friends know we were still alive and hadn't forgotten them. Marv, my oldest son, and Ralph, the son of another missionary, were with me on the trip. When it came time to leave the village and head back toward home, I stopped to say goodbye to the sister of the man who several years earlier had threatened to kill me.

This woman, whom I will call "Maria," brought out a somber, emaciated child and said, "Paul, this is my thirteen-year-old daughter, Elena. She has advanced tuberculosis, and when we took her to see the doctors in the market town, they just sent her back here to die."

Elena looked more like ten years old than thirteen.

"Paul," said Maria, "I want to give my daughter to you. You can get good treatment for her—only you can save her life!"

This was not what I wanted to hear. I knew that Elena's tuberculosis was at a very contagious stage, and I had four young children of my own to think about.

"Please," Maria pleaded, "take her with you. If you don't take her, she will die!"

Elena stood by silently, emotionless, waiting to hear what I would say.

I wanted to say, "No," but I couldn't make myself say it. I felt a very strong conviction that the Lord wanted me to take this girl to Puebla with me, and so I said, "Yes."

Maria gave Elena a small cloth bag with a few clothes in it and told her to go with me and the boys. Still showing no emotion, she obeyed; and we all got in the car and started to Puebla. The four-hour drive seemed much longer that day. Elena was coughing constantly, and I could almost see the tuberculosis germs filling the car and invading our lungs. I was more than a little scared, especially for my children; and this was one time when I didn't know what Dorothy would say when she heard what I had done.

I shouldn't have worried about what Dorothy might say. Again, my soul mate rose to the occasion.

"We'll trust the Lord to protect our family from this disease."

We hospitalized Elena until contagion was no longer a threat; and then we brought her home, gave her her own eating utensils and a separate bathroom and let her sleep in my study. She gained weight, color returned to her beautiful Indian face; and she started to laugh and enjoy life with us. Dorothy taught her to read Spanish and Chinantec. She especially enjoyed reading the Chinantec Gospel of Mark. She became a believer and liked to talk about what heaven would be like.

After only twenty-seven months, our little Chinantec sweetheart departed from us. The best medical care we could provide her wasn't enough to stop the ravages of tuberculosis that had already advanced too far when we first started her treatment. We were just happy we had been able to give her those extra months, and we rejoice in knowing that she is waiting for us in heaven. And we thank the Lord that He did protect our family from contracting the disease, as we knew He would.

In 1967, having completed the translation of the Chinantec New Testament, we packed our six children into a 1964 Pontiac Catalina, hitched up a little two-wheel trailer loaded with all our worldly possessions and moved back to the U.S.A. We spent seven years in California before moving to Cedar Hill, Texas, in 1974.

My soul mate and I have come a long way on our journey through life together. Of course, we have hit a few potholes along the way. The biggest arguments I can remember having with Dorothy took place over the details of a house we were building in Puebla. My soul mate didn't like the way I had done something, and she made the contractor tear it out and do it over. Now, in my old age, I have finally come to realize that if she disagrees with me about something, she is usually right and I am wrong.

As I write, we are close to celebrating our fifty-second wedding anniversary. I have had Parkinson's disease for more than ten years, but I still drive my car and am still able to travel. Dorothy and I just returned from a two-week trip to Mexico, where I finished work on a script for dubbing Chinantec onto a video of the life of Jesus, based on the Gospel of Luke. Dorothy has prepared literacy materials in Chinantec and was able to teach several people to read while we were in Mexico.

This odyssey of two soul mates isn't over till it's over, and we are enjoying every minute of it!

We also enjoy reminiscing over the way our journey began way back in 1949 at that Wycliffe conference in Siloam Springs, Arkansas. Humanly speaking, everything hinged on Lulu Reber's illness, and her asking me to take her place on the program in Dorothy's church; but we both believe that God was in the circumstances that brought these two soul mates together. Amen!

(W. PAUL SMITH is the author of educational film and filmstrip scripts, the book *Bibles on the Moon* and co-author of *One More Mountain to Climb* with his wife, Dorothy L. Smith.)

THE MAN IN MY DREAMS
By Jill Maser

I WAS TOO YOUNG TO KNOW. TWENTY YEARS PASSED BEFORE I REALIZED THAT the man who was ripped from my arms by the KGB on that frigid night in Leningrad is my soul mate.

I don't know his last name. I don't know his fate. But I know that I will see him again. Sometime. Somewhere.

*   *   *

Yuri was about my age, I think. About twenty-two. Classically handsome, goofy-looking in his blue-and-orange black market anorak, complete with fur-trimmed hood. A capitalist who wriggled under the Communist thumb. And, oh, so street-smart.

My Russian professor and his wife had organized a three-week tour of Moscow, Leningrad and points between. I was seduced by the whole idea. My ancestors had fled their tyrannical leaders generations ago. I needed to see my homeland.

The year was 1981. Ronald Reagan and Leonid Brezhnev detested one another. The Cold War was heating up.

We were warned well. Don't attempt to sell anything on the black market. Make trades only. Pack warm clothes. Your hotel rooms will most likely be bugged. The KGB will follow you.

And once again, do not sell anything on the black market.

Tom didn't listen. There's always one in the bunch. He brought his broken Sony Walkman with the express intent to sell it. I was nervous when we hopped off the trolley at Red Square; but the sights took my breath away, and I felt calm wash through my body. I felt connected to the snowy slate beneath my feet, to the psychedelic

70

domes of St. Basil's, to the blood-red wall of the Kremlin. Had I been here before?

I felt lost. Insignificant. Alone. I looked around. I *was* alone! Tom and the others had moved off. I spied them several yards away and hurried to catch up. They were chatting with three young men, each dressed in the popular American winter coat of the day—the blue anorak with a neon orange lining. Matted fake fur ringed their hoods.

Don't tell me Tom's hooked up with some American students. I did not travel halfway around the world to meet Americans.

The tall one sensed my approach and glanced my way. I saw only half of his face; the other half remained hidden behind the oversized hood's edge. He pushed the hood off his head and stared. *My God! He's Russian. I'm in the black market!*

His name was Yuri.

I didn't hear or see the transaction. I couldn't take my eyes off Yuri. He and his friends spoke English—an interestingly accented English that was a mixture of school, American and British English. Who knows what else had been tossed in?

Yuri and his friends wouldn't let us speak Russian. He insisted we call him "George." The KGB might be listening, he explained. I remember thinking, You're not fooling anyone with that accent, mister.

Yuri wanted to be as American as the clothes on his back. I refused to call him George, but I indulged him by speaking English. It was the first of many indulgences on that trip. It was easy to give in to him. I was smitten.

The Russian friends gave Tom three hundred rubles for that Walkman, a veritable fortune. He was stuck with those rubles. He couldn't spend the money on souvenirs—he'd made his declarations upon entering Moscow. Customs agents would sniff him out for sure when we left for the States.

His only option was to buy food and drink. Yuri and his pals must have known that, because they became our fast friends. Whenever our group was out on the town, Yuri and his friends showed up to meet us. We'd wind up at the nearest disco, Tom doling out hard cash for bottles of vodka and champagne.

Yuri and I talked for hours. We soon began to make plans of our own. He became my private tour guide. One day, I skipped the group's planned outing and spent the day riding trolleys and exploring the streets of Moscow alone with Yuri.

We came across a shop selling political posters. My Russian wasn't good enough to understand the nuances of the propaganda slogans. Yuri was reluctant to translate outright, so we concocted a plan to fool the KGB, should they be following us. We'd speak with British accents. We'd pretend we were British students and try to translate the posters together—aloud and in very bad accents. Would our giggling give us away?

We tried it in the bookstore next. Yuri's ever-watchful eye was relaxed. No KGB. I'd never felt so comfortable, warm, free in the presence of a man before. I began to concoct secret plans for smuggling him back to the States. I knew it was what he wanted. I seriously thought of asking him to marry me. Sure, I wanted him all to myself, but I also knew how much he wanted to be in America. It would be cruel to leave him here.

We ate ice cream from a street vendor's cart. We walked for miles through the snow and cold. We scowled at the huge, yellow KGB headquarters building. We were one.

I needed some gifts for my family and friends. I wanted something unique. I had jeans to trade. Yuri offered me a Red Army uniform belt with its distinctive sickle-and-hammer buckle. Perfect.

"How do you know the jeans will fit?" I asked.

"They'll fit."

"I think you should try them on."

Yuri's eyes grew round—with anticipation or fear, I'm not sure. He knew what I was asking. I couldn't help myself. I'm not that kind of girl. I do not jump into bed with just anyone, but Yuri was not just anyone. I didn't realize then just how special he was; but I'm certain of it now.

"I can't go to your hotel." He explained that Intourist hotels are off-limits to regular citizens. Only the privileged citizens of Moscow were permitted to rub elbows with Americans.

"You look American," I lied. I was desperate. There was no denying the hold Yuri had on me. "There's a big New Year's Eve party at our hotel on Saturday. How will they know you're not with our group?"

I could see he was intrigued. I gave him the details. I know now how selfish I was.

Yuri and his friends attended the party. He and I snuck up to my room, but he didn't try on the jeans. We made passionate love without a word. None were needed. We each knew exactly what the other wanted, needed. There was no doubt about it—we knew each other.

We were frantic. It was dangerous. It was delightful. We combed our hair and returned to the party. No one in our group seemed the wiser.

When I next saw Yuri, we laughed that we hadn't made our trade. Our group was leaving for Leningrad in a few days. We'd need to trade before then. We grew quiet, alone with our thoughts, relishing our limited time together.

I spent my last day in Moscow with Yuri. I'd never see him again.

I brought the jeans. He brought the belt. We talked and walked. We ate steaming pierozhki. We window-shopped. We rode the trolley back to my hotel. We were quiet.

Yuri said something. The trolley was loud—had he said that I could or couldn't kiss him? I didn't ask for clarification. I didn't want to know. Since he'd brought it up, damn it, I was going to kiss him.

We stood together on the street corner. I looked squarely into the center of his chest. I had never felt so protected. The strength in his chest and the breadth of his shoulders made me feel enveloped, even though his hands were stuffed deep in his pockets. I touched my gloved palm to his chest. I needed the connection.

I bounced onto my toes and pressed my lips, firmly, to his.

I walked the few steps to my hotel. Alone. I didn't look back. I couldn't.

That night our group left for Leningrad. Tom and I shared a bottle of vodka. He missed "George." I missed Yuri.

*   *   *

Leningrad is beautiful—when the sun is out. In the dead of winter, it only shows its radiant face for about four hours.

The cold was numbing. Foot-thick ice floes in the Neva clinked together with a sound that reminded me of ghostly bells worn by Swiss cows hidden from view by dense Alpine fog. I stumbled through the last week of our tour in a similar fog. I was missing a large part of me.

Our tour included a trip to the forest for a troika ride. The temperature hovered around twenty degrees below zero. We were greeted at the lodge by a group of children in native costume. They danced for us and served us vodka. They escorted us to our open sleigh where we huddled under heavy blankets, squeezed in beside Father Christmas and some buxom "snow bunnies."

The vodka helped ease the pain. The pain of the biting cold. And the pain of feeling so alone. It should have been a beautiful ride. All I could think of was how to remove Father Christmas's lecherous hand from my thigh. I wanted another shot of vodka.

*   *   *

Our tour would end in two days. Tonight we were seeing an opera. Our last night would be free.

I can't remember the name of the theater. I do remember its glory. Exhausted, I trod behind Tom down the ornate staircase, through the lobby and onto the frigid street.

"It's George!" he shrieked.

Yuri swallowed me in his bear hug. My face felt ready to crack— from the cold and the huge smile I had for him. He smelled so good. I squeezed him as hard as I could. I'd never let go.

He had followed me to Leningrad, an eight-hour train ride from his home. Was he insane? He had risked everything to see me again. Oh, if I could only pack him in my bag and take him home with me.

We followed Tom, arm-in-arm, to a nearby disco. Yuri wore my jeans. We toasted our friendship. We warmed our bodies. Yuri and I warmed our souls. I memorized his face that night, for I knew that our time together would truly be over tomorrow. Even if he did manage to escape to the States, would he find me? College students don't stay put. We wouldn't be able to correspond. The mail wasn't safe.

We knew we had to make love again. It was the only thing we

could truly give one another. Love. Sweet memories. No one could ever separate us from those gifts.

I was too tipsy to notice how he got into my room. Again, wordlessly, breathlessly, frantically, we made love.

A knock at the door startled us. Yuri kissed me, zipped his jeans and ran to the door. It was Tom. The KGB was on its way. The floor monitor had tattled. It was her duty.

He turned to me. And then he disappeared. He ran for his life.

Tom was stunned. I was numb.

The hotel was agog.

I went to bed.

I didn't cry. If I started, I'd never stop.

The next night, our last in the USSR, Tom and I drowned our sorrow in more vodka than I can remember. He had lost a friend. I had lost so much more. More than I could fathom.

*   *   *

I never knew what happened to Yuri. There was no way to check. I fear that he was chased down and arrested. I hope he is safe.

I've never forgotten him. I can only hope that he hasn't forgotten me.

I've never had a meaningful relationship since Yuri. No man measures up to him. I don't consciously compare the men I date to him, but in retrospect, that's just the way I feel. Yuri is the only man for me.

I've come to know that he is my soul mate.

There are nights when I feel his presence. In my dreams, I reach out and touch his chest just as I did on that cold Moscow street corner. I still feel safe.

In the last two years, my dreams of Yuri have intensified. I hope this means that he is near. If not, I'm confident I will find him. Somewhere. Sometime. Somehow.

(Jill Maser is the author of *Red Passion*, *Desert Desire* and the award-winning *Concerto Diavolo* and *Unspoken*.)

TWO PEAS IN A POD
By Tel Asiado

I TAKE FRIENDSHIP SERIOUSLY, BUT THE IDEA OF SOUL MATES IS SOMETHING I've never given much thought. Not until four months ago when, through the Internet, I "met" Dorothy Thompson, now a good friend. My interest aroused, since then I have found myself wanting to know more about this soul mate mystique. And as I learned, all indications from descriptions and other attributes suggest that Caithlin is my twin flame, "the other pea in the pod."

Caithlin was one of my childhood friends. We grew up in a close-knit flock of Christian believers whose lives were centered on church-related activities—Sunday worship, choirs, Sunday school, Christian Youth Fellowship, Daily Vacation Bible School and prayer meetings. These were activities we shared until our adolescent years.

After high school, we drifted apart and lost track of each other. She was older than I, graduated ahead, entered college in the big city while I was left behind. Besides, it was best we were not classmates, for if we had been, we would have competed in almost everything and not become friends. Both avid readers, we devoured all the books in our school library. Her aunt was my mentor, my guiding light in my learning years. After my own high-school graduation, I went to another university, pursued a career and lived my own life.

The third quarter of 2001 was a major milestone in my life. After twenty-two years in the computing and information technology industry, I decided to leave my fulltime job to pursue other lifelong interests, primarily writing. I was filled with hopes and excitement for my dream, at the same time anxious regarding what the future held.

As I constantly seek God's guidance for my decisions, I took the challenges with steadfastness in my heart.

However, after a year, things were not as I would have wished. My writing needed more research, initial targets were slipping by, monthly bills piling up, my life savings getting depleted and other day-to-day problems. Add to these turbulent relationships and disappointments with fair-weather friends. Except for three, all my work friends simply vanished, near and far. At the end of each day, I was always hurting.

Why is it that when things are going well, when we have plenty of money, our health is good and life is rosy, that we have no shortage of friends? Ah, it is only when the chips are down, when life looks bleak, that we learn who our real friends are.

Feeling very isolated and dejected, I lived in my own thoughts and dreams. Being an only child, with both parents deceased, I began to long for my childhood joys, friendships and the smell of home. It was in June 2002 I decided to seek out my childhood friends—or anyone from my past. Five people came to mind, three friends and two former teachers with whom I had been close. I only found two of the names, neither of which had email addresses.

But it was Caithlin who dominated my thoughts and whom I pursued until, eventually, I found her home address. She lives in a Great Lakes state of the US while home to me is Sydney, Australia. We are half a world apart.

Thirty-six years is a long time. A lot of things happen.

I wrote to her.

"If you are the same Caithlin who was my childhood friend way back home, please respond."

After ten days, I received a three-page letter written in beautiful calligraphy, full of wonderful childhood and youthful memories. Full of excitement. I felt the same way.

In her letter, she gave me an email address but warned she's not much into the Internet.

Our rapport was terrific the instant we connected. Through email we talked about our high school days and people in it, including old-fogey professors. We reminisced a lot, laughed using online emoticons and struggled to find an answer as to why in heaven's name we had lost touch. We even discussed our old boyfriends and wondered what became of them. It was as if the thirty-six-year span dissolved into nothingness. We read each other's thoughts between the lines.

After about five months, Caithlin asked why we hadn't thought of calling each other. Perhaps subconsciously we had, but we were not ready yet to reveal how our "voices" had changed over the years.

Like her, I was highly thrilled at the prospect of our first phone conversation. I knew from the past that we had strong vibes— common interests, sense of humor, as well as being similar both intellectually and spiritually.

The first call was filled with excitement. Eventually, we got the feel for each other's voice, including our intonation and accent. By choice, she has remained single; so have I. We had both decided to commit to pursuits other than marital life. Talk was good. Time seemed short. I'm certain we would have connected for endless hours if we had both lived alone and could do so without being inconsiderate of other people in our households.

Since then, we've communicated regularly by phone. We talk for hours and never get bored even for a second. Thank goodness for phone cards, or she'd be broke by now.

In half a year and across the miles, as we continued sharing our lives, we felt very special toward each other. We also realized how spiritually and emotionally bonded we have been. We labeled ourselves "two peas in a pod." We also decided that each week of connecting meant one year of catching up; so after five months, by our calculation, we have already caught up on twenty years of our physical separation.

We are always able to tell when the other is happy or sad, at peace or not. If I am down, the phone will magically ring for me. All the time, she knows how I feel, even though we are thousands of miles apart.

Our senses of humor are amazing. Who else can I tease and be certain to get a laugh? And vice versa. Quite often, without mentioning it, I will be listening to a CD of someone while she's watching a DVD of that same person. Or at the same time, we'll discover we're both reading a book about a particular celebrity, except written by two different authors. Occurrences like this have been frequent.

As in many relationships, "familiarity breeds contempt." As we shared our thirty-six years of living separate lives, we had disagreements, some small, others heated, especially where values, relationships and spirituality were concerned. Almost all the time, she remains the temperate and reasonable one. And despite our stubborn and hardheaded natures, another similarity, these disagreements never lasted long. We usually end up apologizing at the same time.

Career-wise, we come from a different background. She pursued a medical profession and I, computing and information technology. While her experience has been of a more human environment, mine has been stiff, rigid and within the cutthroat business world.

I look up to her world, pleased and proud of what she has made of it. Caithlin has a solid extended family, a healthy relationship within her circle of friends and, above all, a rock-solid relationship with fellow Christian believers. She is deeply committed to God and obedient to Christ's teachings. On the contrary, my life has been hurting and downtrodden—career-wise, in relationships, spiritually and financially. But then, I probably wouldn't have searched her out if I had been on top of the world.

Through all my instabilities, I have also tended to be insecure, sometimes selfish in these insecurities; but Caithlin always understands. She is kind but firm in her practice of friendship without expectations, as well as of loving unconditionally. It may not be in leaps and bounds; but through her, I have progressed in the spiritual growth I abandoned after I left college. Perhaps this is another of God's purposes why I found her after thirty-six years.

She has had every chance to let go and leave me be; but through all my woes, she has been there for me regularly, calling from across the miles. She has constantly embraced and prayed for my moods and challenges as if they are her own.

I realize she has other best friends, including her only sister, that I am only one of them. We realize and agree that friendship is sharing, that it's not exclusive and that, in doing so, it grows.

But she and I alone are twin flames, "two peas in a pod," for in finding each other, we feel we have found ourselves in each other, in so many ways.

When I'm happy, she rejoices completely in my joys and doesn't temper it with criticism or advice. She is simply glad to share my triumphs without taking anything away from my moment. My failures make no difference to her, and she never expects much from me.

So do I.

She isn't there to lead me through the dark but to walk by my side. She is there to share the darkness, not to offer advice about how to dispel my perplexities.

So am I.

We want to set each other free, allow and respect each other's freedom and space, to explore our human relationships without entanglement of sex or love. To probe ourselves without having to remember tact or diplomacy. Just to be ourselves.

Caithlin and I believe that after thirty-six years I found her for a purpose.

We thought of meeting this year, but financial concerns on both sides are in the way. We take this as a "not yet" in Almighty God's plan. Anyone who truly cares understands the anxiety that distance conveys, but Caithlin and I know we will meet.

It's just a matter of time.

(TEL ASIADO is a freelance writer and business coach currently residing in Sydney, Australia.)

YOU JUST KNOW
By Candace Sams

I DIDN'T KNOW HE WAS MY SOUL MATE WHEN I FIRST MET HIM. I WAS DATING one of his friends at the time. We were all in college, and most of us were about to graduate. I thought the guy who had all my attention was the one I wanted to spend the rest of my life with, but what I felt for him was different from what I feel for my soul mate. Quite different.

The guy I was dating was more than a bit shallow. He spread rumors about others, which included me, a fact I wasn't aware of until much later. He thought quite a lot of himself—his father, after all, was an industry giant. He was going into the same business and wanted to follow in his father's footsteps. Actually, like most lazy folks in the same position, he wanted his father to help set him up—get him inside whatever loops exist for his future career and place him ahead of others on waiting lists.

But that didn't happen. Sometimes, even if only rarely, Providence actually takes over and insists on skill, hard work and the presence of integrity before putting someone in any position of power. This guy just didn't have any of those traits. So, he bragged to his friends about his father's illustrious career, hoping to trade on that for a place of his own. One totally undeserved. And when he didn't get it, as most of us suspected he wouldn't, it became someone else's fault. Mine, his friend's, anyone else's fault but his own.

While dating him, I saw the foibles and the game playing; but I was young and thought he was meant for me. The one I wanted to be with. He was handsome and had ambition, however misused or abused that trait might have been. I guess that's when I started noticing the other guy. His friend.

Now, this other guy was dating another girl, but she didn't seem interested in him exclusively. She lived near me, and I saw her with other men. Whether her current beaux knew she was sort of spreading her wares around or not, I don't know; but the women who knew her did. I guess that's a comment about the observant qualities of women, good or bad.

Because we sometimes went out in groups, I occasionally saw this other woman with my date's best friend. This other, quiet man. And this other man wasn't obnoxious, like some of the young rakes the girls were dating. He was big and observant, with nice blue eyes and what seemed like a patient nature.

In short, he was everything the guy I dated wasn't.

While I suffered through discovering how my date was gossiping about everyone and saw this other woman fooling around on her boyfriend, he and I managed to find some kind of center ground and began to talk more and more to each other at parties and outings. I drifted away from the guy who was using me and everyone else to get what he wanted and the woman drifted more toward her parties, where she could impress multiple men at as many intervals as she pleased. That left me with my ex's best friend. We were finally unattached and maybe more than a bit hurt by our previous companions' behavior.

When you start deeply caring about someone, you think rockets will explode, planets will collide and all the portents of astrology and God will be staring you in the face. You think they'll be telling you in no uncertain terms that THIS IS THE ONE. But it's just not so. When my boyfriend and I called it quits and the quiet guy's girlfriend ran off to some other man's bed, he and I found time to enjoy each other's company. The conversations weren't commiserating soliloquies about how our loves did us wrong. Rather, we began by sharing a soda in a cafeteria, talking about old school chums and asking each other if we had heard from this person or that one.

By now it was early summer, and we were finding it very lonesome being on our own. Some of our college classmates had graduated, and others weren't attending extra summer classes.

There's something very sad and isolated about college campuses when the summer break starts. I guess we were both feeling the separation from all our friends and our old lives. Everyone we knew had gone on to jobs or elsewhere while he and I continued our lives there at the university.

As the summer progressed, we got much closer. I learned his personality was the exact opposite of mine. Where I was sometimes bold, brash and more than a bit mouthy, he was calm, persistent and thought things through before speaking. I think that's what impressed me most. He had the patience to see the big picture where I could not.

And he was kind to people. Not like that boor I'd been seeing before him. Not like that party girl he'd been with. Folks seemed to like him. He made friends easily. And that's how we started. As friends.

But more and more he pushed into my life and into my head. I wanted to hang on to him. He fit me the way a really favorite pair of old blue jeans would—soft and comforting. There was nothing flashy or gregarious about it. There was no monumental upheaval of souls or overt signals of undying devotion and love. It's just that I started to get the feeling I'd very much rather go on living with him than without him. It wasn't even a very intense feeling at first, but became so over time.

I could talk to him about anything. We could go anywhere and the place we went became the right place. It didn't matter whether we picked up a hamburger and went to the park to eat it or if we made reservations to eat at a favorite restaurant. I grew to discover that it hurt when he wasn't around.

Later that summer, he finally finished his course work and began his final semester. I knew he'd leave and go off to the Navy. That's what he'd always planned to do. I also knew he'd stay in contact at first. There would be letters and phone calls. Then those would trickle down to only birthday or Christmas cards. Finally, he'd go on to another life and leave me behind. And with that thought came the realization that if he walked out of my life, this quiet, unassuming gentle person would take my soul with him.

That kind of feeling is very rare. Having never had it before, I still recognized it for what it was and that I'd never know it again with anyone else. But I didn't have the right to hold someone who wasn't ready to be held. He and I both knew that. He left to follow his dreams, I left to follow mine.

Fate doesn't make mistakes when a thing is real, however. Some years later, I arrived home from work to my small duplex, a lonely repetition of something I did every single day and saw continuing until the day I died. There, parked in my driveway, was a black car I recognized as his. It was a very bright day. The heat in Texas at that time of year can be unbearable. But when I pulled into the driveway, I didn't feel the heat or the loneliness anymore. I just saw and felt him. I knew I had one more chance, maybe the last chance, to keep him in my life.

That was sixteen years ago. As I write, my real soul mate is on a business trip and won't be back until the end of the week. Am I lonely when he's gone? No, because I know he's coming back. He'll always be here with me. When you discover someone is the other part of your heart, the next breath you take and the only person you'll ever really love, you can take the distance and the time apart. You're still together. Inside, where it counts.

Oh, we argue and feud at times. But those fights generally clear the air and make things a bit more right with us. We have different tastes, sometimes different opinions on ethics and personal beliefs. But it's okay. We don't have to agree on everything. Our relationship seems to work best sometimes when we don't. He likes exotic food, I don't. I love to write romances he tolerantly reads because I need the help editing. He does the lion's share of giving, and I take without depositing much back into our lives.

But he loves me anyway. The red rockets don't glare, the stars haven't fallen from the firmament and we don't declare undying love each and every moment. Life isn't like the cover of a romance novel where the bare-breasted beauty is held by the weightlifting mega man.

We hold hands and talk. We share ice cream and like to watch television together. Usually when I'm able to wrestle control of the remote. He'll bring home an unexpected gift of chocolate. I get him underwear. That's the way it is. But there isn't anything deeper or finer in the universe. I won't ever love anyone else. Not the way I love him. And I long ago decided that if he ever has the unholy gall to leave this life before me I won't ever be with anyone else. How could I even try? He'll still be here. Right beside me. In everything I do, each and every day.

It's a slow, steady thing, this soul mate stuff. If you're looking for a crash of lightning to indicate that someone is that one and only person for you, look first to the man or woman who's your best friend. The patient, understanding and generous heart. Look to see what happens in the quiet times when no words are said. It isn't just about sex. It's about understanding someone so much you know what they're about to say or do. The soul will find its own way.

You may not know he or she is the one at first. It may not come to you in a flash. They may not be perfect in physical attributes. Who of us is? I challenge any of you to look at your parents and see them as they were when they were twenty or thirty. Looks fade but not the solid heart. It can stay young forever if you're with the right person.

But how do you really know? I can only say this. If little things they do don't bother you, if you find you can talk to your man or woman without fearing criticism, and they love you even when you screw up, that's a pretty good sign. If they care about you no matter what you look like in the morning, that's even better. And you'll know you can trust them with your every secret and your very life. They'd purposely never hurt you for any reason.

If you have any doubts, and can't talk to your woman or man about them, I leave it for you to decide whether you've found a soul mate. I can really only answer in three words: you just know.

(CANDACE SAMS is an author from Alabama.)

GOD GAVE ME A PRINCE

By Jennifer Anne F. Messing

"Do you need a ride home, Jennifer?" asked the young American gentleman I'd just met. His warm brown eyes looked at me intently.

"Actually, my parents' driver is coming to pick me up," I answered. "But thanks anyway, Michael."

"Can I walk you to the lobby and wait with you till your driver arrives?" He was not going to let go of me easily—I sensed this at once.

"Of course," I replied, smiling at him. He appeared to be a genuine, tenderhearted fellow.

We had both just attended the wedding rehearsal of mutual friends, Andy and Jaylyn, on that sunny afternoon. They were to be married the next day in a garden wedding at this gorgeous hotel, the Century Park Sheraton in Manila, Philippines.

Jaylyn and I were young, single, working Filipina women. Our families had known each other for several years. Andy and Michael had come to the Philippines on short-term missions trips every year for four consecutive years. This year their team came to Manila not only to minister but also to attend the marriage celebration of Andy and Jaylyn. Now here I was, honored to be asked by Jaylyn to be a bridesmaid. Michael was a groomsman.

Michael and I had fun chatting for more than twenty minutes until my driver arrived. Why did I feel excited that I would see him again the next day at the wedding?

The following day Mom and I both had our hair done at a salon—my parents had been asked to participate in an important part of the wedding ceremony. We were all dressed and ready to go at four p.m. When I entered our living room wearing a peach-colored bridesmaid's gown, my dad whistled.

"Wow!" he said. "You look beautiful. Are you the bride?"

I laughed good-naturedly, thinking that I wished I *were* a bride today. But I smiled at Dad and replied, "No, but I've heard that after a second stint as a bridesmaid, you get promoted."

"I've never heard that before," Mom commented.

We all chuckled, got into the car and left.

The wedding march proceeded as planned, and all went beautifully. As I stood watching Jaylyn and Andy exchange wedding vows my eyes filled with tears. While I rejoiced with them for the new life they were beginning together, the tears I shed at that moment were ones of sadness. Wasn't this the way life should have turned out for me, too? Meet a devoted, loving Christian man while in my twenties, fall in love, get married, then live happily ever after? That's what I had hoped for, what my mom had prayed for, wasn't it?

Yet here I was, a twenty-three-year-old single mom. My precious one-year-old daughter, Celine, was at home with her nanny.

I had met Celine's father Alvin [not his real name] when I was twenty, when we were both students at a six-month live-in Discipleship Training School. Students there could not date or go steady with a fellow student for the duration of the course. Attracted to each other, Alvin and I disobeyed this rule from the start.

The school's aim was to help one get to know God intimately and become committed to discipleship through Bible study, mentoring and prayer support. Obviously, Alvin and I were both immature in our walk with God.

Our leaders assured us that God loved us and that they did, too, but at the same time said we needed to discontinue our relationship. We never listened to them; and because we always saw each other in secret, soon we became intimate.

We finished the school and, shortly afterward, eloped. I married Alvin against my school leaders' and—most importantly—against my family's wishes. My mom and two older brothers had seen in Alvin what I was too naive to see: immaturity, ill-preparedness for the responsibilities of married life, even partying and drugs.

On our wedding night, Alvin had a bitter argument with one of his female cousins who lived nearby. Their quarrel became so severe and Alvin got so enraged and out of control that he punched two of his female cousins. And this on my wedding night!

A dark sense of foreboding came over me. What have I gotten into? I wondered.

Only two months into our marriage, our own severe quarrels began. I discovered that Alvin was jealous and suspicious. He watched my every move closely. Since he knew my family disapproved of our marriage, he didn't want me to call or get in touch with them. This hurt me deeply.

Alvin didn't have a job and didn't appear to be trying very hard to get one. Sometimes, he would take off with his friends for several days, and I never really knew where he went.

After six months I became pregnant. When my mom found out, though she had opposed our marriage, she invited us to live in a spare bedroom in my family's home for as long as we needed. She was concerned about my health and the baby's health, plus she knew Alvin still did not have a job.

She also encouraged Alvin to finish college at night, and paid for his tuition.

As my pregnancy progressed, our explosive fights escalated. Finally, two weeks before my due date, Alvin left and never returned. Two weeks later, with my parents' loving support, I gave birth to my first child, a beautiful baby girl I named Celine Marie.

I never saw Alvin again, and Alvin never saw Celine. Several weeks later, I found out from Alvin's friends that he had never gone to college at night as we supposed. He had partied and even had affairs with different women.

Crushed and heartbroken, I don't know how I made it through those early months of caring for Celine. Fortunately, my family gathered around me to offer their love and support.

During the next few weeks, I recommitted my life to Jesus. I repented of my sins, my rebellion against my parents and the immoral relationship with Alvin prior to marriage. Though it was difficult to do at age twenty-two, I told my parents I would live in their home once again in submission to their authority. I also told them I would not remarry without their blessing.

I began to attend church regularly with my parents and Celine. I also became a member of a women's Bible study group.

God began doing wonderful new things in my life. I landed a job as an executive secretary at the Manila office of a French perfume company. While I was at work, Celine stayed home with a full-time nanny.

By the time Celine was seven months old, a few eligible men, at different times, had asked me out on dates. I accepted a few invitations but very cautiously. I kept praying, "Lord, please show me who You want for me this time around. I want Your will for my life." And I sincerely wanted God's will, whether it meant being reconciled to Alvin, being single forever or getting married again.

As I prayed and sought God, however, it became clear to me that He was calling me to a brand-new start in life, not a reconciliation. My pastor's and parents' advice also confirmed this. So, I kept up with my new job, developed Christian friendships and took care of Celine at night after work. A friend from my church gave me the name of a lawyer through whom, she advised, I might obtain a legal annulment. After receiving much wise counsel from my parents, I filed.

One evening I received a phone call from an old friend, Jaylyn. She said she was to be wed the following month to Andy Trogen, a Christian man from Portland, Oregon.

"Would you be a bridesmaid at my wedding, Jennifer?" she asked.

"Sure," I replied, feeling honored. "I would love to!"

*   *   *

Now I stood here, teary-eyed, watching as Andy and Jaylyn exchanged their vows. I prayed that someday I would find a Christian man who would love me and want to spend the rest of his life with me, and also be a father to Celine.

Later, during the reception, Michael came and spoke with me. I enjoyed his kindheartedness and his intelligence. Actually, he monopolized most of my time at the reception. He told me he was going with the missions team to different cities in the Philippines for the next several days. Would I be free to join him for dinner when he got back to Manila, before he returned to Portland?

I told him that would probably be fine. I asked him to call me when he got back to Manila. Then I took a picture of Celine out of my purse.

"This is my one-year-old daughter, Celine," I said hesitantly. I wanted any man seriously interested in pursuing me to know about her at once.

Michael looked at the picture, then smiled. "She sure is cute! She must be a joy to have around." Then he paused, and added, "Jaylyn told me you have a daughter, Jennifer. But I'm glad you did, too. When I get back to Portland, I'm going to keep on praying for you and Celine, every day."

Later, after we had talked, I noticed that Michael approached my parents and introduced himself.

Before he returned to Portland, we saw each other again. Jaylyn and Andy did not leave to go on their honeymoon immediately, so they invited all the groomsmen and bridesmaids for an evening out at Cafe Adriatico. The restaurant's Spanish-style architecture and elegant, quaint interior never seemed more picturesque than on that night. I had a delightful time. I sat beside Michael, and we laughed and talked and got better acquainted. His deep-set brown eyes gazed into mine so intensely…almost as though they were asking without words, "Who are you, Jennifer? You are a mystery to me. I want to get to know you better. I want to know who you really are deep down inside."

During the months after Michael had returned to Portland, I often thought of him, especially while I read my Bible at night. I started to pray more earnestly. Did God have something in store for Michael and me?

My pastor encouraged everyone to maintain total purity before marriage, and he also exhorted us to truly seek God's guidance on whom He wanted us to marry.

"I believe Michael is the man God wants me to marry," I told my parents one evening. "I've been praying, and that's what God is saying."

Since Michael had been gone a few months, and I had not received any letters or phone calls from him, my mom replied, "We better pray harder, then."

I continued to pray about it, as did my parents. My questions and prayers were answered when, two months later, my father received a letter from Michael. He reintroduced himself.

"See, Mom," I said, "I told you. I think God is saying, 'It's Michael!'"

Not long after, I received a letter from him. Several weeks after that, he called long distance. It was December 16th, my twenty-fourth birthday. During this phone call, we talked heart-to-heart. He told me he had been praying for me and Celine almost every day since leaving Manila. He also told me he wanted to come visit me for three weeks with the intent of pursuing marriage.

As he shared this, a growing peace enveloped my heart. I knew that God was moving in my life, bringing His will to pass. Before we ended our phone call, we decided he should come to Manila seven weeks later, in February.

My parents were excited, and they told my brothers and my sister all about Michael. They also told our relatives, our pastor, and other close Christian friends. Everywhere I turned, I found favor and approval. How different it was from my first marriage! So, this is what it's like to pursue marriage with God's blessing, I thought.

Things began to happen quickly after Michael's phone call. The legal annulment of my first marriage was granted. I was given time off from work during the weeks of his visit. The day he arrived, and the moment we met again, my heart pounded. I gave him a warm hug, and we sat and visited in my home that evening. He also met Celine for the first time, and she welcomed him into her life easily.

During the next three weeks, I experienced the most glorious courtship and romance of my life! Michael and I spent each day together. Celine and her nanny were often with us on our dates. We visited my friends and relatives, took Celine shopping, went sightseeing, went to the beach and went out for candlelight dinners.

Of course, we went to Cafe Adriatico once again. This time we chose a table for two in a dimly lit corner. We gazed into each other's eyes and held hands.

"I love you, Jennifer," Michael said. "I don't want to live my life without you. Will you marry me?"

"Yes," I replied, filled with awe and wonder. "Yes, I will marry you."

With joy, I received the engagement ring he placed on my finger.

On October 20th of that year, I married Michael Robert Messing, the most wonderful Christian man I've ever met, with my parents' blessings. With God's strength, we had followed a path of purity—our first kiss was our wedding kiss.

We have lived in Portland, Oregon, since; and we now have two lovely daughters and one son—Celine Marie, Monique Lyselle and Gabriel Grant. Our thirteen years of marriage have been filled with love, passion and adventure.

I have come to discover that Michael and I are compatible in many ways I couldn't have known during our somewhat brief, long-distance courtship across half the world. Over the years, we have grown—slowly but surely—in our unity. We are united on long-term life goals with regards to our careers and finances, desires for our children and home life, dreams in ministry and future missions involvement as well as our fundamental commitment to remain best friends and passionate lovers. There are not enough words to express the many ways Michael has engulfed me in the warm blanket of his tenderness, care, unconditional love and, when needed, understanding and forgiveness. As his devoted wife, I lovingly reciprocate.

This doesn't mean we don't have trials to overcome. Indeed, no marriage is problem-free—but our faith in God continues to help us overcome obstacles. Whenever I reflect on what God has done in my life, I thank Him for giving me a prince.

(JENNIFER ANNE F. MESSING is an author and poet, wife and mother of three who resides in Oregon.)

GOOD THINGS TAKE TIME
By Mary Ball

OOD THINGS TAKE TIME; MINE TOOK TEN YEARS.

1991

On a bright and sunny day I hurried to get my child ready for the jam-packed afternoon I'd planned. I submerged my consciousness in the joys of motherhood partly to avoid the rest of my life, which seemed a shambles.

I dressed my son in dark-blue overalls that wouldn't advertise his gift for getting filthy in seconds flat. A cream-colored turtleneck with dark-blue and maroon cars peeked through the top of the overalls, and his matching tennis shoes completed the outfit. I thought the cars on his shirt were appropriate, since we were going to an antique car show at a park in the small town of Wayland, Michigan.

When I first heard we were going to Wayland I was disappointed, to say the least. I'd already conceded to moving to Grand Rapids from Chicago and could barely handle that without going stir crazy. Now I'd agreed to accompany my husband and his family to spend the day in a small hick town looking at antique cars all day and talking with the cars' proud owners. My husband's father owned an antique car and often displayed it in shows such as this. I still don't know why I agreed to go in the first place, but something told me I had to be there.

My son loves cars and trucks and squealed with delight as my husband and I pulled in to the park at eight in the morning. After locating my father-in-law and letting my son honk the old horn, there wasn't much else to do but smile while passers-by admired the old Chevy and elderly folks reminisced.

I took my son for a walk as soon as I could without appearing impolite. I held his hand through all the "ooh's" and "aah's" for the better part of two hours, reveling in his childhood innocence and delight. We took tons of pictures before returning to "Bomb-Pa's car." He especially liked this one because it was the only one he could touch and actually get into!

We ate lunch there, and I tried to lay him down for a nap—like that was going to happen with the surrounding excitement. I usually put my foot down, not wanting to break his routine, but not today. I looked at the playground on the other side of the park and felt it calling to us. I thought he was going to get whiplash doing a double take when I asked him if he'd like to skip naptime and go play in the park instead. He was off in an instant, and I could barely keep up.

As we entered the playground, I had to pause for a moment because it seemed like I'd entered a new world. The oldies music and other assorted sounds coming from the car show were suddenly distant, and it felt as if the air filled me and hugged me with unexplainable warmth. I began to feel giddy and lightheaded as I pushed my son on the swings and chased him up and down the slide. When we climbed to the top of the monkey bars, we rested and surveyed the entire playground.

I could see all the other parents watching their children from park benches, barking orders to "be safe" and "keep clean." I had to wonder, was I the only one who actually played with my child?

Then I heard the most beautiful sound, almost like music; it was a little girl's giggle and her father growling and playing with her. It took my breath away and filled my eyes with tears as I watched his face light up each time she came closer in the swing. I could see the love, the warmth and the bond between them.

I felt so...at home watching the pair. I couldn't take my eyes off them until I noticed my son tugging on my shirt because he had to go pee. He had probably already wet his diaper, but I wanted to encourage any attempts on his part to sit on the potty.

My body was numb—that father's smile and the twinkle in his eye were burned into my memory forever now, and my question had been answered. I was not the only one!

Somehow, that thought comforted me later in the day when I found drugs in my husband's clothes and felt I had no choice but to leave him. He convinced me he would change and talked me into staying. That night, hazy images of a smiling man with twinkling eyes pushing his daughter on a swing danced through my head and lulled me into a peaceful sleep.

1997

It had been more than five years since I felt that wonderfully warm calm rush over me, fill me and instill me with an unexplained peace. Now it was about to happen again. I was entering the Chicago city limits on my annual visit with friends and family. I didn't get to see much of either, since everyone's schedules seemed to be in conflict. Instead, my husband, my son and I spent our time downtown museum-hopping and sightseeing.

I realized for the first time that I loved watching people. While my husband took our son to the restroom, I sat outside the planetarium on the cement steps and studied the people walking by, the people standing around and the people sitting. For the first time it hit me why I loved going to new places and being in a crowd but not part of it. It was faces—I loved watching faces and wondering what stories they had to tell. There were so many, each with an untold tale behind it. I saw irritation, annoyance, impatience, worry, anger, loss and more. It was all so sad. There were so many sad stories I could see.

The first smile I saw was on a child, though it hadn't been the first child I saw. As I realized the number of children I'd seen that day without smiles, it depressed me even more. I stared at a girl who appeared to be the same age as my son. Her beautiful blond hair shone brightly in the sun and bounced as she skipped up and down the steps. Her father approached and, with a big smile and twinkle in his eye, handed her a lunch. They sat there, oblivious to the pain that surrounded them, lost in conversation, lost in their own world and lost in each other.

For the second time in my life, I felt an indescribable peace wrap me in a blanket of inner satisfaction that I would remember and draw from for years to come. It would be a mental haven to which I could retreat when I could no longer stand to stay in the emotional hell that was my reality.

Throughout that year the best and worst came from my husband as we dealt with my many physical health problems. I became pregnant and was hospitalized four times with massive blood clots in my ankles, legs and lungs. I was on thousands of dollars'-worth of medication; and to add to the mass confusion in my life, I was put on bed rest for the duration of my pregnancy and for a bit afterwards. My husband told everyone how much he loved and needed me one minute then verbally and mentally abused me the next. He was often out at a "job" he never got paid for, leaving my seven-year-old to care for his bedridden mother, who was depressed because she was supposed to be taking care of him.

1998

After the baby was born, things got worse as my husband stayed away into the wee hours of the morning. I wanted to leave, but realistically, I couldn't in that condition. Even as things got better for me physically they got worse mentally, and the only thing that kept suicide at bay was the thought of my children and how they needed me. The only comforts I found in life besides them were my dreams at night and food during the day.

I quickly rose above my already heavy weight of two hundred-fifty pounds to more than three hundred-ten by the end of the year. This only gave me more reasons to be depressed.

1999

My husband had been trying for the eleven years I'd known him (and longer) to get hired by a really prestigious furniture-making company in town, where his father worked. This year, they'd finally agreed to consider his application. This was, perhaps, our last hope, not only for getting the bills paid but also for finding happiness and making our marriage work. If he were happy, if he felt some kind of self-worth and if he gained some self-respect things would get better. I believed this with my whole heart. I had to.

When the envelope came in the mail I ran it to him as if it were from the Publisher's Clearing House Sweepstakes Prize Patrol van. He put it down on the couch and continued to play Nintendo without opening it or even looking at it. I was aghast.

"Why aren't you opening it?" I demanded.

Without turning off the game, he said, "Because I failed the drug test."

My legs gave out, and I couldn't speak. For the first time, I couldn't even cry. He asked if I was mad, and all I said was, "I don't care." I realized for the first time how true that statement was. I didn't care! Then I walked into my son's room to play with him.

As I sat there building with blocks, I heard a voice from some past vision. "You're not the only one." I smiled with tears in my eyes and held my son close, not feeling so alone all of a sudden.

2000

During the beginning of the year, things started taking a turn for the better. I made plans to end my marriage. I started singing karaoke with my mother, which gave me something to look forward to; and I'd lost more than one hundred-twenty pounds on an awesome diet called "I Love Dieting" I'd learned about it on ILoveDieting.com. My testimony was added in the member section because my weight loss was so phenomenal. All my health woes were disappearing one-by-one, and I no longer needed all those prescriptions.

The doctor was baffled but happy with my weight loss and improved health. Still, he absolutely refused to admit that any of it had anything to do with the supplements and herbs I'd been taking. I wasn't too upset when he notified me he was moving to another state and I'd have to find a new doctor.

I found one just in time, as my elder son caught chicken pox. We were a bit nervous being at a new doctor's office and all, but it was close to home and I was glad for that. I was glad, that is, until the nurse from hell walked in.

Remember, I'd seen tons of nurses and doctors over the past few years, but none as cold and uncaring as Miss Jan. She was curt and nearly rude in her comments; and she definitely lacked a decent bedside manner, especially when dealing with a child who was feeling miserable. She was callous about my son's discomfort and barked at him when he dared to complain. Needless to say, it was the last time we went there.

I drove away wondering if she had children; and just in case, I prayed for them. I wondered if she was married. Just in case, I prayed for her possible husband as well. I'm sure her child, should she have one, would need a father like the one I had seen at the park, or the one I saw in Chicago. Yes, her child would need a father with a warm smile and twinkling eyes to overcome the drawbacks of having a mother like that nurse from hell!

Later in the year, my mom talked me into entering a karaoke contest—we went every week now, sometimes more than once. I had planned on entering but didn't make it due to family problems at home that night. My mom did make it but lost to some man. Apparently, a young man (to my mother, that's anyone younger than fifty) had stolen the show. He was so good she didn't feel bad for losing; in fact, she said she'd have felt bad if he didn't win.

Man, was I upset I had missed it. For me, karaoke contests are like free concerts, only better. I feel like the performers actually care about what they're singing.

I wasn't too upset, though, as I also missed competing against this supposed vocal god and embarrassing myself. I sing karaoke because I like to sing, not because others like to hear it! As for the winner, Mom said she couldn't forget how his eyes glowed with excitement.

2001

I was dancing at a karaoke bar when that familiar calm came in on a breeze. Just like before, all the sounds became distant and life's whirlwind seemed to slow down a bit. This time it nearly came to a standstill; and everything went blurry, like a rained-on watercolor painting—everything, that is, except one little spot amidst the night's confusion.

Much like the dance scene in *West Side Story* where Tony and Maria see only each other, hear only each other and know only each other, my sight was drawn to a distant table in the back of the bar. I don't even remember who I was dancing with when that sense of peace took my breath away.

I looked toward that table in the back of the bar because I felt someone staring at me, but I didn't see anyone. A man sat there, but he wasn't looking my way. It was weird how he was the only thing not fuzzy in my vision at that moment. I normally wouldn't have even been able to see that table at all, but the fifty or so people sitting between him and me were arranged perfectly so a clear path of vision existed between us.

I looked at my dance partner but couldn't seem to hear or make sense of what he was saying as he rambled on. After a baffling moment, I was drawn to look again at the distant table; and this time I caught the man as he turned away. I was overcome with both an immense sense of calm and an overwhelming wave of excitement. Through the smoke and haze his face seemed to glow, and I couldn't take my eyes off first his smile and then his eyes. Time and existence froze, and I felt as if I recognized those eyes that seemed so full of love and compassion. I felt myself smile—not a surface smile consisting of lips and teeth but a deep inner smile of my soul.

My whole body and being was light and airy as the bar lit up as if the sun had come out. I knew the song had ended because the couples began leaving the dance floor. I can't remember if I thanked my partner or not. My only thoughts were on getting closer to the mysterious man.

As I approached, I noticed my friend Jason was at the table as well. I walked right on by, as I didn't know what to say or what the heck I was doing; but the pull between me and the man who had touched my soul wouldn't let me get far before turning me around to head back. I had to meet this man, I had to find out what made him so happy and fulfilled that I could feel it so deeply within me; and I had to inquire about this strong and passionate inner peace that radiated from him to me across a crowded bar strongly enough to momentarily stall my universe.

When I returned to the table, Jason was gone, but my friend Jen was there.

"Mary! Sit down for a sec."

Yeah, like she had to tell me twice! I glanced over at the mysterious man next to me, who looked away again. Jen introduced us then left to turn in her song slip; she never returned. This conveniently left us alone. He timidly requested a dance in the most unforgettable and polite manner I've ever been asked.

"If you'd like to, you could save me a dance later."

I could barely speak, so I whispered, "I'd love to."

I found out later that he nearly melted right then and there. The very next song was a slow song, and I asked him if he'd like to dance to that one. His face lit up as he flashed that smile of inner happiness and joy that his whole body reflected; he smiled from deep within and it radiated out. He later told me that while he'd been watching me on the dance floor (and, yes, he looked away each time I looked over at him) he felt I'd smiled from within as well. I guess it was my soul that smiled that night.

I walked to the dance floor on a cloud of happiness and turned toward him to begin our dance. I noticed right away that he didn't grope me or try to plaster his body to mine. He didn't let his hands roam over my hips and butt, either. His right hand rested politely but firmly high on my waist while his left hand's fingers laced mine.

There was an instant connection when we touched hands for the first time on the dance floor, something that grabbed them, brought them together and cemented something permanent between us. We both felt it; it was like some force wrapped silken chords around them, never to be undone.

I instantly felt at home with this man. Then our bodies were tied with the same bond as we were drawn to each other. We came together so smoothly, like a door closing on its hinges; and we fit together like a hand and glove. Some might wonder how, because he's shorter than I, but I don't. We're two pieces of a puzzle that are just meant to be together, and we fit just that snugly.

I felt a bit shy and thought of looking away but couldn't. My eyes were glued to this miracle of a man I was dancing with. I thought it made him uneasy, because he was the one who looked away. Later he said that there was something there, something between us, something so powerful and honest that he had to look away to catch his breath.

I felt a powerful current flowing between us as we danced. I've never taken any dance classes; but when I'm with him, we dance! He dipped me, swayed me, twirled me; and we didn't stumble once. Our legs looked like we'd choreographed the dance. And practiced for months. It's like that every time we've ever danced, and everyone watches with smiles on their faces and in their hearts.

Something is very apparent whenever we're together. My mother told him once that when I walk in the room the sun rises inside him, and she can see it on his face. People say similar things about me and asked when he and I were going to be wed even before I'd admitted to myself that I loved him! Somehow, they plainly saw what I refused to admit at first.

More than one person has said they see that "something" between us when he sings to me. The whole place is captured in our dream, conversation stops momentarily at nearly every table and many look back at me and smile knowingly. It's plain to see the love he has for me, and I for him. It's more than love, though. It's so much more.

I wouldn't accept it at first. How could I? I didn't understand its depth and magnitude. Little by little, it began to make sense. One day, while going through my photo albums with me, he looked at a picture and gasped. I asked him what was wrong; and he looked at me intensely, pointed to a photo I'd taken over ten years before at that car show and softly said, "That's my house."

He began to tell me about how his day had unfolded back then. The car show got there early and blared that oldies music, waking him up. He and his daughter later went to the park across the street from their home, which borders the car show's boundaries. I got tingles when he told me that his little girl was the same age as my son. Yes, he, too, was there that day at the park at the same time I was. He was pushing his little girl in a swing. He said he was so happy that day. I told him I knew—because it had shown in his smile and in his eyes.

When we started sharing more of our lives and our pasts with each other, I found out he nearly left his wife back then, as I had planned to leave my husband. He was glad he had waited until later because he had gained a mass of fond memories. He then shared some of his precious memories with me, like how he had gone to Chicago with his daughter a few years back. He remembered how she loved it, and how they really liked walking along the shore of Lake Michigan.

Then he told me how they'd stopped for lunch and sat on the cement stairs of some museum to eat it. It was just him and her with her golden hair shining in the sun and blowing in the breeze while he watched and couldn't stop smiling. I told him I knew, and that his eyes were twinkling that day as well.

I knew there was something more than I could ever comprehend between us, and I knew what I felt for him. The only thing I wasn't sure of was how he felt about me at first, until one day it nearly knocked me off my feet.

I was shopping in the grocery store and somehow ended up talking to a man named Scott about the 9/11 tragedy. After a bit, the topic switched to family and love. He was going through many of the same things I had in my past marriage. I told him to hang in there because it would get better, and that life has an uncanny way of working things out. I proceeded to tell him about how I met this man who really loved me and how my life was finally turning around.

He said, "Damn! You have that same look in your eye as my best friend when he talks about the love of his life."

Scott told me about his friend, who was so in love with some girl who just danced into his life one night, and how he knew there was something there that was bigger than the both of them from the moment he laid eyes on her. He had known he was in love by the second date, which wasn't really a date but another accidental chance meeting.

Scott went on to relate that his friend couldn't stop talking about how beautiful the girl was both on the inside and the outside, and he couldn't understand why a "fox" like that was even remotely interested in him. Everything about her was so perfect, and he was only a country hick; he was just a short old warehouse rat with nothing to offer her but his love. Scott told me what his friend said in the end: "Everyone's got someone out there, that one special one meant just for them. Scott, she's my ONE!"

As Scott told me how his friend had tears of joy in his eyes he looked at me and realized I was crying as well. I smiled, took his hand, and then softly said, "It's nice to meet you, Scott. I'm John's girlfriend, and he told me the same thing just last night."

I've often wondered how in the world I accidentally met John's best friend in the store that day, or how any of these things happened; but it's not something that can be explained. Some things can be, though, like why I was so devastated each time I'd been dumped by a boyfriend in the past, even when I knew I didn't love him. I now know why I felt a loss, and it wasn't because I lost a boyfriend. It was because my soul was searching for its other half; and after a break-up I was forced to realize that this was not the ONE for me and I was still flopping like a fish out of water through life frantically searching for him. I knew there was someone out there for me; I just hadn't found him yet.

Those images of John at the car show, on those steps in Chicago and at karaoke that night we met were each steps to the happy home I've now found in his love. The never-ending coincidences keep rolling in like thunder before an awesome storm. The nurse from hell was his wife, and her possible child I prayed for was John's daughter. The man who won the karaoke contest I couldn't make it to was John. We've both dreamed of traveling out west on a Valkyrie with black leather saddlebags and a sissy bar, and we both purchased a Bursa for our first gun. We both like camping, the great outdoors, hunting, collecting knives, music, children, the performing arts and more.

My story isn't done unfolding, so I'll never be done telling it; but that doesn't mean I'll ever stop trying. The more I learn and understand, the more I'll share about how I finally know what all those love songs are really about. I'll tell my story about how I've found my ONE, my love, my soul mate. With him I feel an inner peace and calm. I feel as if we fit together like we belong and like we're finally home after traveling far and distant foreign lands.

(MARY BALL is a writer from western Michigan.)

SOUL MATES FOREVER
By Anika Logan

I HONESTLY BELIEVE THAT MOST THINGS IN LIFE DO NOT HAPPEN RANDOMLY, but rather that there is order to the universe. An order, however, that more often than not we fail to fully understand. There is a reason for each of us to be here, a purpose for our life. We are not just born to die; we are born to live and matter and cherish the precious time we have been given.

In the same way, I believe in my heart that we are destined to meet certain people in our lifetime. Our meetings with others are very well-choreographed, in my humble opinion. The sad part is that most people we meet, no matter how special to us they become, are not fated to be in our life for long. Some loves, sometimes the greatest of loves, are intense, unforgettable but not lengthy—short but sweet, as the saying goes.

There has always been a tragic element to my love life—not tragic in a death way, but tragic in that I found myself loving men who could never be mine. This often gives me pause. Even as I write it, I continue to ponder certain questions about the loves I have had and the loves that are yet to come. I wonder if I will ever know the answers for sure, or if there will always be those question marks in my life. Perhaps there are always questions that remain unanswered. Could this be, in part, an explanation for why, as human beings, we yearn to know more and more? No one can really answer that conclusively.

After reading my story, you be the judge of what constitutes a true soul mate. I give you now my love story, my tragedy, my heartbreak and the soul mate who made it all possible.

*   *   *

I stood amidst the throng of people waiting for the passengers to disembark from the plane. I hadn't seen him in five months. My heart beat with such fervor I thought it would jump out of my chest and onto the floor for everyone to see.

I loved him, and I knew he loved me, too. It was all there the last time he was with me, hundreds of miles from his home. We had had only three weeks together; but they were unforgettable weeks, the best I'd ever had.

We'd stood at the airport holding each other close before his flight out. For how long we stood there without speaking I couldn't say. Time did, indeed, stand still when I was with him. I ran my fingers through his hair and kissed the side of his head. Physically, this was as close as we'd ever been. We had talked about our intense attraction to one another, the chemical pull that bound us together, but had not acted upon it. We couldn't—we both knew that.

Many men had hurt me before I met Marc. I was afraid to allow myself to have feelings for a man, petrified to open my heart enough to love again. I had built a locked fortress around it and thrown away the key—permanently. Or so I thought until I met him.

It took a while; but with each passing day, the more time we spent together, the more I felt my heart thawing out. I wanted to trust this man so very much; and eventually, I did come to. I realized that for the first time in a number of years I wanted someone to know me, really know me.

It was uncanny, really. I would walk with him in the park or sit across a table from him at our favorite coffee shop, me with my tea and him with his café latte, and feel some force within me compelling me to bring up a personal topic, to reveal parts of myself to him and, in turn, learn more about him. It was a feeling I had never experienced before, but it felt unbelievably good.

We had more in common than I had ever thought possible. The correlations between our pasts were amazing. I thirsted to know all I could about him and to get as deep into his heart as I could. When I looked into his eyes I penetrated his psyche. I felt something. I was almost scared of the intensity of my emotions.

Ours went deeper than mere physical attraction. We had forged an emotional connection like none I had ever experienced before. My former relationships had been more about sexual fulfillment than emotional involvement, and this was entirely different. This was a bonding of a spiritual and emotional nature.

He made me feel whole; he made me feel right with myself and the world around me. He accepted me for who I was, unconditionally. This was very important to me. It didn't matter who I was last year, or five years ago or ten years ago. Nor did it matter who I'd be next year or in four or five years. The only thing that was significant to him was who I was today, just today.

I loved him for all the good things he brought to the surface of my life. All forms of darkness were extinguished when he was around. I loved him for all of these things. I just plain loved him. I knew that. It had taken me far too long to figure it out.

I opened myself up to Marc, and it was the closest that I had ever come to true magic. The thrill of being in love—truly, honestly, wholeheartedly in love—was phenomenal. My heart felt buoyant, free and joyous. I had had many boyfriends and many casual dates but nothing that came close to this. My life became possible when I fell in love with Marc. I was undeniably blessed. When we talked, when we held each other, I could almost touch the love we shared; it was that tangible. He was my soul mate. I looked into his eyes and glimpsed his spirit and the deepest yearnings of his soul. I was his, and he was mine—no question.

I saw him coming down the escalator. Soon the door would open, and I would run to him. I could hardly contain myself. How I longed to be in his arms again!

The sliding doors opened, and he stepped through them. Our eyes connected at almost the exact same moment. The chemical pull was there, all right. I started moving, quickening my steps the closer I got to him. His eyes widened, and his mouth was brimming with happiness and excitement. His arms encircled me. I was home, where I belonged. This was the only way to live.

He pulled back just a little to search my flushed face. He reached up to touch my cheek. I closed my eyes as I reveled in his caress then opened them just as his eyelashes fluttered closed and his lips sought out mine. I responded in earnest to the sweetness of his kiss. Time ceased to exist. Everything else receded. I loved him. I loved him in a way that I'd never loved any man.

When the kiss was over, he looked into my eyes. I smiled back at him. We clung to one another as tightly as we could. Our eyes communicated what our voices could not yet say.

Finally, he spoke. "I've missed you, Annie."

My heart leapt. "I've missed you so much, Marc, so much you have no idea."

I was choked up with emotions.

He ran his fingers through my hair and traced the outline of my face as if he were committing it to memory.

"Let's go get my bags, and then we'll get out of here," he said, looking around.

We both were suddenly aware of our surroundings. People moved around us in every imaginable direction. The airport was bustling.

Marc took my hand and said, "I want you all to myself. I've been away from you far too long."

"Yes, you have, Marc. I second that."

We walked hand-in-hand towards the baggage conveyor to retrieve his luggage.

"We need to catch up, Marc. Tell me what's been going on with you." I tried to sound lighthearted.

With a serious expression, he whispered, "No, Annie, we need to love."

His pronouncement meant the world to me.

We made love that night for the first time. I had known him three years, and this was the first time we had been intimate. Our relationship, though, was not destined to last. Fate had made sure we found our way to each other, but it would end and I would be destroyed. My heart would threaten to close up forever and never let another man in again.

I could give him everything, but everything would not be enough to keep him with me. He gave me the world when we were together. My heart splintered at the thought of losing him. I died a little inside when I imagined him not a part of my life.

I lived every moment as if it might be my last. Our days together were few and fleeting. On this night, he told me he was so deeply in love with me that he couldn't breathe sometimes. His feelings for me would never change, he told me, no matter what happened in the future.

He lay beside his wife at night and thought of being in my arms. I was the true love of his life, the one—not her. The knowledge of this was enough for me. He would stay with her—I had known that from the start. I could live with the consequences of our involvement because I had experienced true love.

The earth really did move when we were together, just like in all of the classic love stories and romantic movies I knew by heart. They often end tragically, with tears that refuse to cease and pain that cuts deep. They can be defined as brief and passionate but what makes getting up every morning worthwhile. An everlasting love that lives on in one's mind, heart and soul but not in one's daily life.

A hallmark of an unforgettable and genuine love story, it seems to me, is that it end in a devastating manner. Mine was an example.

(ANIKA LOGAN is from Halifax, Nova Scotia.)

LOVE CAN WAIT
By Connie Curry

S HE STOOD ALONE, LOOKING AT THE AZALEAS. THEY WERE IN FULL BLOOM, their color vibrant. She thought of the day, many years before when she dug into the earth, planting them. They were small, fragile, in need of nurturing just as she had nurtured her children so they could grow healthy, strong and independent.

Laura looked up into the blue, warm spring sky; and her back ached. Her hands showed signs of aging, her knees popped and cracked in protest when she kneeled down to pull weeds. She reminisced about years and days gone by. She thought of sacrifices she had made. Her children had been her life, her love—and her sanity.

Laura was born with beauty, good health and a sense of humor. Yes, she had been a lucky woman and a good mother. Her heart was always full of kindness for others, and she brought so much laughter into a room.

The children were stable, happy, healthy and wonderfully independent now; and Laura had become a grandmother.

Sometimes, she would look in the mirror and remember those days of youth and wish for her soft, flawless skin. Her eyes still sparkled, but the lines around them reminded her of now; and she knew those days were gone. She thought about the aging process. Although age encroached at a slow pace, it still seemed cruel. Many times she wanted her youth back. Laura knew her heart could make her feel young again if she had a path to guide her.

It had not been planned. It was by chance that day many years earlier when she was walking down the street and Phil appeared. Life was tolerable, easy and full of routine. She immediately knew it was him. That walk! She became mesmerized. She watched him come toward her; his soft blue eyes and his smile brought back so many memories of school days. He had become a man, and she a woman. They had gone separate ways and now had new lives.

Life was tolerable, easy and full of routine. They both had jobs; duties and love at home...separate homes, with children who needed security. But their eyes met, and memories came flooding back. He touched her face with the back of his hand. She took in his scent. Her heart fluttered; and she recalled the many times, so long ago, she had felt that same touch. They looked deep within each other's eyes, and words did not have to be spoken for them to know the waves of passion flowed again.

She saw emptiness in his eyes and wondered about his life. He was no longer a boy but a man...an unhappy man. He had aged with perfection; but his soul appeared empty, lonely, and his happy, free spirit was gone. She recalled days of so much laughter—endless carefree days when she would watch him laugh. He would sit, watch her and roar with laughter as she chattered with many hand gestures and energy. They had adored each other and were more than lovers. They had been best friends.

They were immediately tempted by the forbidden, and they fought for morality. They knew their love from many years gone by was real, but it had reappeared too late. Their souls melted and ached for each other. What could they do? They knew, without speaking the words, that life must go on as is and maybe another time would come for them to be one.

They walked away, in different directions and back to reality. He had stirred so much emotion in her. She dared to look back. He was more beautiful than ever, and she knew to turn around would test her strength. Reality was at home, so onward she walked with a heavy heart.

Today, as she stood taking in the scent of the flowers and feeling the spring breeze blow through her hair, she wondered about the new future that lay ahead. The quietness was new to her. For many years the house had been full of laughter, and doors slamming, children bickering or playing, errands and demanding schedules.

Laura smiled, thinking about the day she planted a pine tree seedling for her daughter Abby. She looked up now to see the top of the tree. Like Abby, the tree had grown, survived and was strong and able to stand alone. Laura had done her duty, wholeheartedly, and had many wonderful memories. Her heart was full of love.

Her husband was gone. Her life was quiet now, and the years of fast-paced schedules and obligations and the needs of others were gone, too.

Phil and Laura had waited thirty years for this day. Their lives were now less complicated, and they had made the right choices and chanced their sacrifices. Their love had prevailed.

Today was a new chapter in the life of Laura; and as she thought about it, she smiled. She saw dust whirling in the sky and heard his truck as she recalled his words.

"We did the right thing, Laura. We waited. We did our jobs as parents. I have never known true love, until you. You are my soul mate."

He was finally coming for her; and her heart felt warm, secure and young again. She knew he felt like a boy again, too. So alive.

Phil approached her; and when she looked into his beautiful, gentle eyes, she knew he saw the youthful beauty of years past. He did not see the aging woman; he saw the vibrant, beautiful girl. He felt promise and love. He touched her. She smiled, and she knew life was good again. The loneliness was gone, and the wait was over. All those years seemed to disappear; and like the azaleas planted so long ago, she felt new life taking hold.

She walked to the truck with him at her side. As they headed away into their new life, she looked back at the azaleas. Like the children, they would survive and bloom again next year.

The wait was over, and the dance had begun.

(CONNIE E. CURRY is a freelance writer/columnist from Delaware, Ohio.)

SEALED WITH AN E-KISS
By Leslie Dennis

THIS STORY TAKES PLACE A LONG TIME AGO, BACK WHEN BULLETIN BOARDS ruled the Internet and 2400-baud modems were considered lightning-fast. Prodigy and AOL were the leaders of online communication, and I had just gotten out of a long-term relationship with a controlling man. I was simply looking for something fun to do in my spare time.

My cyber-life began on Prodigy, back in the dark ages of '91. There was no real-time chat, however. Messages were left on bulletin boards and emails were sent between members for a small fee. I wasn't looking for anything online, and I certainly wasn't looking for a relationship. It just sort of happened.

I hit it off with a charming man named Michael. We were complete opposites, and he was twelve years older than I; but something just clicked with us. We exchanged emails at first; then we began snail-mailing each other cards and gifts. Then the phone calls began...

I was young and naïve at that time, and knew absolutely nothing about cyber-relationships. Of course, it was all brand-new anyway, so I guess I knew about as much as anyone else online did. I got to the point where I became dependent on receiving Michael's daily emails and/or calls to me. The fact that he lived in Massachusetts and I lived in Louisiana was the only barrier that kept us from being in a real-life relationship.

My days were filled with thinking about Michael and fantasizing about going up to New England and visiting him and what a wonderful time we would have together. I started checking airline prices and trying to figure out when the best time to fly in would be. Then, during one of our email sessions, he admitted he had been seeing a local woman for the past few months.

To say that I was shocked would be putting it mildly. Never had I felt such a betrayal; and all the while, he was telling me what we had wasn't real since we lived so far apart. Oh, he was always so practical!

The kicker came when he told me he and his new girlfriend would still love for me to visit. What? I remember thinking that my poor foolish heart would never mend after that episode.

I never got to meet Michael, and I left Prodigy that very day. I'd received a copy of AOL from a local friend—this was before AOL started junk-mailing their software to every household in the country. I remember logging on and thinking how wonderful it was to talk in real-time to people. This was definitely a step up from my Prodigy experience.

Being online was still costly at that time, and you had to pay by the hour to use the service. One month my AOL bill was more than $500! Obviously, I was addicted, but it offered so much more than Prodigy! I could wake up in the middle of the night and turn on my computer and know there would be someone on I could start a conversation with.

My dating life had all but ceased to exist, replaced by my new addiction. I turned down nice guy after nice guy in order to log on to the Internet every night. It didn't take long before I found myself in another cyber-relationship.

His name was Peter; and ironically, he was from Massachusetts. What was it with New Englanders and me? I couldn't find someone a little closer to home?

This relationship was one I tried to stave off from the beginning, telling Peter I was not interested in anything more than a friendship with him. Well, that lasted all of a month. Before long it was emails, cards, gifts and phone calls, just like it had been with Michael.

Peter was a year younger than I when we met, making him twenty-five at the time; yet he fancied himself worldly because he had gone to college in Maine. Now, I may be blond, but I know that Maine is only one state away from Massachusetts (and here I thought I was a bit worldly having gone to boarding school in Florida, college in Texas and vacationed in various ports of call around the globe). But, alas, I was in love, so I bit my tongue.

It wasn't long before Peter was trying to engage in hot chat in private rooms and over the phone. I can honestly admit that I have never in all of my online life engaged in cyber-sex. Not because I'm a prude but rather because I was always editing the dialogue. Hey, I'm a writer, what can I say?

I'm also a night owl. I would stay up talking to Peter for hours, and he would always chastise me about how tired he was at work the next day. I always caught the blame for that, even though he did the majority of the talking. It didn't help that he lived with his parents and they weren't very tolerant of his late hours.

I began making plans to fly to Boston to meet him. We had been talking online for more than four months now, and our feelings had grown by leaps and bounds. I booked my flight a month in advance so I could get the cheapest airfare; but when I told Peter, I think it must have become too "real" for him to handle. He goaded me into a fight that lasted more than three hours on the phone, until it was clear there was no changing his mind. He wanted to break it off.

I had no choice but to comply, even though I had already paid for my plane ticket. My former roommate from boarding school lived in Boston, and I had made arrangements to stay with her during my visit to New England. I wrote Peter and told him I was still going to visit and reminded him of the dates. He never wrote back.

As soon as my friend met me at the airport, she told me, "Peter called and wants you to call him when you get settled in."

My heart leapt! I was so excited I don't think my feet touched the floor the whole trek through Logan Airport. I was actually going to meet the man I had fallen in love with! No matter that he had tried to break it off a few weeks earlier.

Finally, the day we had arranged to meet arrived; and I drove my friend's car up to Peter's parents' house to meet the "whole fam-damily," as he called them. On that brisk October afternoon, with the fall foliage in Technicolor bloom, I finally met my cyber-love.

We had a great visit and got along extremely well, but things weren't the same as they'd been online. In person, you notice faults that hadn't been apparent over the modem.

Peter was far from perfect, but my feelings for him hadn't changed. I found his obvious inexperience with women endearing. Yet he wouldn't let me get close to him. I still have no idea why, since it was painfully clear he was desperate for someone to love him. In a virtual world, he was chivalrous and gallant; but in real life he was as insecure as a young boy. With a heavy heart, I left New England and Peter. I tried to contact him when I returned home, but he never answered my emails or calls. For all I know he is still living at home with his parents.

After that, I threw away everything even remotely connected to AOL and vowed never again to get online. I got back into the dating scene in town and made lots of new friends. When spring rolled around, I decided to clean out a lot of old junk. My dog Jessie, a golden retriever mix, came bounding out of my bedroom with a piece of paper in her mouth—she's always "fetching" something and bringing it to me. I took it from her and was about to throw it away when I noticed the word *Delphi.com*. Remember, this was 1993 and dot-coms were just starting to be recognized. I put the paper up and decided to have a look at it later.

"Later" just happened to be that very same night. I was talking to a friend on the phone, and he mentioned Procomm Plus for DOS (a very archaic communications program by today's standards) and how you could use it to dial into various online services. I had never used the program before, so my friend came over and hooked me up. After he left, I grabbed the Delphi.com paper and called in.

It wasn't nearly as sophisticated as AOL and you had to put special characters in front of your text in order for the commands to go through. I wound up in a chat room called "Fools," and immediately I was hooked. I hadn't realized how much I had missed the cyber-banter during my self-imposed exile from virtual reality. "Fools" had been appropriately named, too—it was full of wacky, zany people, and I was having a blast!

After about an hour, a person with the moniker "Wolf" came into the room. I'd make a joke and he'd match me one better so I would throw another one out there. It was getting late and the room cleared out until there only Wolf and I were left.

I had been so busy playing around I hadn't learned the proper way to exit a room. It was then Wolf wrote: "Looks like it's just you and me."

That simple line—from a "Wolf," no less—made me nervous, as I'd heard it many times before as a prelude to a come-on. I started typing in every possible command to leave the room (which also showed up on the screen):

Exit
Quit
Leave
Byebye

Nothing worked.

Then across my screen, I see:

"type: /bye"

So, that's how you did it! Duh! Now I felt more comfortable, knowing I could just leave; and the fact he'd told me how to accomplish it raised him a rank in my book. We wound up talking and kidding around for a few more hours, and he even emailed me the entire list of commands for navigating the site.

The Wolf's name was Brandon, and he lived in Louisville (I was so thrilled he didn't say Massachusetts) and he had the most incredible sense of humor! Thus began a wonderful friendship. Neither of us tried to monopolize the other's time. If we happened to run into each other online, we'd say hello and visit for a bit in private messages, then we'd go on about our business. We had exchanged phone numbers and would call each other now and then and just shoot the breeze. Like I said, it was a great friendship.

He knew how I felt about Internet romances and was always lending a sympathetic ear when I would go on about some guy who wanted to get serious online—he was a wonderful listener. He was my buddy, my pal. It wasn't until nine months into our friendship that I received this email: "Leslie, I love you. I'm sorry, but I can't help the way I feel. I know you weren't looking for a relationship and neither was I, but you're all I think about."

It was signed simply: "aml, -b" (All my love, Brandon).

I checked and saw that he was online. I sent him a private

116

message and wrote: "NO NO NO! Please don't do this!"

He didn't reply. Minutes later, the phone rang. I answered it, and there was a long pause on the other end, then I heard "I love you, Leslie."

I liked the way he said my name, "Lezlee," with a sexy drawl. Of course, I hadn't realized how much I liked it until that moment. But I was not about to go through another online, long-distance romance. My poor heart couldn't handle another break!

"Let me fly you up here. We'll meet and then take it from there," he told me. "Leslie, please. I'm not Michael or Peter, give me a chance."

We agreed to meet for the upcoming Thanksgiving holiday, and I was so nervous on the flight up there. On the plane, some poor man beside me had the misfortune of having to listen to me blab the whole time. I recall him trying to get a word in edgewise and telling me something about where Kentucky and Indiana bordered was called "Kentuckiana." I asked him why it wasn't "Indiucky." He was very quiet after that. I'm sure he thought I was a complete airhead.

As soon as I got off the plane, Brandon walked up to me and gave me a stuffed lion, saying, "See? I wasn't Lyin' (Lion)." Did I mention his adorably corny sense of humor? It was so sweet, and he was exactly as I had imagined him for so many months—we had exchanged pictures, but sometimes photos can be misleading. All my apprehensions faded away as we hugged.

We had a great Thanksgiving. I met his family and got to go to Churchill Downs, where a horse I bet on actually won!. Since it was getting close to Christmas, we bought some ornaments and decorated a tree in his small apartment. It was so cozy and romantic being there with him, like a dream. And I didn't want it to end.

I dreaded getting on that plane and leaving him behind. I was so afraid once we got back into our real lives, away from each other, the magic would disappear. Unlike my trip up, I didn't say a word the entire flight back.

As soon as I got home, he called to make sure I'd arrived safely and told me he missed me. He was always so thoughtful like that. November turned to December and then the New Year rolled around. It was 1995, and Brandon and I were racking up enormous phone bills.

"I want to be with you, Leslie," he said, "so I've decided to move down there."

I couldn't believe he was going to pack all his belongings up in that little Honda Prelude and travel eight hundred miles to Louisiana. But on Valentine's Day 1995 Brandon arrived at my door to hand-deliver a dozen long-stemmed red roses. I couldn't believe he had actually left all he knew behind just to be with me. My heart filled with so much love that day I swear it nearly burst.

Two years later, on November 1, 1997, we were married; and not a day has passed that we haven't said, "I love you."

It's true what they say: "A woman will run from a mouse, but smile at a Wolf." Now I know why.

smile

(LESLIE DENNIS is a writer from Louisiana.)

ETERNAL LOVE

IN THE TRANQUIL HOURS OF NIGHT,
I walk in your soul,
You live in my heart.
With each beat,
With each breath,
We are one.

Dawn merges with day.
I melt into you,
You capture my spirit,
Our hearts swell with passion,
Our bodies weep with ecstasy.
We are eternal love.

My Warrior, My Beloved, My
Everything,
I'll love you endlessly

— Margaret Marr

PART TWO
KARMIC SOUL MATES

"Some people come into our lives and quickly go. Some people move our souls to dance. They awaken us to new understanding with the passing whisper of their wisdom. Some people make the sky more beautiful to gaze upon. They stay in our lives for awhile, leave footprints on our hearts, and we are never ever the same."
— Flavia Weedn

REUNION

I read love poems in dog-eared volumes
on a quest for the one that speaks of you and I.
I weep for the losses, and cheer for loves shared
and sweet. Yet no words written by any poet's pen
give life to my heart's abandon.
It was yours from the day you danced
into life, miles and years away. I did not
know you but for a little girl's dreams and
twinkling eyes. That was you, tickling my soul.
You were back!
Different paths and many loves later
we felt a hand as familiar as our own
extended across an ocean of tears.
Grasping tightly to this gift, we journeyed
to waterfalls and the past, a friendship
in spirit, in faith and in trust.
I believe in miracles, for here you are,
close enough to warm my skin
and unfold my layers of fear.
We share memories of a life celebrated
on the pages of time, though our story is yet
to be written. Perhaps someday.
You are as much a part of me
as the blood that runs through my veins.
You are that necessary. As I read love poems
and search for what we have found, my eyes
twinkle. I am at peace, with you once again
tickling my soul.

— Lori Williams

MY HERO
By Jeanni Brosius

S HE LIES ON THE SMALL, PLASTIC-COVERED BED. I SWEEP WHAT IS LEFT OF HER auburn hair from her face. Quietly, she opens her eyes and turns to gaze out the second-story window. It has been three months since she walked down the stairs without assistance, and longer since she has played outside with her children. The only fresh air she inhales is through the sliver of an open window.

Her eyes reflect a distance I cannot begin to understand. The distance of her life, perhaps, memories or even hopes and dreams she knows will never happen. Laughter emanates from the front yard. I reach up to close the window.

"No," she says.

I hesitate and turn to look at her.

"I love the laughter. It is a sign of life."

I smile and take my position next to her bed. My position. That sounds strange to me. My position has changed from co-worker, friend and even soul sister to that of caretaker, babysitter and actress. I have to mask my hurt, my sadness so as not to upset her. I must maintain a positive and upbeat attitude that no longer exists in my heart.

We are too young to be dealing with such an evil force as cancer. My God, she is only forty. She is supposed to have her entire life ahead of her. She is supposed to grow old with her husband, see her children graduate, plan their weddings and then enjoy her time as a grandmother. How can this happen? This isn't the regular course of life. Or is it?

"I'm thirsty."

Her voice brings me up from my despairing thoughts. Reaching for her glass of water, I turn the bent straw around and place it under my index finger. Holding it to her dry, cracked lips, I notice where her eyebrows and eyelashes once grew. The treatment seems to be killing her along with the cancer.

Each week, her husband takes her to Little Rock for these treatments. He stays the night with her. He holds her hand as her skin is punctured with needles, places a cool cloth on her head after she vomits and soothes her tears with his reassuring voice. He loves her. He needs her. She needs him. I have no idea where he finds the strength.

Tomorrow is their nineteenth wedding anniversary. They will spend it with him at her bedside, loving her with his entire heart, already missing her. We know it is a matter of time, but that is something we just don't talk about. It has been swept under the rug or placed high upon a shelf where no one looks. It is something we can't comprehend.

"Hi," he says to me as he takes off his coat and flings it over the bedpost. "How is she today?"

"She's fine," I lie to him. She isn't fine and never will be. She is dying.

He bends down and kisses her on the forehead. She opens her eyes and smiles. How can she smile? The scent of death is in the air, and she is smiling. He smiles back.

"Sweetie, I'm going to go home now. I'll be back tomorrow. We'll finish reading our book." I pack the tattered copy of Erma Bombeck's *Four of a Kind* into my bag.

My friend always referred to me as the "new Erma Bombeck." I always laughed and slightly blushed when she would say it to someone else, but inside it made me feel very special. I'll never be another Erma nor will I ever have the strength or the heart of my friend, who is dying before my eyes.

I squeeze her hand and smile through an invisible veil of tears. "I love you, sweetie."

"I love you, too, Jeanni. Thank you."

Each time I leave her house I wonder if it will be the last time I see my friend alive.

Closing the front door behind me, I fill my lungs with the scent of the season. The neighbors have a fire in the fireplace—the aroma of burning wood escapes from their chimney and floats through the neighborhood. The cold wind bites my cheeks; the sky looks like snow. Perhaps it will, and we can sit her up by the window so she can watch her kids pummel each other with snowballs.

By the time I get home it is dark. My husband greets me at the door.

"How is she?" he asks.

"She is fine." There I go, lying again.

He puts his arm around me, and I bury my face into his gray sweatshirt. I cry. Stroking my hair and holding me, he cries, too.

As I hear my son trotting down the stairs, I pull away and wipe my eyes with the backs of my hands. My husband turns toward the stove and pretends to finish making his tea.

"Hi, Mom."

"Hi, Baby." I put my arms around his ten-year-old body, wanting to hold him close to my heart forever. There is nothing that makes one more aware of life than death.

Later that night, preparing for bed, I try to get hold of my emotions. I try so hard to be strong for her and not let her see me cry. Her sickness penetrates my heart; our souls are one. We feel each other's pain. Why do I kid myself into thinking she isn't aware of my pain? She knows mine as well as I know hers.

A restless night leads to a groggy morning. I force myself out of bed to spend another day attending to my friend. An overwhelming feeling of sadness fills my heart, and I know. I feel her soul departing.

She's dead.

Without hesitation, I drive to her house. Her husband meets me at the door; tears stream down his unshaven face. I drop my bag and throw my arms around him.

"She isn't hurting anymore," he says.

"No, she isn't." Months of hidden pain reach the surface as I hold him while he cries.

I pull away and leave him in his mother's arms as I take the long journey up the stairs for the last time. Peering around the door frame, I see her. She is so peaceful. She is smiling. I smile through

the tears as I bid my best friend—my soul mate and my hero—
goodbye.

As I leave the room, I place the old, tattered Erma Bombeck book
on her nightstand.

(JEANNI BROSIUS is a nationally syndicated columnist, National Public
Radio commentator, author, speaker and journalist at the Batesville
(Ark.) *Daily Guard.*)

BACK WITH ELI
By Avis Townsend

WHEN MY HUSBAND DAN AND I BOUGHT OUR FARM SEVEN YEARS AGO, WE brought with us four dogs and two horses. I knew we'd need cats, also, not just to scare away mice but because we'd always had them. A leukemia epidemic had gone through our last neighborhood, however; and we had no kitties to take to our new home.

Shortly after we moved in, a petite female cat approached me in the pasture, meowing like she'd known me for years. I discovered she lived in an abandoned tractor bucket and marveled that she'd been smart enough to survive the coyote attacks that had taken the lives of most of the farm cats in this new neighborhood.

She let me pick her up; I adopted her but took her immediately to my veterinarian to be vaccinated and tested for leukemia. When she was given the all-clear, testing negative for any diseases, I was relieved. She was kind and colorful, and I named her Sweet Pea.

She adapted to the house quite well. Before I could have her spayed, however, she presented me with three tiny kittens—Pinky, Murphy and Eli—born under a bed in the spare room upstairs. I now had my cat family. The household was complete.

As the kittens grew, I had them spayed and neutered. Four cats was enough, I reasoned.

I loved them all; but Eli was the special one, and everyone noticed it. Eli and I became close—so close, in fact, we could almost read each other's minds.

"That cat won't leave your side," Dan commented more than once.

My son was more sarcastic. "You got some Velcro on you? I've never seen you without that gray one stuck to you."

No matter where I was, Eli was at my side. As he matured, his gray turned into a beautiful silver; and I called him my Darling Silver Eli, much to the groans and annoyance of my husband and children. When I watched TV, Eli watched with me, tucked in the crook of my arm, lying on his back with his feet in the air. When I was outside weeding, Eli sat on the edge of the garden, meowing and "talking" as I did my work. When I did my barn chores, he'd stand on the stall boards, meowing and chatting as I shoveled. We had many conversations, and I knew he understood me, always meowing an answer as I discussed things with him.

He tried talking to everyone, but not everyone understood. When I took him to the vet to have him neutered, Dr. Monti said, "He's some kind of cat. He talked to us the whole time he was here."

"That's my Darling Eli," I told him.

Because of the coyotes, each night I'd round up the cats and make sure they were all in the house before dark. I wasn't about to take any chances. Dogs were in, also. As for the horses, I bought them Jack, a donkey, to keep the coyotes out of the pasture. I had seen one run under the fence and chase them into the barn. It was shocking to know the coyotes were brave enough to come so close to the house. Donkeys are known for keeping vermin at bay. After Jack came I saw no more coyotes in the pasture. Things were pretty good.

Eli was about three years old the day I had to take my van to the car dealer. I had expected to return home before dark, but it was well after eleven when I pulled into the yard. I called for the cats. Everyone came running—except Eli. He didn't answer, so I assumed he was already in the house. In the pit of my stomach, however, I felt something was wrong.

But I was tired from my long day and didn't want to think that Eli was out there in the dark. Also, I didn't want to think about the fear that was building in the back of my mind.

The next morning, the lack of his meowing was more than noticeable; and I began to panic. I went outside and began calling. No Eli.

He'd been known to hide in the woods, looking for unsuspecting chipmunks; so I went to the tree line, calling and calling. No answer.

Deep inside, I knew he was gone, but I wouldn't accept it. Looking back, I think I knew it when I'd come home in the dark and he didn't answer me. I couldn't face the fact that I'd let him down.

Day after day I called his name. I cried. I sobbed. I became so upset I retched.

"You have to quit torturing yourself," Dan scolded. "He's gone. It wasn't your fault."

"It was. I should have left the car dealer. I should have put Eli in the house before I went away. I was so stupid."

I called to him for a year—not every day but now and then, when the night was still. I'd go out to the mailbox and call, waiting for that familiar "meow" to answer me, all the while knowing it was useless.

The date he disappeared, July 18, will be etched in my mind forever. I hated that date. It was the day I let down my best friend, the day I let him be killed.

As the second anniversary of his death rolled around, I became more sullen. On July 17, just before going up to bed, Dan said, "I miss Eli. He was one cool cat. I wonder whatever happened to him?"

Tears filled my eyes. "How can you mention his name? You know he was eaten!"

Dan just shook his head and went up the stairs. I stood in the kitchen, remembering the feline friend I'd lost two years before. I had begun to turn out the lights prior to following him when I heard a familiar meowing on the back porch. I was puzzled. All the cats were in for the night. Had one of them gotten out? Who was it?

I flipped on the outside light; and there on the porch was a little gray kitty, half-grown, with a silver glow about him. He was the spitting image of my darling Eli. My hand flew up to my mouth, and I sucked in a great gulp of air. I stood there for a minute, shocked, before I flew out the door and scooped him up. He purred and slithered around in my arms. I carried him in the house and set him down. He walked around the kitchen like he'd been there before.

I went to my chair in the living room and sat down. He followed me in, tail carried proudly in the air. He jumped in my arms and did a flip upside-down, feet in the air. He looked at me as if to say, "I'm back."

The dogs sniffed him, as did the other cats; but they didn't treat him like a stranger. It was as if they knew him already. It was as if I knew him already. Could it be my Darling Eli, back in another body?

I carried him upstairs and rushed to Dan's side of the bed, rudely waking him with running feet and a flick of the light switch. I shoved the kitten in his face.

"Remember how you said you missed my Eli? Well, he's back."

He squinted in the light, trying to focus on me and what I was holding.

"What are you talking about?"

"It's Eli. He's back. He's back, reincarnated. I knew he'd come back. I knew it."

Dan looked at the silver form I was holding and shook his head in disbelief.

"He sure looks like Eli, but I think you're crazy," he said, rolling over and pulling the sheet up over his head.

I carried my new friend back downstairs. We talked for hours. He meowed when I talked to him, answering me like the old Eli.

He's all grown up now and is a beautiful silver, just like my first Eli. I named him Eli the Second, but we know he's the original.

We talk every day. He doesn't enjoy going outside alone, however; and when he does he's at the door in minutes wanting to come back in. I don't think he trusts the coyotes, not even in the daylight. "Been there, done that" is his motto.

Life is back to normal. My friend Karen, a believer in reincarnation, says I'm much calmer now that Eli is back in my life. My kids just roll their eyes. I think they're jealous.

We were meant to be together. He is my soul mate. I know he returned home to be with me.

As I type in his story, he calls to me from the other room.

"Yes, I'm here," I tell him. Though I can't see him, I know he has just lifted his head and meowed to let me know he's okay; and now I've answered him he'll go back to sleep. I know, also, he's going to live a long time. We'll spend the rest of our days on this earth together, and face new adventures when we pass on.

Sometimes I wonder what might have happened if I hadn't called him so many times; and now and then I feel guilty, though he seems as happy now as before. Did my incessant calling—my constant mourning—pull him back to me before he was ready? A pet psychic I met once told me that our animals will return when they're ready, whether it is immediately or twenty years in the future. They may walk to us from out of a field, like Sweet Pea, or we may find them in a pet shop, along the roadside or in a box at a flea market.

Being reunited with Eli has shown me that life goes on, that soul mates can be found in any species; and when we find them we should grab them and hang on for the ride, no matter how long or how fleeting.

(Avis Townsend is an award-winning author and columnist from western New York.)

MY FIRST SOUL MATE
By Bonnie Johnson

1954

DURING THE TIME OF DIAPERS AND DROOLING, I MET MY FIRST SOUL MATE. I was two. John was four. We would play happily on the kitchen floor while our moms had their coffee and shared the local gossip.

By the time we were five and seven we had become inseparable. I knew even then that John and I had something special. We had a certain connection I felt with no other person. We loved one another dearly, although we didn't tell each other until we were adults.

1958

John received a bicycle built for two on his seventh birthday. We often rode for hours. Sometimes, we wouldn't return home until dinnertime.

During the fifties Farmingdale, Long Island, was a child's haven. Farms surrounded our home in the woods. The land around us was filled with inventive games waiting to be discovered. Ranches with apple orchards and horse stables dotted the landscape. In winter, we sleighed and skated in the park up the street, exploring its valleys and caves during warm weather.

In those days, parents didn't worry about their children being abducted. We were free to disappear for hours at a time. We spent many of those hours climbing trees, gathering apples, playing in the pumpkin fields and finding new ground to explore. We felt like Columbus, constantly discovering new territory.

1960

After a winter storm, packed snow and frozen ponds begged the neighborhood kids to go to the local golf course and sleigh or skate. During the summer, the ponds became a golfer's nightmare; but in winter they gave us glorious opportunities for creative fun.

The bumpy hills made us laugh as we skidded our way down with two or three kids piled on a sleigh or stacked five to a toboggan. We became daredevils, adventurers, explorers. We loved the excitement.

One day we went riding on John's sleigh with me on top of him. We whirled over huge bumps. I shouted happily all the way to the bottom of the hill. Then John stood up, covered with snow down his coat and in his mouth and hair. His sleigh was still halfway up the hill, slowly sliding towards us sideways, out of control. We'd gone halfway down the hill on John's belly.

I couldn't stop laughing. John, although stunned, thought it was pretty cool and suggested we try it again except with me on the bottom. I changed the subject.

1962

John and I took a long walk to find a pond all to ourselves on which to skate. The small lagoon we picked had an island in the middle. The walk took us more than an hour. The island was edged with beautiful trees and overgrown bushes.

The water wasn't always solidly frozen, which was the case on this particular day. John skated off without me, speeding towards the island.

"I'll race you," he yelled. He was off in a flash. Then he was gone!

I jumped up with one skate still waiting to be put on. I screamed, "John!" I saw nothing! I heard nothing! I was so frightened I wet my pants as I ran out onto the ice with one unshod foot. I couldn't see him anywhere. I didn't know what to do.

When I got closer I saw his coat. I lay down on the ice and reached out to grab him. I felt as if my arm grew ten feet long. In a trance, I acted on instincts alone. Somehow, I managed to pull him up. With his head finally above water, he helped me to help him onto the ice.

John had a broken arm; he was soaked to the skin. We hiked the long, rough journey home. He was still coughing up water and phlegm when we reached his front door. His mom took one look at us—John holding his dangling arm, me crying uncontrollably—and she hurried us into her warm home. She undressed us in seconds and tucked us into thick, soft blankets. John's dad called my mother to come pick me up as my friend was hurried off to the emergency room.

1963

At thirteen, John considered himself "officially" a teenager. I still had two years to go to make it "official," but it might as well have been five. I was as developed as my mother's washboard, and it didn't look as though that would change anytime soon. I was still interested in boys, though.

John was very interested in girls. He was also interested in boys, although I didn't know this at the time. He kept it well hidden during those years, even from himself. Though he dated many girls he was never with any one of them very long.

John invited me to all his teenage parties, which he held in his playroom. For some reason, his classmates accepted me. The parties were small, and the kids usually played spin-the-bottle, a game of which I wasn't too fond. I usually had to kiss the smelly boy who lived up the street.

Mostly, we would listen to records as we danced the new dances we had practiced. Having been blessed with two left feet, the Twist was the only one I could do without feeling the fool. Yet John would often take me as his partner; and we'd dance to all the music, both fast and slow. Magically, I seemed to be able to dance with him, for he had a way of making me feel special and a part of something great.

1967

John headed off to college. He was so bright he skipped a grade during his elementary years, then again during high school. I, on the other hand, was having a rough time. At home, my parents treated me strictly and harshly. They stayed drunk, and they fought all the time. As I dealt with all forms of abuse I cut many days of school to go to the beach or to a friend's house to goof off.

Shortly before John left for college, my brother married and left home. My brother and sister were the only ones in my family I felt safe with. After my brother got married, my sister didn't stay around much anymore as my parents' alcoholism progressed. I felt abandoned and alone. When John took off for Boston I became wild and soon ran away from home to escape the family turmoil.

I joined John in Boston, at his dorm, with a girlfriend who had run away with me. We stayed for three weeks, getting into all kinds of mischief. I was with John once again, though, so I felt safe.

1971

By this time I had not seen John in four years. I left Boston to go back home to live with another girlfriend. John went on with his studies. He, of course, graduated with honors. We lost contact shortly after I returned to Long Island. I then proceeded to try and sort out my life and my troubled soul. John, I was sure, was off to do great things.

1981

It had been fourteen years since those wonderful, fun-filled three weeks in Boston with my best friend. Our contact had been severed. I had no idea where John had gone since then. Neither did my family. I had moved to southern California nine years before as I tried to put my life together. I carried too much unresolved pain from my childhood to be successful, however.

1982

Life was very real these days. Lessons became awfully painful. With all the challenges and mistakes, the fears and anxieties, I barely hung on to my sanity.

I was a young, single, twenty-nine-year-old mother with a beautiful seven-year-old daughter. I struggled to make ends meet. I asked all of life's questions young people ask. I carried emotional baggage it would take many years of heartache, for both my daughter Bonnie and me, before I was able to let go. For the moment, life was hard, life was scary.

From the time Bonnie was three I dragged her from one town to another as I repeatedly tried to make a new start. I had enthusiasm. I had determination. But I had no direction. I felt lost and alone. I was filled with intense fear. Now, my daughter and I were about to make another change, another move. Once again we packed to go where I thought the grass was greener in hopes of a long-awaited stable life.

While we were staying with a family member my parents phoned me. They had received an address with a phone number from a mutual family friend. My long-lost soul mate had been found. I was elated! I was hopeful! I was so excited!

When I called him, I felt peace, comfort and direction for the first time in fourteen years. He asked us to come and live with him in Houston, Texas. He wanted me to work in the restaurant he managed. I couldn't pack fast enough.

Shortly after that call with my long-lost friend, Bonnie and I headed off once again to make yet another new start. This time we headed to Montrose, Texas, a small gay community on the outskirts of Houston. This little town had many single people of all backgrounds with different sexual preferences. They even had their own boulevard, with many clubs where friends could mingle and party.

It was here, while we lived in John's beautiful apartment, I found out he was bisexual. Yet it didn't bother me, for the platonic relationship we shared was deeper than any sexual relationship I could even imagine. After all these years, we seemed to pick up where we had left off. It felt like we had only been apart for a weekend.

There was much for us to share. Bonnie fell in love. She, too, became close with John. They had their own special connection. For this, I was grateful. It gave me great joy and peace in my heart to see them together. I loved to watch them joke with each other. John was crazy about my daughter. He beamed at how beautiful she was. He loved her laughter and wit.

John offered me a job at an exclusive restaurant in Riveroaks, a rich area outside Houston. For years, as he put himself through chiropractic school, he had managed the health food restaurant that attracted the rich people from the area.

He was also a successful massage therapist. He had clients such as the Houston Ballet Company and the Houston soccer team, when there was one. My favorite client of his was the band ZZ Top. One day when I came home from work, I saw a limousine outside. As I walked up the stairs, the entertainers passed me on their way down, long beards and all.

Riveroaks reminded me a lot of Beverly Hills. Filled with lush mansions and acres of sculptured landscapes, this town reeked of money. I finally started to make enough to get stability, something I'd never had. The food was excellent. The building was quaint. It was built at the turn of the century, and had collected a few ghost stories over the decades.

Shortly after we arrived in Texas, an apartment became available downstairs in John's building, so Bonnie and I took up residence. We didn't have all the beautiful furniture he had, but it was a start. I had a job where I was making decent money. I enrolled Bonnie in the local school and bought a car. Life seemed to pick up. Maybe the grass *was* greener here in the overwhelming heat of Texas.

1983

After a particularly long, strenuous day at work, John and I came home to fall down onto his couch dog-tired. The babysitter dropped Bonnie off shortly after. She was filled with nine-year-old wonder and boundless energy. She jumped around and made us laugh with her little jokes and sweet ways. We enjoyed her high spirits even though we felt bushed.

Bonnie desperately wanted to go to the movies to see the latest scary flick. John kept telling her, "No, hon, not today."

She persisted. Suddenly, my beautiful child climbed on the couch, spread her arms wide and proceeded to sing at the top of her lungs,

"Nobody Knows The Troubles I've Seen." John scooped her up and covered her with kisses, tickling her at the same time. I laughed so hard I fell off the couch. Needless to say, we went to the movies that day.

Soon the good times would end, the long-awaited stability begin to crumble. Ten months after we arrived in Texas, Bonnie and I had to move back to California because of a series of unfortunate events.

The health food restaurant had been signed over to our boss's wife during a divorce settlement. She brought in her own crew; we were laid off on the spot. She gave us no warning. One day I went to work to find out I didn't have a job anymore.

I had nothing to fall back on. I tried a few other restaurants, but it was the same old story. I just couldn't earn enough to make ends meet. Soon after that, I sent Bonnie back to California to stay briefly with her father. I had to return my car to the original owner. Then I followed my daughter to California.

1987

By the time Bonnie was thirteen I began therapy and tried to sort out my life as my daughter was being introduced to hormones. We hadn't heard from or talked with John much during the years. When we did, once again it was as though we had talked last only a few days before.

With each call, I sensed something was terribly wrong. I began to fear for my dear friend's life, and I voiced it to his mother, living in Florida. John became angry with me for this, yet my dread soon proved true.

1990

A rough year, indeed, this one was. I lost both my mother and my father within eleven months of each other. Then I found out, through my brother, that John had died in Florida at his parents' home just two months before my dad.

My dear friend had contracted AIDS. Now he was gone. I never had the chance to say goodbye. I never saw him again to say how sorry I was. I was never able to tell him how much I loved him. I didn't have the opportunity to tell him what sharing our lives all these years had meant to me.

He never saw me grow up. He never saw my daughter blossom into a beautiful, wise and loving young woman. For all of these my heart breaks still. I miss you, John! And I love you!

(BONNIE JOHNSON is a freelance writer, mom of a beautiful twenty-eight-year-old daughter and friend to the elderly.)

YOU SEND ME

By Nikia Billingslea

HE REACHED OUT TO ME FROM ACROSS THE ROOM. AT FIRST, I DIDN'T KNOW what was going on. It was as if someone were calling me from inside my head, because I know I did not hear anyone speaking my name. I sat thinking I was crazy as the group of middle school-aged girls around me talked, oblivious to my dilemma.

From time to time, I looked around the room at the clusters of students, who ranged from thirteen to eighteen years old. At twenty, I was going to play the role of adult for the first time in my life as a resident assistant in a college prep summer program.

Just as I was ready to shrug off my unease as performance anxiety, I saw him. A young man sat in a corner by himself; his eyes drew a straight diagonal line to me. I couldn't tell if he was mad or if he thought I was funny. The one thing I was sure of, he stared at me as if he could see the thoughts in my head. I thought of the line "He looked right through me as if I wasn't there."

It wouldn't have been so bad if he weren't so fine. His skin and hair conjured visions of Hindu princes, shiny black coils kissed his reddish-brown skin. Eyelashes long enough for me to notice from across the room framed his brown eyes, and his lips were the tint of blackberry flesh. My first reaction was to look away and convince myself he was not looking at me. The last thing I wanted was for everyone to witness a student flirting with me.

They had told me he was trouble, but they did not say he *looked* like trouble. I could thoroughly understand why other counselors had defied professional ethics to get a touch-taste of him. But I was not about to join the list of the damned so I turned my head to ignore

139

him. When I moved to get the girls settled in their rooms, I stood and looked around, but he was nowhere to be found. Good, I thought.

A week went by; and I hardly saw the young man, whose name was Guy. When I did see him, he was totally unaware of my existence—or so I thought. I breathed a sigh of relief, but I could not help noticing there was something different about him. It was easy to see why he so intimidated the director and teachers. He was very confident and well-spoken for a seventeen-year-old high school graduate. Every other day he carried a new book: *Another Country*, *Song of Solomon*, *On the Road*, *The Trial*. I was impressed.

One night after dinner, I was talking with two other counselors, Edith and Monique. They were as giddy as schoolgirls as they related their conversations with Guy. For his summer project he had chosen the topic of female sexuality, and the women on staff were his willing subjects. Edith and Monique could barely contain their excitement as they told me about their conversations in private rooms with the young man.

He told Monique he knew how to bring a woman to orgasm twenty-two times in one night. Edith, who was a virgin, told us how he took her hand in his and explained how he could satisfy her merely by massaging certain pressure points. She was beet red from the neck up.

Just as Edith finished her story, he walked up and asked me if I would mind answering a few personal questions. I was definitely curious, but I was also cautious. I wanted to feel him, his presence, so badly, but I told him no. He persisted; and my coworkers insisted that I should, saying it would be fun. Reluctantly, I agreed to answer a few of his questions.

We met in a private room in the basement of the dormitory. I sat across from him at one of those big, heavy oak library tables. He wore the same half-smile, half-scowl that had been on his face the day he sat staring at me.

Sitting there with him felt like something I had done before and would never tire of doing—ever. He began to explain his project, and I wanted to feel the vibrations of his baritone in my chest always. When I threw some sass at him, he would do a verbal sidestep and come at me with another question. We had a good word-joust for a while until he stopped, looked directly at me and accused me of being full of it.

From that point on he made a point of taunting me every chance he got. Whether it was mimicking me in a room full of students and staff or taking my keys and pretending to go to my room, he became the inextricable grain of sand in my shorts. I loved it and I hated it. He knew exactly how to affect me, and made me feel what I had never felt before: excited, agitated, challenged—and aroused. Everyone was a spectator to our spiritual courting and emotional foreplay, except the director.

I tried to stay out of his way, tried to be professional; but he would not allow it. One day we were loading buses for a field trip. In an attempt to avoid him at all costs, I chose to sit with the counselors. Unfortunately, we were ordered not to sit in a cluster but to station ourselves in the front as well as in the rear of the bus. I chose the front. Who decided to get on last? Who sat next to me? I protested aloud about it, but neither he nor my coworkers paid me any attention. It seemed as if they wanted this young boy to get me fired.

I refused to look at him, but he talked to me anyway as I stared out the window. He wanted to know when we would be able to talk and get together again. Feeling as if I had no other choice, I turned in my seat to face him and told him, "I can't see you, or spend any time with you. I shouldn't even be sitting here with you while you're trying to get with me. I am a counselor, you're a student! I think you're a nice and intelligent young man, who can have any young lady here you want. What's wrong with all of the pretty girls here? Why don't you try to talk to one of them?"

He told me he was not interested in any of them, said that I was wrong for cutting him down like that. But I insisted that any further social interaction between us would be inappropriate. He passionately disagreed, but I would not give in. In an effort to appease him temporarily, I told him to make the best of the moment because the likelihood of it happening again was virtually nonexistent.

Weeks went by, and I was relieved. The residential program was coming to an end, and all of the students were working on their projects and getting ready for the big talent show. The buzz was that

Guy could rap really well. As a fan of hip-hop music, I looked forward to seeing his skills.

He seemed to disappear a week before the event. I relaxed a little but was disappointed. His teasing and subtle mind games had become a much-anticipated reprieve from the mind-numbing antics of thirteen-year-olds who tried to sneak into each other's rooms.

The night of the talent show was chaotic. It was the last night of the program; some children were already packing up to leave, and emotions were running high. The corridors, the steps, the commons area, even the staff office were stages for tender farewells. I tried not to look as if I was searching for him, but I was. I wanted to talk to him one more time, for one last time.

When I finally saw him, he was onstage blowing up the spot. He was a phenomenon, basking in the glaring light of a small college theater. The walls could hardly contain his energy as he flowed, angrily agile, on the microphone. He reminded me of my cousin, who had been shot and killed when I was in high school.

I admired his vitality and resilience because for the entire six weeks he had been under constant scrutiny and criticism. In the midst of the adversity, he had something that gave voice to the turmoil in his still-maturing mind. I could relate to that. I could relate to being scrutinized and dealt with adversely.

After the show, I went straight back to the residence hall. I was overwhelmed with his performance; but I was afraid that if I talked to him, I would not be able to conceal my admiration and desire for him. So, I left.

Some other force was in control that evening. As I headed back to my room, I heard someone calling me. He had run across the campus to catch up with me. Yes, I was happy, happy he needed to see me as much as I needed to see him.

I turned around, chicken-necked a little, ready to defend myself against wanting him. But I did not get the usual mocking Guy. With a very sincere look on his face, he asked me if he could call me sometime. I started to remind him of my position in the program, but he interrupted me and announced he was aware of how I felt about my job but would I mind if he called me *after* the program. Part of me felt the need to keep up the charade, and the other part of me wanted nothing more than to smile from ear to ear.

I agreed to give him my number, but he did not have a pen or paper. When he memorized my phone number, I was sure the whole thing had been a joke—that he had just wanted to see if I would give it to him. Before he walked away he said, "By the way, I like that *Temple of My Familiar.* You have good taste."

I had no idea what he meant by that. I thought he was talking out the side of his neck. It was not until a week later, when I was packing to go, that I noticed I had Alice Walker's *Temple of My Familiar* lying on my desk. I could not help but laugh to myself, realizing he was not as much of a puzzle as everyone thought. His world made perfect sense, and I would not mind being in it.

When I finally moved back home at the end of the summer, I had a message from him. He wanted to get together. Once again he had proved me wrong. So, after many weeks of protecting myself, I let go and made up my mind that the next time he called I would follow my heart.

One evening I thought about him, and the phone rang. Over the course of our relationship, he would, without fail, answer my mental pages; but my insecurity kept me from calling him when I felt *his* energy. There was one time, however, that he called out to me so intensely I answered.

I was riding around in my car when I got a compelling need to see Guy. A phone call would not suffice. I had to *see* him, and I did not know why. As I pulled up to his aunt's house he was coming out, back first, with a tote bag and an armload of clothes. He was arguing with his aunt and so upset he did not notice me until we nearly collided on the sidewalk. When he turned and saw me, there was a look in his eyes that was altogether relieved, angry, sad and tired.

I opened the trunk of my car for him to stow his things, and we got in without speaking. After riding around for a while, I asked him what he planned to do. He said he had friends he could stay with and that he would be okay. I felt grateful—he seemed to be fine, but I wondered how he would have been if I had not shown up. How would he have felt walking down the street or riding on the bus like a transient? Divine force definitely worked through me for him.

I felt that the experience pulled us together, because for once I felt like he needed me. I needed him, too. To say we had a lot in common is an understatement.

Both of our mothers grew up in the same neighborhood, and had served time in jail. There was a pain we shared we tried to heal with each other. We could openly talk about the feelings of fear and helplessness we felt as children as we watched the adults in our lives self-destruct before our eyes. As we fumbled toward adulthood we were company for each other.

One night, when we were sitting in the driveway of his gay friend's house in Malibu, we discovered another connection between us. Three years before I met Guy my cousin was murdered; he was the closest person in the world to me. I was devastated when my grandmother called me at college to give me the news of his death. Guy told me he used to hang out with my cousin, who was older. As a matter of fact, they were B-Boys together, rhyming, break-dancing and spinning vinyl in neighborhood garages.

Neither of us could believe we were so close but had never actually met. I would like to think that my cousin put Guy in my life to fill his place. Guy was a blessing to me; because before my cousin was killed, I was afraid to do anything or express myself creatively. After he passed, I made a declaration to live my life fully and be a vehicle for the expressions of creativity he had been so gifted in but so briefly able to share.

Guy also encouraged me to reveal my talents, despite the excruciating pain it caused me at first. He became my guru and guide.

Over the course of the years, I became less self-conscious of my need for him and became more aware of the ways in which he could use positive input. Like a lot of underground dwellers, he did not have a place to live—he kind of floated around from house to apartment to shelter, from family to friends. He had as much talent as he did temporary residences. My boy could write, sing, rap, drum, play bass guitar and command an audience with his oratorical skills. For years, I watched while he moved from one project to another, like a hummingbird, not always finishing what he initiated.

But I was always encouraging, supportive and honest when he asked for feedback.

We used to go hiking to get away from the incessant critical voices in our lives and return to ourselves. Our favorite place was in the mountains near the Pacific Ocean. About five years after we met, I admitted to myself that I loved him and saw him as more than just a friend or little brother. On one of our excursions, I told him what was on my mind.

At first he did not say anything; but when he did speak, it was with great clarity and brevity. He took me back to when we first met and reminded me that he had always been in love with me. He painted our future on a canvas of balance and unity that was so pretty, with us creating new thought and healing with our love. To my utter astonishment, he cried.

I had not known he felt as strongly as I did. There was not a word I wrote or a note that I sang I didn't think of the encouragement and support he had always shown me. With only a moment's pondering, I could replay all of the gestures, words, even looks that now dispelled any doubt I might have about his sincerity.

It was not easy. Although my mother, who moved to another state, loved him from the moment she saw him, the rest of my family did not approve. They thought he was a rogue. I would not deny that he was, but he had goals and a vision I believed in. His family echoed the sentiments of my family. It seemed that, other than his mother, his cousin O.G. from the West Side Piru set in Compton was the only one who had faith in him. I could not believe a person's very own family would openly disapprove of *him* rather than the person he wanted to be with.

But we went forward anyway. In the midst of his struggle with the past I would often find him outside of poetry readings I attended, high on something—mushrooms, acid, marijuana, cheap alcohol, never crack. Thank God. Those were the times my love for him was tested, the times when I wondered if I was creating this soul mate fairy tale.

Seeing him try to kill the life in himself, the way our parents tried to shut off their feelings, disgusted me. Unlike him, I could not relinquish control over my body to any chemical or herb for any amount of time. Too many nights I drove him home after one of his shows, pulling over every other block to let him release the toxic liquid tearing the lining of his stomach away. Sometimes he could not even hold it in that long. My car still has traces of his binges in unreachable corners.

My disgust and his shame would create an unbearable space that would drive us away from each other for weeks and even months at a time, but never permanently. Eventually, I would begin to feel the pull, practically seeing what he was doing when we were separated. I would stubbornly wait until he called. He'd always tell me exactly, or at least very similarly, what my premonitions had revealed to me. We would both be drawn back into our private space.

Our best times were spent when I was house-sitting for a friend. Her pad was plush and romantic, complete with fireplace and backyard patio draped in fragrant vines. I would happily play wifey while he sat back and enjoyed being pampered, doing manly things like running to the store for last-minute items or taking out the trash. But that was one of very few times in our relationship we had time to spend exclusively with each other without his boys walking in and out of his room or my family barring him from the house altogether. It was the one time in my three-plus decades on this earth that I made love to someone I truly loved.

When we were not dealing with his demons and reuniting, we dealt with my issues of having to prove how unlike my parents I was going to be. This was at the expense of my true convictions. I thought by surrounding myself with upwardly mobile, college-educated African-Americans I would be able to evade feelings of inadequacy and inferiority. It was no secret to him when I had been around my so-called friends. The vibe hung around me like too much cheap perfume. After they bragged about their boyfriends playing basketball overseas and proposals from high school sweethearts, they loved jamming me up about how much of a loser Guy was.

But even that left an impression on me, and by the time I got with him my heart and spirit were heavy because no one seemed to be able to see the qualities in him I saw and loved. Being with him was like a deprogramming, because although my so-called friends were well-meaning, smart and ambitious, they weren't particularly endowed with vision. They saw the world as it is, not as it could be or should be.

He never let me forget that it was important to hold on to the image of a better world, with people who arrive at a state of expanded consciousness. If I randomly echoed one of my friends, he would get incredibly angry and call me out on it, admonishing me for buying into vacuous rhetoric. I would pout and sulk, embarrassed for being found out, but even more for subconsciously absorbing ideals that were clearly not my own.

Reluctantly, I appreciated his caring enough to say anything. I appreciated his interest. Despite our individual dysfunction, I sensed that we each desperately needed to see the best in the other to have faith in ourselves—the positive side of co-dependency, I suppose.

The day he told me he had gotten another woman pregnant was devastating. I never was deluded enough to think I was the only one all of the time, especially as much as we were on and off; but for some reason I thought he cared enough about us to be protected. For hours we argued, him defending the fact we were not an official couple when it happened, me trying to make him realize that, if he knew he was eventually going to reunite with me, the least he could do was protect himself and us from AIDS or a big oops like this one. He was more willing to see me as a jealous girlfriend than accept that his actions could have grave results.

The extent of his self-destructiveness hit me like the Chicago hawk in January, so I bounced. I left the country for two years, because I was certain he could not come up with the money to follow me. At that point, his boys were shutting down the cooperative living space, he had lost his zillionth job and his world was spinning out of control. This time, I promised myself, I would not be there to rescue him. For once, I was going to try and rescue myself.

We corresponded with snail mail. His letters were so sweet my hands stuck to the pages, and my heart leaped across the oceans. I could not give any other man a fair chance because I was convinced the creator gives us only one soul mate per lifetime.

While I was away, Guy was my church and my sanctuary. There was no light without my memories of him. Day in and day out, I replayed them in my mind, and his letters confirmed me. I even began to relish the drama we had to together. No man had taken me through what he had. In my homesick delirium, I thought our history,

147

however flawed, was everything because we still wanted each other.

Then the letters came about how he got a job as a youth counselor, a car, an apartment, even a scheduled hip-hop tour. His world was coming together without me. I thought, great, now his head is clear maybe we can do something when I get back. My time abroad was up, and I was ready to resume something wonderful with my man and partner.

But he left out the girlfriend he was with, nor did I consider that his life was coming together because I was not in it.

After seven years of knowing for certain he would be there for me in spirit or in flesh, I was confronted with resonating silence. When none of my phone calls were answered, I felt abandoned and alone, even more alone because the space he no longer filled reminded me of my cousin who was gone, too. I fell into a pattern of self-destructive behavior—being promiscuous, trying to smoke my way beyond the situation and replaying every single moment until I was too mentally exhausted to do anything else. The days and minutes blurred into an abstraction of striations and curved lines, circling in on themselves, back to an unseen source.

Then I received a phone call.

At four in the morning, he called to tell me he needed to talk to me face-to-face. I sprang out of bed and waited on the porch for him to pick me up, not knowing exactly what to expect. In the midst of the madness, I could only smile when I saw him again. The years we had not been together and the girlfriend that created the space between us did not take away from our knowing. Before driving off we embraced, allowing our energies to commingle. I could feel it all inside him, and I knew immediately that the only person suffering was me.

We took a ride, caught up on family, friends and jobs. Then began his reliving the last few years of our relationship, out loud and in detail, from his perspective. Without any regret or anger in his voice, he admitted to his mistakes and pointed out the part I played in breaking his heart by leaving. I sat, silently crying, trying not to feel the sadness of loving someone so much yet unavoidably causing him the greatest pain. Yet I did not want to take it away because he seemed better and stronger for it, seemingly more determined not to take love for granted.

In the approaching morning, we made angry, passionate, forgiving love with each other like grown people. When my body experienced the strongest climax ever, I was released from him. I half-asked, half-told him he had no intentions of resuming a romantic relationship; and he very honestly told me no. After all of the pain and disappointment we had caused each other, I understood. Neither did I regret our last time together.

Whether or not he shares his life with me or another woman, I am proud of the man he has become. Through our relationship, he evolved; and neither of us is today the same person we were when we met. Sometimes, at a book signing or a community event, I feel his presence; and he emerges somewhere out of the crowd.

A soul mate unhesitatingly takes the journey of spiritual growth and has a profound understanding and desire to relate to his chosen path and his partner's. There is no one with whom I have shared as close a bond, but I do not believe he is the only person the creator has put on this planet to connect with my spirit. Our paths unfold beyond the scope of our perception; but always our spirits find home in within our personal space, with others, or more preferably within the vast womb of the universe.

(NIKIA (Knee-kia) BILLINGSLEA teaches English in California at Los Angeles Southwest College.)

STAR MAKER
By Katharina Katt

M Y APARTMENT DOOR BUZZER WENT OFF, AND I SWEAR I JUMPED, MY adrenalin giving me a high no drug ever could. I checked my hair and makeup in the mirror. I could look better, but there was no time, it was late.

The apartment complex was quiet. It only got that way late at night. He stood at the entrance waiting for me to come let him in. I grabbed my key and rushed out my door and down the stairs. I had envisioned him a million times in my mind. He had sent several pictures in the letters we had exchanged. Our long distance phone bills were bulging at the seams, but he was here. I nearly tripped on the stairs, trying to get a glimpse of him before I fumbled with my key in the lock. I didn't expect what I saw.

His pictures certainly didn't do him justice. He was taller than I imagined, with broad shoulders. I like that in men. The kind of man a woman loves to cuddle up to. His long dark hair, almost black, lay straight from his temples but curled at the bottom. If a vampire prince from the books I read could step into reality, I believe the vampire would have hard competition from him. Evergreen eyes looked back at me with that look I'll never forget. Tenderness. I smiled and quickly unlocked the door, rushing up the stairs in front of him to open the apartment door as well.

Once inside we sat down on the couch, not sure how to start. It wasn't just the attraction—that wasn't why he was here. We had started as friends and were now meeting. We both blushed and giggled like schoolchildren, though our ages were much past that.

"I didn't expect you to be so tall." I was still dwarfed by him, even sitting down. I am rather petite and small, almost child-sized in many regards, but I am still more than five feet tall. I guessed he was at least six feet; but my ex-husband had been six feet, and I am sure he was shorter than Wesley. Ah, yes, that was his name. I loved to whisper it over the phone to him; he made such a lovely purring sound when I did. It always sent joyous shivers down my spine.

"I didn't expect you to be so small," he remarked back, smiling at me.

We sat apart on the loveseat. It was a small apartment, and I had never had much company over so the loveseat was all I needed. He touched my hair gently, playing with the curls at the end as we talked. I don't know if all women love this, but I always will.

"I was afraid I wouldn't be able to see you. I mean, I thought I would die on that operating table without ever seeing you."

I nodded. He had told me when he went for emergency surgery they removed a tumor. It was a life-threatening case, and I had wanted with all my soul to be there when he woke up from it so he could have someone holding his hand when he opened his eyes. Why couldn't I be rich so I could go to a loved one's side when I wished?

"I wanted to be there. In spirit, I was," I told him.

He smiled at me, and as time passed I moved closer. We just cuddled there together, our arms wrapped around each other. Talking about life, as we always did. It was so different, having him in person. I knew his visit in town was short, perhaps only for the night; but for this moment, he was here, with me.

Since my divorce, I had not been with another man; and honestly, any attempt at dating had proved to be a horrible experience. It was Wesley I came home to on my computer screen and whose weekly calls I waited for.

He had taken a taxi here, and I knew he was staying the night even though we had agreed sex was not an option. I felt better when he reassured me of that, cuddling there on the couch; and I was sure we would be up until dawn talking.

Dawn did come, but we were kissing instead of talking. It had been so long for both of us. I guess we got carried away. I trembled when he touched me. I felt terrified at the same time.

"You don't have to," he whispered in my ear. Oh, his voice was music. So deep and manly. He was my Greek god turned to life. When I didn't answer, he repeated it again to be sure I heard him.

"I want to," I said, blushing. He touched my cheek, and it gave me courage. I wanted to go to the bedroom. I kept it dark there, and honestly, I didn't want him to see how overweight I'd become. I know I'm beautiful otherwise, but I didn't want him to see me like this. Not my Greek god.

"But I want to see you," he urged. "You are beautiful." He touched my stomach, and I failed to suck the fat in.

"This is a sign of femininity. You are a mother. You bear the signs, and I think it is beautiful."

I melted. Could he give me more of a reason to fall for him? Not only did he say he thought I was beautiful, but he touched and caressed me as if I were.

It was late into the morning when we lay together, in my bed. He had finally agreed to move there when I could stay awake no longer. I slept an hour or two in his arms.

"When will you be back?" I asked, not wanting us to be apart too long.

"I don't know, but I'll call you tonight when I get home."

He did call that night, saying his plane had arrived with no delays and that he got home safely.

"I have a wonderful idea," he said. "Come visit me for a week. I have a big house and it's just me here."

I wasn't working, so I jumped at the idea.

"I'll pay for the tickets, don't worry about that. Just dress in something you know I'll like."

The day couldn't come soon enough. I had a late flight, but it was the soonest he could get me in. It seemed I was the only one waiting at the airport curb when he drove up. He got out to stash my bags and picked me up, swirling me around and holding me. I laughed and smiled and kissed him gently. We put my bags in the trunk and hurried home. The snow on the ground was thick, more so than where I lived.

He lit some candles around the house, setting the perfect mood for romance. He cooked for me and wouldn't let me lift a single finger. I was his guest, he insisted. I treasured him all the more. I had always wondered what it would be like to find someone as giving as myself. I actually was not sure I could get used to it.

The next night we sat on the couch, and he played recordings of his music on the stereo. He isn't a musician but a composer, as a hobby. The music sounded Celtic, some lively and cheerful while others nearly brought a tear to my eye. I became an instant fan, and he gave me some samples to take home with me. He was really an engineer—his last project had been putting a satellite up into space. He was very proud of that.

"Would you like to see it?" he asked, jumping up from the couch with enthusiasm.

"We can see it from here?"

"Oh, yes!"

"But…it's cold outside. I need a coat."

He pulled me upstairs by the hand, me in my bare feet and a short-sleeved shirt.

"It's okay, don't worry about it."

He stopped at the door and grabbed his long coat, wrapping it around me, and had me put on his shoes that were twice as long as my feet. We stepped out onto his front porch and looked up into the night sky. The stars were so bright. It was beautiful. He went out into the street and looked around in the sky for the satellite.

"There—there it is!" He pointed. I joined him, snow falling into his shoes, which I had a hard time keeping on. He wrapped his arms around me as we looked up into the sky. I could see the moving star he pointed at, and he explained the different paths it took. He always knew where it was.

"And any time you miss me, just look into the sky for my star."

I kissed him and smiled, the shivers from the cold starting to take me.

"All right, we can go back in." He had noticed my shivering.

I tried to take a step but lost a shoe in the snow. He caught me and carried me inside. I fancied him my "star maker," and he seemed to like it when I told him so.

We listened to more music, and then he asked me something strange I will never forget.

"Do you believe in soul mates?"

We often had deep discussions on various things like this, but the timing made it awkward.

"I don't know—maybe." I really didn't know what to say about it, but it stuck in the back of my mind.

The week didn't seem long enough and was over too soon. He was packing for another business trip as I was packing to leave. We weren't sure when he would be back, but we made plans to move closer together.

"Will you wait for me? I don't know how long I might be gone."

"Just write me still, and call. I will wait for you, and hope you the best."

He smiled, kissing me tenderly.

I watched his car leave before going to my terminal. I didn't know if I would ever see him again. He did call, and write. Yet the calls and letters grew shorter and less frequent. I had no idea why. I heard later that he married, and in a way I wish him happiness. For me it's an end—to many things.

I feel I'm missing half of myself now, the half he made complete. I remember his question about soul mates, and I am convinced if I ever had one it was my star maker.

(KATHARINA KATT is a magazine advice columnist as well as an author of erotica and dark fantasy.)

NOT CYBERFRIENDS, BUT SOUL MATES
By Lisa Easterling

I HATE THE TERM *CYBERFRIEND*. IT SOMEHOW CHEAPENS THE VALUE OF A relationship, demeans the depth. Does meeting through computer technology make friendship somehow less real? Cyberfriend. Spacebuddy. Virtualpal. No, I know better.

Glenda joined RCW in early November 1999. She was so much fun to be around. I found myself laughing often at her messages and feeling a little sad when she was away. She seemed to have a lot to deal with emotionally, and I remember thinking how strong she must be to juggle it all. I remember her posting a cry for prayer then shortly thereafter a message that she was just tired and might as well give it up and leave. I remember feeling a little arrow go through my heart at that moment, and I sat down to write to her:

Dry your eyes, sweet sister mine
And let the stars within them shine
Lift them now so you can see
A glimpse of friendship's love in me
And I am only one of those
Who gladly shoulders all your woes
For you're among your family here
Dear angel, you've no need for fear
So place your trust into our hands
And know that we will understand
Let us help you bear your pain
And love you till you laugh again

I sent it to her and added that if she unsubbed I'd just have to add her back and that was all there was to it. She relented and stayed.

We began to email back and forth and then started spending time together on instant messenger. She had a really hard time understanding how I could care so much for her. I had a hard time understanding why she thought I was so special. We grew to love each other very quickly. We had a few rocky spots, mostly just meshing our very different personalities; but it seemed that with each rough time we came through stronger than before. Our misunderstandings could always be handled over the phone; listening to the compassion in each other's voices drew us ever closer.

We marveled at God's love for us, that He would bring us together this way. We had both been burned by "best friends" in the past and were all but sworn off ever having another one. God had other plans for us.

As we grew closer, it became increasingly difficult to handle the emotional side of being so far apart, without much hope of it ever changing. We've prayed together on the phone, in IM boxes and in emails, trying to hold each other together. Usually, it's only one of us at a time struggling with the distance, and on those days we just hold each other a little more tightly in our hearts.

Soon after we became best friends, I wrote a poem from my heart to hers:

DIAMONDS

Heart pounding, I touch my chest
As though my hand might caress
This, somehow
I can't even be sure what it is
I've never felt the strength of such stirrings
Never known such complete and selfless love
From a woman, not unlike myself
So pure, this closeness, so true
And so untouched by immorality
Clothed in a joy I can't express I cry
I let them fall, the diamond tears

Let them fall into her waiting hands
Watching as she clutches them to her heart
Placing them into a sapphire velvet bag
Tying satin ribbons with trembling fingers
To keep forever
She looks at me, passion in her deep blue eyes
And smiles
A smile that touches my soul and leaves me breathless
This love
No words, nothing my lips could speak could capture
     this
I reach out, if only in my heart, to touch her cheek
To smooth her hair, to seek her eyes
I search her face for some way to tell her
What can only be spoken heart to heart
I pull her to me in an embrace so intimate
It scares us both but neither pulls away.
Two women, girls grown up, reaching into each other
For understanding, compassion, completion
Love flows like a life-force between them
Both bodies shaken by the exchange
Pearls of sweat forming on two joining brows
They embrace, oblivious to time
Their eyes lock, each reading the other's thoughts
No need for words
Tears slide past knowing smiles
Cheeks touch again, blending a river of pure emotion
Gently rocking, two friends move as one in the dance
Pure love forges a bond unbreakable
Invincible and everlasting
As strong as the passion between us
As gentle as the breeze that whispers past
Consumed with pure joy, we are reverent with awe
At God
The only plausible author of such love

We planned, we dreamed, we laughed, too excited to breathe

sometimes at the thought of what it would be like the first time our eyes met with no screen between us, the first time we hugged each other, the first time we could say "I love you" face-to-face.

On Sept. 7, 2000, in an airport in Maine, I walked into the waiting arms of my best friend for the first time. There are no words to describe the range of emotion, the depth of feeling that passed between us that day. We spent nine glorious days together, talking, laughing, crying, cuddling, adoring being together. I fell even more deeply in love with her and her family.

They drove to our home in Florida the following February. Glenda's husband Mark interviewed with an ambulance company located within a few miles of my home. They then began exploring options, with plans to eventually relocate to this area. Our six weeks together went by all too quickly, but what memories we made. The relocation is still in progress, and we eagerly await the time when miles no longer separate us and we can continue and grow in our friendship and see each other more than twice a year.

Day by day, we've grown closer to God and to each other. We seek Him daily as our friendship grows and we grapple with mixing our personal approaches. Glenda reaches out, whereas I tend to hide. My love for her has given her wings to fly and believe she is lovable. Her love for me has shown me it's okay to need, okay to cry. I still grapple with letting the tears fall, but her tenderness has a way of reaching past my resolve.

I will never falter in my gratitude for the precious gift of our coming together. I love her beyond what I can find words to describe. She is a gift I will cherish forever. Cyberfriend? Not even close. She is my soul mate, as though something within each of us has always known the other in ways impossible to describe. Somehow, I know in the depths of my heart that we have always been friends.

> We were children together
> Singing and laughing
> You were younger than I
> But not so far removed
> We played together
> Games no one else seemed to know

We knew each other inside and out
I understood what frightened you
I knew what thrilled you
You knew what I couldn't express
You waited patiently for me to trust
Your eyes twinkled with mischief
Just as they do now, years later
We were children together
If only in our dreams

(LISA EASTERLING is a freelance writer from sunny Florida.)

SOUL MATE'S SONG

They say two halves make a whole,
and that explains so much.
Like why I feel a rush of love
from the mere act of your touch.
And when I think about it,
as I'm sitting all alone,
I realize that you're the one
who makes me feel I'm finally home.

We must have been separated
way back at time's beginning.
Although I didn't know it,
all my life I have been searching.
I think that you're the one for me—
I guess you'd call it fate.
What to do, now that I've found you?
My darling…My Soul Mate.

It's not a feeling you can force,
you're born with it in your soul.
And for reasons so unknown to me,
until I met you I wasn't whole.
I didn't even know it,
Just accepted my lonely fate.
Then you came along, singing my soul's
    song,
and I knew I'd found my mate.

We must have been separated
way back at time's beginning.
Although I didn't know it,
all my life I have been searching.
I think that you're the one for me—
I guess you'd call it fate.
What to do, now that I've found you?
My darling…My Soul Mate.

— Ellen M. DuBois

A DIFFERENT KIND OF SOUL MATE

By Vanessa K. Mullins

I MET ANNE ABOUT TEN YEARS AGO WHEN SHE STARTED WORKING FOR THE same company I did. At first glance, I knew I wouldn't like her. She was too perfect—blond hair, beautiful smile, cute figure. The kind of woman you just know is going to be a bitch. How wrong I was.

After awhile, she was promoted to a management position similar to mine. We attended meetings together; and afterwards, we would go someplace to talk. The more I got to know Anne, the more I found out my first impression was so very wrong. Anne was very friendly and full of life. She became the first woman friend I ever had.

Eventually, both of us were laid off from our jobs. Anne ended up moving in one direction; I moved two hundred miles in the other. But when we'd get together, it was as if we had never been apart. And every time we had to go back to our own homes we would cry like babies, because we knew it would be a long while before we would see each other again.

As often happens in life, sometimes it's hard to get through the day, so Anne and I call each other. We tell the other one our problems and find that she has had the same experience at some point in her life. This makes it easier to know what to say and easier to provide help through the bad times to get back to the good.

When I need someone to talk to or cry to or to just listen to me complain, I call Anne. She's always there for me. It doesn't matter what it is, or even what time it is, she gives me a safe place to go for comfort.

She helped me through one of the toughest times in my life. She was there for me, angry when I was angry, hurting when I hurt. And eventually, she was happy for me when I finally got it all back together. Her friendship never wavered. She was my strength when I had none.

Years later, when I found out Anne had cancer, I found out how much a part of me she truly was. I knew that if something happened to her that I would never be the same. I also knew that if I lost her, it would be like losing a piece of myself. Thank Heavens, she beat it. To this day, I thank God that I still have Anne in my life.

Through our years of friendship, we have helped each other with divorce, death, new marriages and the births of our children. These experiences have brought us closer emotionally, even though our physical distance is farther apart. It is through one of these hardships that Anne and I learned just how very connected we are.

Anne's mother passed away after a lengthy illness. I had never met her mom and didn't know much about her except that she had been sick for a while. That same night, I had a dream with a beautiful young woman in it. She told me her name was Kathleen and then proceeded to tell me she was Anne's mother. She was lovely and very happy in my dream and not sick as last she had been to Anne.

I had never really talked too much with Anne about her mom, and when we did, She had always called her "Mom," so I didn't know her name. I actually forgot about the dream...until a couple of days later.

That night, I had a very vivid dream that stuck with me throughout the entire day, and I kept going over and over it in my head. In the dream, I was in the water, and Anne came floating by on her way to Pontiac, Michigan. I told her she should get a boat. Then I awoke. Though it meant nothing to me, it stuck.

I called Anne later in the evening to see how she was doing. To cheer her up a little bit, I told her I had a silly dream about her. I related the dream to her. She got quiet for a moment and then told me why.

It seems that her mother's favorite song was "If I Had a Boat," off a CD by Lyle Lovett titled *Pontiac.* Anne told me that earlier in the day, she had been thinking about her mother and playing this song over and over. (What makes this even more amazing is that I am not a country music fan. Never heard of either the song or the CD.)

We both had chills.

I then asked her what her mom's name was. She told me Kathy. Chills ran through me again when I remembered the dream from before with the woman Kathleen. I told Anne about that dream. Somehow, in some way, both Anne and I believe that her mother came through my dreams to let Anne know she was all right now—no longer in pain and happy.

As I mentioned earlier, a few years ago Anne had a cancer scare. I worried for her. I cried for her. And though I tried to be strong for her, she was the one who helped me through it. I knew that if I lost her, I would be losing a piece of myself that could never be replaced. We're still that close and no matter what happens in our lives, I feel it will never leave.

We have other moments, too. Quite recently, in fact. Anne had been given some letters her father wrote to her mother, and diaries from when he was in the service during WWII. Her father passed away many years ago. She decided to write something about her life with him and what she has since learned about him from the letters and diaries and wanted my opinion on what she should do. I told her this would be a wonderful tribute to her parents.

A week or so after speaking to her about this project, I learned through another friend about a book dedicated to servicemen and women. Immediately, I thought about the letters Anne had and knew I had to call her and tell her about it.

I told Anne that I thought the writing she was doing would be what the editor of the book was looking for. It took a little convincing, but finally she decided to submit her work. She undertook the project and included some of the letters from her father. The piece she wrote was absolutely moving. Within hours, the editor of the book accepted her submission. Her story is one of the most touching things I have ever read.

Later, we talked about it. We decided it was serendipity. Anne had these letters, I talked to someone about it, learned about this book and she had a place to pay tribute to her father.

Both Anne and I feel a spiritual connection to each other that neither time nor distance can break. We always know when the other needs us, and we are always there for each other. We both believe each of us is a part of the other that was lost in some previous time that in the now time we've found. So, in that sense, we are soul mates. I could not imagine living my life without her being a part of it.

A lot of people feel soul mates are those who also become lovers or couples or however you define it, but that is not our case. Both Anne and I know we are best friends—and soul mates. She does not replace my husband or my three children, who are also lost parts of my soul found again. She completes my soul in a different way.

(VANESSA K. MULLINS is a writer currently residing in Michigan.)

A BOWL OF STARS
By Victoria Heckman

Author's Preface

Dear Reader:

As you begin this story, you may think to yourself, what is this fantasy doing in a collection of true soul mate stories? It is not a fantasy, and it all happened just this way. However, its magical quality comes from its setting: Renaissance Faire. If you have never been, then let me assure you that as much as possible everything—customs, etiquette, social status, costume, food, entertainment, even the creation of a personal character—is done "in period." We speak an antiquated English, we behave differently—not necessarily better, mind you! And magic happens at Faire more often than not. So rest assured that this tale is true, with all the charm and fire that meeting a soul mate entails.

*　　　*　　　*

WE WALKED, MY MAID AND I, ALONG THE DUSTY MAIN STREET OF Donnybrooke on market day. The sun beat relentlessly, and although Willow had tucked up her overskirt, it would have been unseemly for me to do so.

Willow trailing as we made our way, I greeted merchants and examined goods, always searching for a new ingredient for my potions and herb collection. My long hair streamed down my back, and I regretted again marketing without a covering. Willow's market bags remained empty, as neither of us was inspired to buy in the heat.

We had reached midway when a shimmering of the air in front of me revealed a striking man. As a weaver of spells myself, this was not alarming, except for the pure white energy he radiated. I stopped mid-pace.

He wore a long black jerkin and breeches, and his smoothly muscled chest peeked from an open white shirt. His long dark hair streamed about his bearded face, and rich brown eyes met mine.

My heart skipped. Stunned, I grasped my skirts as the whirl of marketers continued around me.

The air, ripped open, shivered shut; and time and space resumed. He smiled at me and continued past. I stumbled on with Willow but was compelled to turn and gaze on him once more. He was looking back at me as well, and our eyes met again.

"Goddess," I said to Willow.

"Yes," she said.

"I have to see him again. I must look upon him!" I pulled her the way he had vanished and found him seated under a tree, making a purchase from a stall. He smiled as he finished his task, seeming unsurprised that an herbalist, for that is how I present myself, and her maid would be struck dumb at his presence. He joined us, and we walked together.

I am powerful in my own right, sought after by nobles and peasants alike for my skills with herbs and potions. Even the queen has called upon me; but I was helpless in his presence, unable to leave his side. His touch sent flames along my skin, his gaze caused my heart to pound and his kiss—yes, we did kiss, though I have never acted so rashly in public before—weakened my knees such that I had to lean against him to remain upright.

By day's end, with the market empty of shoppers, the vendors closing their stalls, I knew I could not leave him. I sent Willow home in a carriage.

"Who are you?" I asked.

"I am the navigator."

"Where are you from?" We walked, oblivious to the night sounds of the town—the raucous laughter of men and shrill voices of wenches spilling out of the swollen taverns. I clasped his arm, the need to touch him constant and burning. Less than a day, and I was consumed by him.

"I am not of here."

I knew the moment he said these words that he spoke not of distant lands and churning seas, but of the stars. He was a Celestial Navigator. In my learning, I had heard of these beings, mortal and yet not, made as much of myth as of bone, but I had never given them much thought.

Now, this being of pure light and truth had appeared to me. No, had come for me. I would embrace him and all his teaching. The power of the heavens was his. Through him, it was mine for a time.

I half-longed to take one of my own potions and cease my need for him. I knew then that my powers were weakening, that I was slipping inside him, but I did not care. I burned for him as I have burned for no man.

I also knew in my heart that he would leave—I knew not when. I stayed, embarked on an exquisite odyssey of love and pain.

We lay together for the first time that night, though not the last. I was no innocent maid, but in our love our souls as well as our bodies joined; and I, potent beyond most, was afraid and reduced to clinging to him as he murmured reassurances. Our hair, mine the red of fire, his the richness of night sky, mingled as we cleaved.

And so, the days passed. I did not go home. I cast aside my household duties, sending a message boy to Willow. I did not know when I would return.

Summer days were long and hot, and we often spent them riding far afield, talking of nothing and everything.

"You are a way-shower for me," I said one day as we lay, spent from love, by the side of a stream.

"As you are for me," he replied and laced his fingers in mine. Sunlight glinted off his dark hair; and I saw the underside was lighter, nearing white, as if bleached by star shine. I had to touch its spun silk.

He was as hungry for me as I for him, and our lovemaking increased until it was a powerful window between his world and mine. I had visions. I trembled with love and exhaustion. He channeled spirits of my loved ones until we were both in tears and I begged him to stop.

We were nearly inseparable; and yet, there were times we were physically apart. This troubled me, as I had quickly grown to depend on his light and energy as one depends on food and air. In truth, I had almost ceased to eat and sleep.

When he left me, he disappeared into taverns for hours at a time. Not only was he gone from my side, but his spirit left me as well. Where it went I knew not, but it was like slashing my arm and feeling the life's blood run out of me.

"You left me, and your spirit went, too," I said one day after another such absence when, weak and shaken, I could bear it no more.

"I drank ale, that is all."

"But you left. I was alone." I hated the tremble in my voice.

"I didn't take my spirit from you."

"Then where did it go? I could not feel it. I was lost." I began to cry. He held me close, as always.

Through my earth-magic I discovered that when his earthly body consumed ale or smoked the sweet weed the tavern men seemed fond of, his spirit grew weak and, to protect him, closed in on him, helping him conserve it, keeping him safe.

The times he left wore my spirit thin. I could not tell this demi-god his entertainments were weakening him, but I could see that they were. His mind clouded and his glow, his health of spirit, suffered. He saw it as harmless; but I, not only with my link to the powers of the earth but also with my unbreakable bond to his inner light, saw the damage.

Selfishly, I rejoiced, thinking his weakness would keep him by my side. One day he would be too weak to return to the stars—too weak to leave me. I wanted that. I wanted him to stay with me. I hungered for him more each day, my love ever growing, my need never waning.

One morning I awoke early and watched him in sleep, long lashes resting on clear, pale skin. His glossy hair fell about his chest, and I saw his beautiful body had grown thinner and had lost its luminescence. He had been to the taverns every day since the portal had ripped open and he had stepped into my arms.

I have no need to touch to heal, or even to assess, and so I placed my hand above his chest as it shallowly rose and fell. The veil I had let cloud my inner sight fell away, and my heart fell with it.

I had blinded myself this fortnight. I had wanted him with all-consuming lust, and now I was close to my goal. He was nearly mortal—his celestial spirit ill. He would soon be too weak to travel the stars, to navigate the wonders I had barely thought about before but now needed beyond imagining.

I did not want him this way. I wanted him whole and perfect, able to stay his course on his path. His path was not mine; and I had no right to shift it with potions or powers, even in the name of love.

I had to let him go. At the pain of this truth, I cried out and he woke. He held me in love, as always; and as my hot tears met those cooling on his chest, I felt his heart beat more surely. That night, after he slipped away to the tavern, I stepped into the starlight and birthed a terrifying spell.

"Goddess! He is your child. He is of you. I cannot save him alone. You must save him!"

With each plea my fingers wove skillfully, my powers reaching up and out, a rainbow of surging energy, until the exchange of light and power erupted in white columns—from stars cradled in velvet sky to star-worshipper rooted in earth. Animals had long since flown; but trees shook and moaned, the magic gale whirling stick and stone alike.

"You must speak to him, he will listen to you. Make him see that he is strong without these mortal vices. Make him see that he is right and perfect. Take him home!"

I shook my fists and railed at the heavens for delivering the answer to a prayer I did not know I had asked. I stumbled in the moonless night, the chill smelling of metal and ice. For hours, I asked, begged, bargained. Then I made my most difficult sacrifice.

I released him.

I looked up once more. "He will listen to you. Make him see that he is enough," I whispered. Spent, I sank to my knees.

When I finally made my way back to our lodgings, he was there asleep. I pressed against his side where I had spent so much of our time, and he curled around me without waking. I breathed his musky scent and memorized his face. The soft skin of his body I committed to my touch.

His lips were warm under my cold ones when I kissed him the last time. I drifted to sleep. I awoke just after cockcrow, and he was gone. His pack, his cloak—but most devastating—his spirit, his life-giving energy, had vanished.

And yet, as I lay there on the pallet, tears streaming into my hair, I felt a ring of warmth grow around my heart. My tears dried as I listened to the beat of two hearts and felt the strength of his love.

At night, I lie outside on my chaise and watch the bowl of stars overhead and wait for his return.

(VICTORIA HECKMAN is a writer, actor, director and teacher currently residing in Hawaii.)

HEART OF A WOLF
By Barbara Williamson-Wood

I'M DRIVING DOWN THIS LONELY HIGHWAY, LEAVING THE ONLY WORLD I'VE ever known far behind. Frightened by the unknown, I try to keep my wits about me. The lights from my vehicle illuminate the white lines, causing a hypnotic trance to overtake my senses. I feel his presence with me, as I have on so many other occasions.

There is a truck stop a mile down the road. I am relieved, for here I can get some rest and focus on him...

You cannot run from your destiny, my daughter. I can hear these words pounding in my head over and over. It's as if my grandfather were standing next to me.

Instead, he is within me. In the very bowels of my soul I feel him.

Turning into the rest area, I pull my truck into an empty space and park. No one here, thank goodness! Now I can relax. I reach down and light a cigarette then get out to stretch my legs and clear my head.

The night wind feels good as I stand under a blanket of stars. Suddenly, the hairs on my neck start to rise. Without physically moving, I am running...running on all fours. I am a wolf and can see through his eyes. My paws are hot and sore as I come to a widening turn in the road. I see flames dancing in the wind. I pin my ears back to be on alert as I move in closer...

It is a truck in flames.

*　　　*　　　*

It was my truck that was burning, and I could see men carrying a body out the wreckage. It was me. *Open your heart to the wolf and become one. He will show you the way.* Again I could hear the voice of my grandfather. He taught me the old ways. Grandfather was always right, it seemed.

I found myself standing back by my truck, still dazed by the vision I'd just had. Something wasn't right, I thought as I stared out at the empty road. I turned to get back in my truck when, out of nowhere, a wolf appeared. He lowered his head once then raised it quick in the direction of the road ahead.

"Okay! Okay…I will stay here, my brother."

The wolf vanished in the darkness, and I climbed inside my truck.

I really need to move on. I thought again about wanting to leave, though my body ached; so I closed my eyes and drifted off into a much-needed sleep.

It wasn't the beams of sunlight that woke me, but the noise of many vehicles driving past.

"Miss." Someone tapped on my window. "Miss, are you all right?"

I sat up and rubbed my eyes for a moment then rolled down the window.

"Yes, Officer, what seems to be the matter?" I asked him

"Seems there was a terrible wreck down the road. A semi over-corrected the turn up ahead and rolled over. To make matters worse, another vehicle ran into it, and they both went up in flames."

"How bad is the accident?" I asked.

"Pretty bad, Miss, both of the drivers were killed instantly," he said.

The officer hurried to talk to another motorist up ahead. I leaned back in my seat and lit another cigarette and knew instantly I had been spared again. My soul mate—my guardian, the wolf—had guided my path to safety.

A keeper of my soul—that is what the wolf is to me. Since I was a child, I have found great comfort in the presence of this formidable creature. By the time I was a young teenager, the Wolf Spirit and I had become one. I could see as the wolf, feel his pain and sense dangers yet to come.

As the years went by, my awareness and ability to communicate and call upon him at will became easier. My wolf brother showed me how to feel the pain of others and to use his eyes to see the world more clearly.

173

Some may call this just intuition, but that is only because they do not understand my ways. They believe what they want to believe. They see only with their eyes and not with their hearts.

Soul mates we are, for life, and can never be separated. When I feel discouraged he comes to me and gives me comfort. He allows me to feel through his heart, see through his eyes. The greatest knowledge is this: Grandfather is my soul mate, my spirit guide. He is the wolf!

Years before my grandfather died, he told me how he walked the path of the wolf. When he was just a young man, a wolf saved him from sure death in a winter storm. He was out hunting elk in the big mountains when he became lost in a blinding storm. Grandfather said the storm was so bad he could not see in front of him. Night was setting in, and the temperatures continued to drop. Unable to move, he fell in his tracks.

He cried out for help, but no one came. No one except for a wolf. The wolf led him to a cave and lay with him during the night and kept him warm. While he slept, he dreamed of a wolf. He told me, "All I could see were the eyes of the wolf and how much at peace I felt looking into them."

Here I am today, far away from my home in the mountains; and yet, I find tranquility. For I only have to look through the eyes of my soul mate, my partner, my brother.

No one can walk on this road of life alone. There is always someone. A force out there guiding every footstep whether you are aware of this or not. A soul mate is just that, someone to guide your soul through this earthly passage until you take your place…as a Soul Mate.

(BARBARA WILLIAMSON-WOOD is a Native American author from the Rockies.)

DON'T MISS THE BLESSING
By Kim Ripley

MUST A SOUL MATE BE A LOVER? MUST A SOUL MATE BE A SPOUSE? Certainly not. This in no way diminishes the value of lovers or husbands and wives. Rather, it gives new meaning to the word *friendship*.

True friendship goes beyond an idle chat in the grocery store. It goes beyond sharing a car pool at your children's school, and it goes way beyond exchanging recipes or batting a few tennis balls around on a Saturday morning. Soul mates have a true spiritual connection.

A soul mate can pick up a conversation that left off several weeks before. A soul mate will open a birthday or Christmas card and immediately pick up the phone, just to connect. And a soul mate will finish your sentences, feel your pain and revel with you in your glory. This kind of friend has joined with your heart and soul.

Are soul mates constant companions? Not always. In fact, many are spread miles and miles apart due to jobs, family and finances. Some soul mates go years without physically connecting, yet their souls are joined and the bond remains strong. Others are blessed with close proximity and enjoy each other's company frequently. Our soul mates make us strong.

A soul mate is the one who, when life has handed you all the lemons you can take, and bitterness and sourness run rampant within you, will attempt to add the sugar and make the lemonade. A soul mate is the one who, when you've made grave mistakes, assures you he or she loves you no matter what. A soul mate believes in you.

Do soul mates come together by coincidence or is it part of God's plan? I believe in His plan, and think soul mates are part of that plan. Others may not agree, and believe instead that soul mates are part of one another's destiny. They were simply meant to be.

It doesn't matter how you came to be soul mates, only that you have been blessed with this wonderful gift. For while I truly believe there is a soul mate in this wide, wonderful world for every man and woman, I know for certain that many have yet to discover just who their soul mates are. And for those folks, I offer a tiny bit of advice.

Sometimes, that which you are actively seeking has been there the whole time. Don't overlook anyone in your quest to find your soul mate. Little old lady, homeless man, mailman, store clerk or the lady who dresses the windows in the department store—all are viable options.

How and when will you know? You just will. You will know without a doubt that your hearts and souls are joined. What should you do in the meantime? Ah, this is where it gets complicated.

While searching for your soul mate, be certain not to avoid anyone. Chat with the waitress in the diner. Ask the man in the auto shop how his family is doing. Strike up a conversation with the lady on the bus or the teenager with the pierced eyebrow and tongue.

Blessings come in many shapes and sizes. Blessings defy the law of age, color, creed and gender. Be open to the blessing. Your soul mate will!

(KIMBERLY RIPLEY writes from New Hampshire and is author/facilitator of Freelancing Later in Life.)

I'LL NEVER BE GONE

Before I left you (just for a while)
you kissed me, and
I felt your lips tremble.
Perhaps you heard my words,
though they were secretly spoken.
"It's a crap shoot until you are dead,"
then off I went.
Perhaps you thought angels' halos had
all   vanished.
Well, so have the tulips, my love.
Yet, I am not gone—
never gone.
Perhaps for nights at a time
I hibernated between sheets
not dozing till dawn.
Maybe for hours I sat and talked
to some unseen voodoo priest
like a phantast who doesn't
need to sleep to dream.
Perhaps I've grown some
loved some even died some
Maybe the raindrops
are the only virgins left.
Still, I'm not gone, love
I'll never be gone.

— Lauretta Ali

DESTINED FOR EACH OTHER
By BriAlyse Rochelle

I HAD JUST JOINED THE ARMY RESERVE UNIT IN MY CITY AFTER A TWO-YEAR active duty tour. I did not know anyone yet and was a bit reserved in my manner (not always the case). As we all headed into the Mess Hall to gather in our groups, I saw a man walking in front of me. He had a sign on his back, put there, I am sure, by one of his friends as a joke. Of course, it was a "kick me" sign. So, I proceeded to give him a swift kick in the behind.

He spun around, shocked that someone had just kicked him and surprised it was someone he had never seen before. I just smiled and said, "I always do what I am told" and walked away, never letting him know there was a sign on his back.

Not surprisingly, the rest was history—or was it? Did our history somehow start long ago, somewhere in my childhood?

We talked one night about our growing up stuff. He had lived in a small town about twenty miles from where I grew up. I talked about the alleys where we used to play kickball and learned, much to our surprise, that he had dated a girl a block away—he is nine years older than I. We might have seen each other when I was nine or ten, neither knowing who the other was—or was to become. We never met—on a conscious level, anyway—at that time.

After I graduated from high school, I joined the army about the same time he did, still never meeting. We were both stationed at one base at the same time. There was a particular day when there was an ice storm, and everything except one cafeteria was closed. With no school for the day and nowhere else to go, a bunch of my friends and I went to the cafeteria for a few drinks. Guess who else was there as well—same day, same time and same place!

Yet still we did not talk, because we did not meet.

When Christmas came around, we all went home for the holidays. We ended up on the same flight and still didn't come face-to-face. It would be almost two years before we would meet in the Reserves at home.

After that day I kicked him, I never gave him much thought. However, I found myself hanging out with his group of friends more and more. These were the black sheep of the unit. They weren't that bad, but they were fun to be with. Mildly dangerous is always attractive, for some reason.

I went to my first summer camp with the unit and found I had a sexual attraction to the man I had kicked and the feeling was mutual. We spent two weeks together at camp finding all kinds of places to meet up.

I must tell you this was a "first" for me; never in my life have I gone out with someone just because of the sexual attraction. I always dated with the agenda of finding a husband. So, for me, this was my first fling. That was all it was, just two weeks of keeping busy and having some fun—no strings, no commitments, just fun.

After the two weeks of summer camp ended, I went back to my normal life. Much to my surprise, this man came into the place where I worked tending bar and asked me out. We went out for some very nice dinners and movies. He politely took me home and dropped me off at a decent hour and with nothing more than a kiss goodnight. I felt a little confused, especially after the two weeks we had spent together. This is the pattern of our relationship to this day—we do it all kind of backwards!

Easter drew near, and he invited me for a weekend at the beach. I thought it was a great idea and went. I had never done this before, either, going away for a weekend with a lover. We had the most beautiful weekend together. I knew then that I could very easily fall in love with this man.

But something just didn't click. I thought I overheard snippets of conversations about him being married. I never really gave them much thought at first. I never gave a thought to us ever being together—like I said, it was a fling thing happening.

But after that weekend together, I had to find out. I had to know the truth because I knew I would fall in love with him if we kept seeing each other. He sensed there was something on my mind. He never imagined what was about to happen.

He came to my house, expecting to tell me good news; but it wasn't going to be like that. I asked him if he was married. He apologized and said he was, and that he should have explained that part of his life before this. I never gave him a chance to explain. I didn't give him a chance to tell me his news. I simply told him to leave and that we would not see each other again.

You see, I was all of nineteen years old, with no inclination to be involved with a married man. I had no time for triangle affairs that always ended up with someone getting hurt at someone else's expense. I did not need that in my life when there were so many other opportunities out there waiting to be found.

We did have to be together at least once a month at Reserve meetings for, unfortunately, we hung out with the same group. Although it was uncomfortable at times, I never felt awkward. I thought we had separated on good terms.

I smiled and said hello all the time and talked—or tried to talk— to him, but the only responses I got were growls and grunts. This was a first for me. You know how after you've stopped seeing somebody and you come face-to-face with them you feel awkward? Well, I never really felt awkward. I did everything to be nice to him. I wanted to be friends. When all I got were growls and grunts, I just ignored him and talked to the others. There wasn't much I could do about it, so I just talked with the other guys and got through the meetings just fine.

In July of that year the Reserve unit had a weekend camp at a nearby park, which meant camping without going home in the evenings. So here we (The Black Sheep Group) were, all sitting around our little fire. Everyone else had fallen asleep with the exception of him and me.

We had some strained (on his part) small talk. He asked me why we just couldn't be friends. I gently chuckled, knowing I had tried to be friends. I said I didn't know. I told him I had tried to be friends with him and all he did was growl and grunt when I tried to just say hello.

It got silent for a few minutes; then he spoke again. He told me he knew why we could not be friends. He was in love with me.

It was at that moment I knew I would be with him the rest of my life. I don't know how I knew, for I can't say that I was head-over-heels in love with him; but something deep inside me knew.

Unbeknownst to me, he had changed his life and circumstances. Before we got married, we made a commitment to each other that we would make our marriage work. We would do whatever it took to keep it together. We both knew marriage is not easy and not full of fairy tales and fantasy; but that it actually takes two people willing to put in the work of making the marriage a strong one. We both grew up in a world where couples broke up because it was the easiest thing to do and because divorce has become so commonplace. We were and are committed to working within our marriage to keep it. To each of us, our marriage is worth the effort and more.

We now laugh at our beginnings, especially the Easter Weekend trip. He will never take me to the place we were on that trip because of what surprise might be waiting when we get back. That is what we laugh at. I now know he came over that day to tell me he was changing his life and wanted to spend more time with me. That is what I never gave him the chance to say. And I still think, to this day, it was the right thing to do. No matter that popular opinions say otherwise.

All the times our paths crossed over the years, they had never intersected until the right time. Our hearts may have seen each other at those times, but our eyes never did. Why, so many times, were we in the same places and never saw or met each other? I feel we were destined to meet. It had to be.

Of course, our hearts knew the timing would be off in all circumstances until the "sign." On the earliest occasion I would have been far too young to even blink an eye at. The second and third times, our lives were going in other directions for the moment. But when the "sign" came, it was finally time for us to meet the one we both had been looking for.

If I believed in either past lives or reincarnation, I would have to say our love has been growing, that we have been meeting and meeting again for all time. Our souls are combined both in this life and in eternity. It is a peaceful and beautiful thing to know that, no matter what happens in this life, we will meet again. And we will meet again, for soul mates never really part. They are eternal.

(BRIALYSE ROCHELLE currently resides in central Pennsylvania.)

SOUL MATES AND LOVERS
By Kristie Leigh Maguire

OUL MATE. LOVER. ARE THE TWO TERMS SYNONYMOUS?
When you hear the term *soul mate*, usually the first thing that comes to mind is *lover*, the one and only person in the whole universe who makes you complete and brings two separated hearts together to form one, beating in unison.

Does a soul mate necessarily have to be a lover? Can a soul mate be a friend or someone you've never even met physically? Is there only one soul mate for us in the whole universe? Are we only allowed one soul mate for our whole lifespan? Is a soul mate someone who has lived with you in a past life? How do we recognize a soul mate? How do we find that soul mate in this huge universe in which we live?

So many unanswered questions to ponder.

Perhaps there is a guru on some distant mountain peak who can shed some light on soul mates, who can give us some pearls of wisdom, who can tell us exactly what a soul mate is and how to find that soul mate.

If so, I have never discovered this guru.

I think we are left to determine our own meaning of the term, and what *soul mate* means to you as an individual. It could mean different things to different people. To some people, perhaps there is only one soul mate per lifetime. To others, there may be many soul mates over their lifespan.

I believe there is more than one soul mate for each person. I believe that *soul mate* is not necessarily synonymous with *lover*, although it can be. I believe that soul mates are people who lived with you during past lives. I believe that the spirit recognizes these people and is drawn to them, rejoicing upon finding them again after a separation of who knows what duration—time is irrelevant when one is not tied down to the earthly plane.

How do we recognize these people who have shared our past lives? I believe that it is soul recognition. The physical body changes while the soul remains the same, living on in different bodies lifetime after lifetime while striving to "get it right" in order to go on to a higher plane.

I believe that we are reincarnated with the same group of people over and over. The problem with finding this group of people is that they are spread far and wide and may not even be the same sex they were in the past. That is the lifelong struggle—finding your group of people, hunting those soul mates flung all over this big wide universe in which we live. Some may not even be found in the present lifetime, and we will have to wait until another reincarnation to find them. Some may never be found again.

I had a reading once where I was told I was reincarnated this time with a different group of people than usual in order to overcome a very traumatic experience in my past life. Perhaps that is why I feel that I am always searching for something elusive to me, knowing that I am searching but not knowing what I am searching for.

I think I have found a few of my soul mates from past reincarnations.

I had a friend once who was my soul sister. Our spirits recognized each other when we met. I felt as though I had known her before—a feeling of déjà vu upon our meeting. I do not have a sister, but this friend became the sister I never had and had always longed for. Was she my sister in a past life? Was she my mother or maybe my father? Was she my brother? Was she my husband or maybe my lover? Perhaps she was my child. I do not know. This is a mystery to be pondered. I do know that we were kindred spirits who found each other again.

I met two more of my soul mates while living in Saudi Arabia. Again, our spirits recognized each other. We became very close, perhaps not soul sisters but very close friends with the feeling of having known each other before. Perhaps we were cousins in a past life, someone not as close as a mother, father, sister, brother, husband, lover or child but still kindred spirits.

I believe that my husband is a kindred spirit from a past life. I believe we lived together in the days of the Old West, that we traveled by wagon train from the East to the West together. Was it as husband and wife then or some other relationship? Again, I do not know; but I do know we were together then.

Once when my husband and I were traveling in the West, I just knew that if we could go to Inscription Rock I would find my name carved there from when I had lived before. I wanted so badly to go see my name, to discover my identity from that past life. Circumstances did not allow us to go to Inscription Rock; therefore, it still remains a mystery to me who I was in that lifetime.

I believe my daughter is also a kindred spirit from a past life. She is more like my sister or my friend than she is my daughter. Our souls recognize each other from before. Was she my daughter in a past life or was she my sister? Maybe she was my mother. Again, I do not know—I just know we have lived together before.

My granddaughter is new to my group of kindred spirits from past lives, as I was to the family into which I was born this time. At a reading I attended once I was told my granddaughter is a pure being of light, never incarnated before. She was born to this earthly plane to experience things first-hand. I believe this. She is very sensitive and full of curiosity.

I have a friend whom I've never met physically. Our only contact is through the Internet, yet we feel as though we have known each other before. Our spirits recognize each other even though we have never met. Is this as close as we will come to each other in this lifetime? I do not know. I just know that we are soul mates, that he is a kindred spirit from some past lifetime. Perhaps it will take another reincarnation for us to come together again.

Life is a mystery. There is no guru on top of that distant mountain, no guidebook to tell us how to live. We ponder the deeper meaning of life while in a constant subliminal search for that elusive group of people who are our soul mates, hoping beyond hope to find them, to make our lives complete.

(KRISTIE LEIGH MAGUIRE is the author of *Desert Heat, Emails from the*

Edge (The Life of an Expatriate Wife) and co-author of *No Lady and Her Tramp.*)

BIRDS OF A FEATHER

By Linda Morales-Kennon

IT WAS FINALLY FRIDAY NIGHT, AND IT HAD BEEN A LONG WEEK. NOT ONLY HAD I put in my forty hours at work but every night after work I had gone to Audrey's house to meet with her and the rest of her political campaign staff to discuss the latest numbers in Assembly District 5.

Audrey Winslow was a good friend of my mother's; and when she found out I had a communications degree and was looking for some volunteer work, she approached me about working on her campaign.

"One thing about it, you'll get to use your writing skills and you won't be bored. If you like, you can go to some parties with me. I hear the Trial Lawyers throw quite an elegant reception for political candidates," she said.

Since my divorce, my social life hadn't been all that great. Going to a few parties might be just the thing to get it pumping.

I liked Audrey. She was what used to be called a buxom woman, with curves that were just a bit more ample than they should be. But her dress size wasn't what people first noticed when they met her. People were attracted to her warmth and sincerity. Her facial features were nicely proportioned; she had longish blond hair worn loose and flowing and big, expressive eyes that were an unusual shade of blue-gray. Her smile made you feel like you'd known her all your life. Her manners were ladylike, but there was an undertone of old-time movie queen glamour and sensuality in her demeanor.

Since I was always running by her house with some new flyer or brochure for approval, we ended up spending a lot of time together. We hit it off right away, and she expressed a genuine caring and fondness for me. My feelings for her were the same. There was comfort in just being together. We often read each other's mind, and we picked up on those nonverbal cues that sometimes communicate more powerfully than words. We were more than buddies and much more than friends. We were birds of a feather.

We began to share confidences, and many evenings our conversation would take on a more personal tone.

"Lauren, I've been married three times," she told me one night after dinner. "Now, at fifty-four, I'm just learning to find myself and what I want out of life. And after all the experimenting with marriage and relationships, I've finally decided that what I don't want is a man. That's not to say I don't like men—I'm certainly not into women—it's just that I just don't want a man in my life right now!"

She went on to say that, if she won the election, she planned to devote all of her time and energy to pushing through legislation that would have statewide impact. She had been anointed by the party to run; and if she succeeded, she was going to make a difference.

Audrey and I thought a lot alike about so many things. One of them was politics. The other was men. Since my divorce I had dated; but for the last two years, there had been no steady man in my life. As an almost-forty woman with a marriage behind me and no children, I had become a workaholic. The way I looked at it, advancing in my career was my ticket to a better lifestyle. So, my career came first, except for my immediate family, and I liked it that way. I felt pretty much the same way Audrey did about a man—I didn't want one at this point.

Still, the thought of meeting someone at one of those political functions did spark some occasional daydreaming. Coming back down to earth took just under ten seconds.

My first-ever political party was on a Friday night in early August. It was sponsored by the Teamsters Union.

"It's a Western theme party, and this is not a highbrow crowd," Audrey said. "So, if you've got jeans and low heels, wear them. You'll be dancing all night. And come by my house so we can drive over together."

I searched through my closet, pulled out my best Calvins, a plaid fitted shirt and those fringed boots I had bought on the spur of the moment and thought I'd never wear. Just before heading out the door, I grabbed a hat that had a western look to it. There, that completed the picture.

Audrey was right. I did dance all night. On the way home, she asked me how I liked the party.

"Pretty nice crowd, good food, and I met a lot of interesting people," I said. I told her a couple of the men who kept me on the dance floor had asked for my phone number.

"You did give it to them, didn't you?" she asked.

"Well, I gave it to Eric Peterson," I replied.

She shrugged and said he might be a good match.

"Good match?" I asked. "You know I'm perfectly happy with things just the way they are."

"Well, it never hurts to get to know a good-looking, intelligent man who has connections in the right places," she responded.

As we pulled into her driveway, I dismissed her last remark and said, "Goodnight, Audrey, talk to you tomorrow."

In the weeks to follow, Audrey and I went to a number of political events. There were B-B-Qs, picnics, cocktail receptions and elaborate sit-down dinners. Most of the time, I got ready at her house and we drove to the event together. It was fun talking and kidding around on the way home. Almost always there was a guy or two who would ask for my phone number. Audrey would often ask, "Okay, was it the tall lanky one or the short stocky one who wants to see you again? Don't tell me, I already know. Both want to take you out, but you didn't give your number to either one."

The money in Audrey's campaign chest had grown considerably. She received contributions from almost every organization, union and business that made them available to political candidates. One Friday night she called about eight o'clock and asked if I'd go with her to pick up a contribution at a bar on the east side of town. She was kind of secretive about the whole thing; and on the way there, we didn't talk much. I sensed this must really be something special.

Then, finally, she said, "Lauren, I know I can trust you, but I have to ask you to keep the details of this little trip to yourself. The fewer people who know the better. We're on our way to a dive bar to meet the secretary-treasurer of the state AFL-CIO, and he's going to give me a hefty contribution."

As we pulled into the parking lot, I couldn't believe we were actually going in. It was a raunchy-looking place with a lopsided neon sign that blinked LIVE NUDES ON STAGE. Who would want to meet in a place like this, especially someone who was going to give a political candidate a campaign contribution?

None of this made any sense to me. We were used to going to events where there were a lot of people around and campaign contributions were made very openly. One look at Audrey told me she was thinking the same thing; but as she pushed open the swinging door, she didn't say a word.

We were barely inside when a tall, thin woman in a dark-blue business suit approached us.

"Audrey?" she asked. "Right this way."

We were escorted to a corner of the bar opposite the stage. There was a table of about twelve people talking and drinking. We were introduced to everyone, but it was obvious the person Audrey had come to see was the one right in the middle of the action. He motioned for her to go to where he was sitting. As he did, the woman next to him quickly got up and took another seat.

The waitress came to take our drink order.

"Vodka and soda," Audrey said.

"The same," was my choice. This was the first time I had seen Audrey order a drink. Diet Coke or ginger ale were her usual, even at cocktail receptions.

As Mr. Powerful stood up to offer a toast in Audrey's honor, he removed his black suit jacket and placed it on the back of his chair. The outline of his arm muscles were obvious through his white shirt. Loosening his tie and raising his glass, he looked directly at her and said, "This lady's going to be Assembly 5's next representative and we're going to see she holds that job for many years to come."

"Hear, hear," came the response; and with it, a lot of clapping and cheering.

"That was quite a party," I remarked on the ride home.

It was a few minutes before she said anything.

"What did you think of him?" she asked.

I didn't have to ask who she was referring to. I didn't quite know what to say and I hesitated for what seemed a long time.

"What's the matter, Lauren, you usually have an opinion. Tonight, you don't seen to want to tell me what you're thinking." Actually, she was right, I didn't want to tell her, but she pushed.

"He's attractive, Audrey, and he's powerful. That in itself would be quite a combination, but more than that, he's also charismatic. What more can I say? He's got it all."

"But?" She could read me too well.

"But…I also think he's a manipulator, he's just a little too smooth, and I think he's someone it would be best not to get too close to."

I could tell she didn't like the last part of my response. I wondered if she wanted to know him better than she had let on. The next morning, I didn't have to wonder any longer.

I answered the phone on the third ring. It was Audrey. Mr. Powerful had a name, and it was Vic Simmons. What's more, he had invited her to meet him up north for the weekend.

"Lauren, pack your bags for some fun and flash, you're coming with me," she said.

"Oh, Audrey, I don't know. I'm not sure I'd fit in, and what if he wants to be alone with you?" I asked.

"Lauren, he extended the invitation to you as well. Besides, I don't want to be alone with him. Better that you come with me so people don't get the wrong idea. I don't want my political career to come to an end before it even gets started."

My wildest dreams couldn't compete with the reality that was to come.

When we arrived at the America West counter there were two prepaid roundtrip tickets waiting for us. Our flight was scheduled to leave at ten a.m. The plane ride was pleasant, but Audrey and I didn't talk much. Maybe it was the excitement of the trip, or maybe we were both just too absorbed in our own thoughts about the weekend.

The flight was short, just a little under an hour. It seemed as though we were no sooner in the air than we were landing.

"Ms. Winslow?" a uniformed older man asked as we reached the arrival gate. "Right this way, please."

We were escorted to baggage claim and then to a limousine. It would be another half-hour to our host's condo.

191

Vic's smile was warm and his manner charming as he greeted us at the door. He was dressed casually but elegantly in pleated taupe trousers, an olive green silk T-shirt and Italian loafers.

"Audrey—and Lauren—thank you so much for coming. Please come in and make yourselves comfortable. I've planned lunch here, I hope that's all right."

The condo was spacious and beautifully furnished in hand-painted Italian antiques. Windows surrounded every single inch of living space so there was a panoramic of view of blue sky and mountain peaks. Vic's houseman, Alfred, took our bags upstairs as we followed our host into his sumptuous living area. A tray with champagne-filled flutes was ready and waiting. I liked the way the rich lived. Most of all, I liked sampling the way they lived.

Conversation over lunch was pleasant and light. Vic and Audrey mostly discussed the campaign. After lunch, he gave us a tour of the condo. The bedrooms and baths upstairs were just as spacious and elegantly furnished as the living areas downstairs. Throughout, there was a warm golden glow and, with that, a feeling of comfortable richness. Outside, adjacent to a small guesthouse, was a palm-shaded cabana and pool. The grounds were aromatic with scents of jasmine and gardenia.

"I can't tell you how glad I am to have you both here. I've taken the liberty of providing a few things to make your stay more comfortable, but if there is anything else you need, please let me know," Vic said.

As I excused myself to go up for a nap, I couldn't help asking myself if this guy was for real.

I noticed my clothes had been unpacked and my toiletries neatly arranged on the large black marble vanity in the bathroom. Alongside them were assorted baskets of designer soaps, perfumes and bath oils with a note that said "Enjoy!" It was signed with a large V.

Before I climbed into bed, I looked out and saw Audrey and Vic in the pool area. They were sitting very close to each other, and I could hear faint echoes of Audrey's hoarse laugh. Still not sure how close they actually were, I dozed off thinking what a striking couple they made.

*   *   *

Gently shaking my shoulder, Audrey said, "Lauren, wake up. We've got to get ready. Vic's taking us to Patina's tonight. Dinner reservations are for eight o'clock. And I've got a surprise. He's invited Steve Cassen to be your date."

"Who's Steve Cassen?" I asked.

She said Steve was one of Vic's staff members. "I know you're going to like him. He's handsome, quite a snappy dresser, makes great conversation, and he'd be a fantastic catch. All the campaign groupies make a play for him, but so far, he's managed to stay single."

As I got out of bed and headed toward the bathroom to shower, I glanced over my shoulder and saw those familiar wheels turning in her head.

Audrey was absolutely stunning in her royal blue sequined evening gown. As we walked by several tables to an intimate corner booth, every head turned to her. Was it because she was so breathtakingly beautiful or because she was on the arm of one of the most powerful men in the state? Suddenly, none of that seemed to matter as we reached the booth and my eyes locked with the most beautiful blue ones I'd ever seen.

I heard Vic say, "Steve, I'd like you to meet Audrey's friend, Lauren Hunter."

"So nice to meet you, Lauren. Vic and Audrey have told me so much about your work on the campaign. I've looked forward to meeting you for some time."

Steve was everything and more than Audrey had said. Suddenly, my head was reeling, and I felt like Cinderella at the ball. Only I didn't have to worry about midnight.

Steve asked if he could take me to brunch before Audrey and I flew home the next day. Since I wasn't sure about the plans Vic and Audrey might have made, I whispered to her that we needed to visit the ladies room.

"Please excuse us, gentlemen, Lauren and I have to visit the powder room," she said. As we headed toward the restrooms, she gave me a knowing look. "Don't tell me. Let me guess," she said. "He wants to see you tomorrow."

"Audrey, how did you know? Did you and Vic put him up to it?" I questioned.

"No, Lauren, we didn't. Certainly you know me better than that. Anyone can see he has an interest in you. He's been hanging on your every word all night. Vic said Steve's acting like a smitten schoolboy."

"So, is it okay to accept his invitation?" I asked.

"No problem, Lauren. It appears that I have a schoolboy of my own to deal with."

I went downstairs around eleven the next morning and found Audrey and Vic having breakfast on the patio.

"Good morning," I said.

"Morning, Lauren, how about a cup of coffee or juice?" they said in unison. Before I could answer, I heard the bell and saw Alfred heading toward the door. Steve came in and walked out to the patio, cheerfully offering his good mornings to Audrey and Vic. Then, turning to me, he said, "Ready, Lauren?"

Our conversation was casual as we drove outside the city limits to a large two-story house that had been converted into a restaurant. Claire's was known for its romantic atmosphere, beautiful gardens and superb menu. Once inside and settled, Steve smiled, leaned toward me and whispered, "Lauren, I want to see more of you."

Could he hear the millions of thoughts clamoring inside my head? Clearly, I just wasn't ready for this. It was very hard not to show it.

"I'll be spending a lot of time in Audrey's district on campaign business. All I'm asking is that we date over the next few months and see what happens," Steve said. "I've never felt like this about anyone, and all I know is that I want to get to know you better. After that, who knows? I realize we just met, but I want you in my life, Lauren."

"Steve, you're a great guy and I'm flattered. If I were looking for a relationship, I couldn't hope to find someone more appealing than you. But right now, I just can't commit to what you're asking," I said.

The look on his face was one I hadn't seen in quite some time.

Vic arranged for a limousine to take us to the airport. Once on the plane, Audrey made the first attempt at conversation.

"You've not going to see him, are you?" she asked.

"No, Audrey, I'm not."

"I somehow knew you wouldn't," she responded.

"We've had our talks, Audrey. You know how I feel, how I think and what's important to me. Right now, there is no place in my life for Steve or any other man."

"You're making a mistake, Lauren. You've got to know that. Steve can make all of your dreams to come true! I saw you at Vic's. You want the good life. Steve can give that to you."

"You're right, Audrey. I know he can. And as important as it is for me to better myself and my lifestyle, I need to get that accomplished without a man's help. You've got to know that or you don't know me."

She dropped her eyes and nodded in confirmation. Deep down, she did know; and although we saw Steve from time to time at campaign events, we never spoke of him in that way again.

*   *   *

Audrey walked into campaign headquarters just as the media announcement came over the TV screen. She had defeated the incumbent in District 5. I'd never seen her look so radiant and alive as her supporters made way for her to get to the stage. In the midst of cheering and whistling, she graciously offered a toast to her campaign workers and began her acceptance speech. As she finished, she glanced my way. Her smile told me our journey together would continue on past that night.

In the coming years, heartaches and pain shaped our paths; but there were also good times and successes. Ten years later would still find us birds of a feather.

(LINDA MORALES-KENNON is a writer currently residing in Las Vegas, Nevada.)

HALF OF ME

Dancing in the wind
playing a favorite song
My lover calls to me
from the secret world beyond.
Sifting through the memories
for a love so dear to me.
Just waiting for tomorrow
to face uncertainty.
Living for the moment
because the future looks so grey
Stealing time from destiny
helps get me through the day.

— V.K. Mullins

PART THREE
COMPANION SOUL MATES

"The best and most beautiful things in this world cannot be seen or even heard, but must be felt with the heart."

— *Helen Keller*

YOU ARE MY LOVE

You are the essence of comfort and acceptance
Forever encouraging and loving me
For who I am and who I wish to be
Radiating your love like the warmth of a favorite
blanket.
I am wrapped within your heart.
You are like the ocean's tide
Constant and beautiful, yet forever changing
I watch in wonder at your many hues
Like that of a glorious sunset
The colors of you are infinite.
You are the one I need to seek
When I experience a newness in life
I want to share it with you and only you.
Like a sturdy oak I lean on your strength
When I feel like a weeping willow.
You are eternal
You are woven into my soul forever
Etched into my life.
You are My Love

— Ellen M. DuBois

I MARRIED MY BEST FRIEND'S WIFE
By Larry James

FINDING YOUR SOUL MATE IS LIKE DISCOVERING THE MISSING LINK TO YOUR heart. When that special someone enters your life, has similar values, ideals and beliefs and lives them as well, you discover that the two pieces of the relationship puzzle fit perfectly together. There are many souls you connect with in this life. With some you feel an immediate bond you know will always be there.

I first met my soul mate when we were very young. Ours is a story of four people who loved each other, had fun together then were separated by time and distance. Twenty-six years later, two of them were reunited under very unexpected circumstances.

My best friend Ted Charveze and I were both very active in the Topeka, Kansas, Jaycees. We spent a lot of time together. He was best man at my wedding. His wife Sandy, my wife and I were all close friends.

After six years of doing things together as couples and enjoying each other's company, my family moved to Tulsa so I could take a position of management with a major real estate firm. About two years later, Ted and Sandy moved to Scottsdale, Arizona, to be close to his mentor and to take advantage of a better opportunity to promote his work as a jewelry artisan. Even though we had all been close friends, we all moved about the same time and did not know where the other had gone. We lost contact.

Nineteen years passed. One day while cleaning out some drawers, my former mother-in-law found an obituary notice from a year earlier saying that Ted had died. In spite of my divorce several years earlier from her daughter, we had remained friends. She sent me the obituary notice along with a note to inform me of his passing. I had not known.

The notice stated that Sandy was living in Scottsdale. I called to express my sympathy. She told me that not only was Ted gone but her twenty-five-year-old daughter had died suddenly less than a year and a half before. In addition, her mother-in-law, father and a sister had also died. She had been grieving for a long time.

I never called again, although I did send her a copy of my *Life Skills* book. She wrote a brief thank-you for the book and made it clear she was content to be alone.

Three years later, on her birthday, I received a message on my voice mail. It said, "Hi, Larry. I was just thinking about you. Thought you might like to talk sometime. Call me if you want to!" Click! There was no name, no number and a voice I had only heard once in about twenty-six years. After listening to the message over and over, I decided that it might be Sandy so I called. It was.

Since the last time I had talked with her, I had been in a relationship that ended abruptly. A year passed, and I had spent most of my time focusing my energy on working on me. The first six months I saw a therapist, who helped me work through the pain of a changing relationship. I discovered in the first therapy session that I had no guidelines for one. I had always done the best I could, but it never seemed good enough.

I became a full-time student of relationships. I read every book my therapist recommended. I began writing a daily journal. It was a painful process. As I started to feel better about myself, I wrote my own relationship guidelines. I gave them to my therapist for review, and he encouraged me to write more and publish them.

At the time Sandy called, my first relationship book, *How to Really Love the One You're With: Affirmative Guidance for a Healthy Love Relationship*, was about to be released. We talked for about twenty minutes. She was beginning to date again, and I told her I would send her a copy of my book when it was out.

On December 20th I sent the book. The day after Christmas I called her. We talked for about an hour about the book and relationships. Four days later, I accepted her invitation to go to

Scottsdale for a brief holiday.

We were both very nervous about meeting after so many years. We talked about our fears, and the conversation defused our anxiety.

We spent a lot of time talking about the "good old days" when she and her husband and my wife and I had spent many happy times together. We acknowledged that even back then we'd had some kind of special attraction for each other, but neither chose to pursue it because we were both married to someone else. We visited some of her favorite places to eat and had a wonderful time just talking and getting to know each other again.

We discussed how we both enjoyed being alone. We were very clear that neither she nor I was interested in a relationship at the time. We were learning to be ourselves, and could be alone without experiencing loneliness.

We both truly enjoyed each other's conversation; and as time passed, we got to know each other better on the phone. Several months later I presented a "Relationship Enrichment LoveShop" in the Phoenix area and took time to see her again.

Sandy's daughter lived in Topeka, which was a four-and-a-half-hour drive from Tulsa. Whenever she visited there, I would drive to Topeka to see her. She also made several trips to Tulsa.

The hours we talked on the phone, for months never suspecting we would ever be together, was a time of building the foundation of trust that healthy love relationships need to make them work. Finding the right person is more about being the right person. We were preparing for love. The walls of resistance were coming down.

We talked openly and honestly about our feelings about life, relationships and each other. We discovered that we could express our own individuality and still choose to be together. The fears of our wounded hearts melted away. When two whole people come together, they enhance each other's lives more than one can alone.

As time passed we became aware we were growing in love and toward each other.

A soul mate is not someone you need to be happy. A soul mate is someone you share your happiness with.

After an eighteen-month long-distance relationship (and

hundreds of dollars in phone bills) we began to talk about being together, not really sure we wanted to give up our independence. Several months later, I moved to Scottsdale to be with her. She admitted to me later that when she saw me pull the big U-Haul truck into her drive she said to herself, "Oh, my! What have I done?"

I married my best friend's wife on June 8, 1996. God smiled on both of us that day. We are both confident that Ted smiled, too, and that we have his blessing.

Since then I have written two more books on relationships and am on staff with Dr. John Gray, Ph.D., author of *Men Are From Mars, Women Are From Venus.* Sandy made the connection to Dr. Gray by attending his seminar and giving him one of my books. He has endorsed all of them.

Sandy and I are a team. Whenever she can, she travels with me to present my Relationship Enrichment LoveShops across the country. We are committed to having our relationship be the kind of example we can be proud to share with others. We continually search for new and creative ways to keep the romance, passion and the fire of love burning. We, like other couples, have our ups and downs; and we have learned relationships are something that must be worked on all the time, not just when they are broken.

Soul mates? You bet! A great relationship? Definitely! Trust is the foundation of a healthy love relationship. There can be no trust without conversation, no genuine intimacy without trust!

Sandy is my very best friend. She supports my dreams, accepts me for who I am and loves me unconditionally. We were truly meant to be together. With so much time passing, it is truly a miracle we were brought together at all. This soul mate journey took more than thirty years!

(LARRY JAMES is a professional speaker, author and relationship coach from Scottsdale, Arizona.)

THE QUINTESSENCE OF ROMANCE
By Richelle Putnam

I ADORE ROMANCE—THE KIND THAT SWATHES MY BODY IN GOOSE BUMPS AND hurls a roller-coaster sensation into my gut. I have pined for long-stemmed roses, rich chocolates, romantic music, candlelight dinners and passionate lovemaking.

Each year, millions of women devour romance novels and tearfully view romantic films that squeeze our hearts for weeks, months—even decades. We yearn for one extraordinary moment in our otherwise boring life to be cast beneath a spellbinding blue moon. There, bathed under vast starlight, cuddled in our lover's warm embrace, we wish to lose ourselves in hungry eyes and quixotic dedications.

Face it. We're romance addicts.

Nevertheless, as silver strands crept into my thinning tresses and life's trials and triumphs creased new roads over my face, my former conceptions transformed into what I believe to be the true meaning of the "quintessence of romance." As I wade through precious memories, I pray a new understanding to this perplexing obsession pervades your understanding as it did mine, and that your mate becomes one eternally attached to your soul as well as your heart.

In October 1997, lab tests confirmed my husband's liver cancer and the probability that I'd become a widow in my mid-forties. Further findings revealed the cancer had originated in his colon, had metastasized to the liver and was rapidly developing. If he didn't immediately commence the strongest chemotherapy regimen, death would strike in mere months.

From that point, I touched my husband every day, if only a simple pat with trembling hands. Chemo quickly drained away the life he fought desperately to retain. He couldn't endure tight hugs and certainly didn't desire passion. Yet, at night, when the children lay snug in their beds, we'd retire for another sleepless night of clinging to each other, wondering how many sunrises we had left together.

My husband's mouth, which had once bestowed kisses and spoken romanticisms and witty remarks, now oozed from painful ulcers. Because of his inability to eat, weight shrank from the strong limbs that had caressed me, and his thick silver mane thinned as if with the mange. His tanned complexion, usually shiny from overwork and activity, turned pallid and chalky. I beheld his deteriorating image, and I loved him more than I ever imagined possible.

His energy dwindled—it was on a wish and a prayer that I bought Gatorade, hoping to regenerate it a little. It worked. Finally, we found something he could eat and enjoy—O-Charley's Caramel Pies—and each week I'd purchase a few. God had granted hope through a simple meal of Gatorade and caramel pie. Gratitude overwhelmed me, and I wanted nothing more than to shower devotion all over my husband.

When we were together, I composed myself nicely, appropriately; but in his absence fear, anticipation, anger and grief shackled every muscle and emotion. Anguish encased me. Never once did tears fall because of lost candlelight dinners, romantic music, flowery words or passionate lovemaking. I would have gladly sacrificed it all, and more, if my husband could remain with me for a few more years.

It happened on an oppressive day, one that squeezed sorrow from me. Feeling lost in vacant air, I paced throughout my home moaning, almost hyperventilating. In our bedroom, on the back of a chair, it caught my eye—his dirty shirt. The one he had donned every day when he arrived home. I trudged to it and fondled the material, feeling the coolness, sniffing his body odor of motor oil, lingering cigar and caramel pie. I smashed it to my breast and embraced it like a lost lover. Tears splotched the deep maroon color, and I romanced my sweetheart with my soul and spirit. That's how powerful love can be.

I hadn't searched my Bible for wisdom, which was unusual for me, being the daughter of a preacher man, a firm believer in an omnipotent, omnipresent God. Yes, I had lifted prayer after prayer, unceasingly, reverently, confessing willingness to accept His supreme will; but I had been unable to concentrate on His word. However, in a state of panic, incapable of calming myself, I knew what I had to do.

My pink Women's Devotional Bible stared from the kitchen shelf, and its power magnetized me. Slowly, I opened it to the first page and read, "Presented to my loving wife, Richelle, from your loving husband, Tim," dated August 24, 1992.

My stomach wrenched, and I burst like a thin balloon filled beyond capacity. No more perfect prayers, no more reverent requests. I plummeted to my knees and screamed to my Father.

"Please. Please don't take him. I want to grow old with him, to see our children's children born, witness him escort our daughter down the aisle and shake our son's hand when he publishes his first comic strip." My insides tightened with each confession and I dared to go further. "If it is your will, Lord, that his life be taken, change it, please change it. You're God, the Almighty, my Father, who can do all things. Please save my husband. Heal him, Lord. I'm begging you on my knees. You can heal him, if you will."

My honest outpouring brought forth a restful feeling. I poured a steaming cup of coffee and perched on a barstool, opening my Bible to the day's devotion, Philippians 2:27: "Indeed, he was ill, and almost died. But God had mercy on him, and not on him only but also on me, to spare me sorrow upon sorrow."

I froze, stunned and wide-eyed, examining the two sentences over and over. It was hardly a verse most would memorize; however, to me it was the essence of God Himself revealing His will, purpose and intent through His word. He had performed a miracle.

I possessed a new faith and hope, one that allowed me to adore and nurture my husband with confidence and faith, something he had yet to regain. I would smile at him victoriously, knowing he'd survive tomorrow, the next day and the next.

Cancer had sliced his fuse very short, and minor things easily angered him. My newfound faith and hope weren't my husband's. He absconded emotionally, pulling away from sympathetic attention. I watched him drift out of physical and emotional range; but my love continued to embrace him and soft replies, possessing no hint of discontent, whispered sweet nothings to him. I romanced him from afar.

Don't get me wrong. I wasn't a saint, by any means. Many times I wanted to yell, curse, question his actions—and one day I did.

It was Christmas Day 1997, two months after his diagnosis, three chemos behind him. It was a difficult time, as holidays always are when life's uncertainties consume any happiness or gaiety. A Christmas feast adorned our huge dining room table, and family and friends had joined our festivities. I had planned a special blessing for dinner, an emotional one—too much so for my husband. He blurted out, "Get on with it." Needless to say, my heart shattered at his outburst; but it was his detachment that made me bleed internally.

After everyone uttered gracious goodbyes, I slammed dishes into the dishwasher. Anger hung in my throat, and my stomach was tied in knots. I knew guilt feasted on him and he regretted his flare-up, but his harshness had ripped into an already open wound. Teary-eyed, I confronted him.

"You don't need or want my concern or love and I don't know how to act anymore. I have tried so hard, so terribly hard, but nothing I do matters." I finished, regretful that my honesty added injury to his already pained body and thoughts.

He listened, not saying a word. His glassy eyes gazed deeply into mine. He seized my hand, pulled me into his arms and broke into pieces. We cried, embracing each other, wiping each other's tears. It was the most romantic moment of my life.

It's now December 2001, and my husband's cancer has been in complete remission more than two years. Since then, psoriatic arthritis has struck my spine like heavy stones. Often the pain is so intense it's difficult to move, much less make mad, passionate love. So does our romance suffer? Not on your life.

My husband, without my knowledge, located a rheumatoid specialist for me, purchased metallic massagers for my back pain and has surprised me with medical articles on debilitating arthritis. He communicates to me information colleagues have shared with him on chronic pain. Midday he'll call just to say "hi" or ask how I'm feeling.

I pray that if you ever find yourself mourning lost romance, yearning for soft music, sweet romantic words and lovemaking, you will snuggle in your warm bed with your soul mate, just grateful to be at each other's side.

(RICHELLE PUTNAM is an author and creative writing teacher in Meridian, Mississippi.)

THE MESSENGER
By Sandy Breckenridge

IT WAS A BEAUTIFUL SUNNY DAY IN SEATTLE, WHICH IS UNUSUAL FOR THE 4TH of July, a day for fireworks and celebration honoring our country's independence. Little did I know that I was soon to receive a very special message from a most unusual messenger.

It was early in the afternoon, and I was busy refinishing some old windows on my back porch. All of the doors and windows throughout my home were open, letting in the light and the fresh air.

My life was going through some major changes. Only a month before, I had struggled with a relationship I knew needed to change form. A few days earlier I had said my goodbyes.

I have always heard that when one door closes another opens, but I didn't know if I was fully prepared to step through the new door that presented itself. You see, I had finally realized that the dearest male friend I had ever known was the soul mate I had been looking for my entire life.

What a shock this was! I had always thought of myself as an intuitive person, but I didn't see this one coming. It was as if, until now, I'd had a veil pulled over my eyes.

Needless to say, I was filled with bliss at this new awareness, but also scared and unsure at the same time. People say that the chance of someone single in their mid-forties finding true love is like finding an old vintage "oat penny" in a jar full of pocket change—highly unlikely. What do they know!

I knew in my heart that my friend Kirk was a soul mate, but my head was swimming with some fear I couldn't fully understand. So, I did what I do when I need to process so many emotions—I worked on something tangible in the physical world that needed to be fixed.

As I refinished the old window frames, I noticed layer after layer of different-colored paint. It seemed like I was going through the generations of a family tree as each layer was exposed. Each of the paint colors shared a story about different cycles in my life. As each layer emerged I had some sort of revelation. I can't really tell you every thought that went through my mind, but each one was revealing at the time.

There came a point when I was so full of thought I knew I needed to take a break. I decided to walk into my magical dining room, where the beautiful stained glass windows surrounded my favorite plants. It was at that very moment something unusual caught the corner of my eye.

I have always had an affinity for butterflies and love to watch them outside, but this was the first time I had ever seen one indoors.

Wow! I thought. This is the most unusual-looking butterfly.

I have seen monarch butterflies up close, but never one like this. As I crept closer to take a better look, I was in awe. This butterfly was very large—black, white and orange, and incredibly beautiful. He seemed quite calm—much calmer than I was, for sure.

I wondered, Now, what does a person do with a butterfly in their home?

I was concerned he was going to die if he stayed inside any longer. It is unnatural for a butterfly not to be free. I wondered what to do.

Just then I heard thoughts in my head telling me to fill myself with love and then to place my hand beside this radiant butterfly. So, I did just that. As I felt this incredible sense of love oozing from my being, I pressed my hand close to him against the window pane. To my amazement, he gently crept over to my hand and stepped right into the center of my palm.

I was motionless and in shock. How could a butterfly as beautiful as this one come inside my home and end up in my palm?

Just then I heard another thought, and this time it seemed to be coming from the butterfly!

Trust, dear one. Trust your life and trust your heart. Here you are with the door open, and the light is shining the way. I am here to show you that you now have your independence. Do with it as you wish. In going through the door before you, your life will have more freedom than you have ever known before.

This was so weird. Incredible peace filled every inch of my being. I just knew this butterfly was sent to me as a messenger, to tell me everything was okay, that my love for my wonderful friend and soul mate Kirk was perfect so not to fear.

I slowly walked the twenty-five or so steps through my dining room and out onto my front porch. The butterfly contentedly lay in the palm of my hand, not about to leave until he knew I had received my message. At the point of mutual acknowledgement, I raised my hands to the sky and watched as the butterfly elegantly ascended.

I stood there for a while and watched him circle the yard, as if he were smiling back at me, saying goodbye. I thought, What a magical messenger, indeed.

From that moment on, I have never turned back.

(SANDY BRECKENRIDGE is an accomplished intuitive currently residing in Kauai, Hawaii.)

TAKE IT AND FLY

By Margaret Marr

I STARED OUT THE WINDOW OF THE TEXAS HOTEL ROOM; THE SKY WAS CLEAR with a few wispy clouds floating around.

The drive from North Carolina had been long and tedious. I was tired, scared and nervous as I thought of David. My fingers faltered on the blinds, and I released the slats and turned from the window. In a few hours, I was about to meet with a man I hadn't seen in more than fifteen years.

What would he think of me now?

Would he still be attracted to me?

Or would he be disappointed?

I wandered over to the couch and sat down, drawing my knees up to my chest. My mind floated back to high school...

David and I had chemistry class together; and every day I knew he was coming before I saw him, because he carried a lot of keys hooked to his belt. They jingled as he walked.

When he'd arrived at the classroom door, he'd look at me and smile. I couldn't help but smile back. It was always as if someone had turned the sunshine on in his heart and the light spilled out of his eyes and smile.

I suspected David had a crush on me back then; but since I was involved with a college guy, I didn't pay much attention—except for one day when he was absent from class, and the teacher told us he was in the hospital recovering from an asthma attack. I looked at his empty seat, felt a stirring I didn't understand at the time and wished I could go visit him to cheer him up. But my parents were strict, and I wouldn't have been allowed to go.

David never told me how he felt. I married my college guy after high school and went to work in Cherokee as a craft shop cashier. I was pregnant that summer; and David worked across the street from me, although I didn't know this at the time. Later, he told me he had watched and longed for me; and that I was so beautiful it hurt him to look at me, knowing he couldn't have me.

He left Cherokee and joined the Air Force. His military career took him to faraway places, taught him many things and matured him beyond his age. Through it all he thought of me on and off...never forgot me.

The phone in my hotel room rang and brought me out of the past. I smiled as I answered it.

"Hello?" My heart skipped a beat when I heard the voice on the other end. It was David.

"You're there! I can't believe you actually came."

I laughed. "Of course, I'm here."

"I'm at the job center, but I'll be there in a little while."

We hung up, and I returned to my place on the couch to wait.

Six months earlier I'd been working on a novel when I got a notice I had a new message in my Hotmail box. It was from "David," and I wondered if it was the same guy I'd attended high school with. I thought, surely not, so I didn't open the message right away. I was in the middle of a chapter and wanted to finish it before I went to bed.

Around midnight, I finally got to my email and it *was* the same David. I read his message with a smile on my face. He told me about all his accomplishments as if he were trying to impress me. I couldn't help but think of that song by Toby Keith, "How Do You Like Me Now?"

Well, I was impressed, but more than anything I was proud of him. He was a poor boy from western North Carolina who got out and made something of his life; I, on the other hand, hadn't made it to college. My twelve-year marriage had ended in divorce, and my heart was broken beyond repair by a man I'd met on the Internet. I'd made many foolish choices in my life, and the only hope I had left was my writing career. I didn't want or need another man in my life.

But something about David kept pulling me toward him. We

started exchanging emails on a daily basis and grew closer. Things got too hot, too fast, and I ended up writing him a tearful letter telling him we had to put an end to it before it got out of hand. I was scared out of my mind because I didn't want to endure another broken heart or give it to another man with no guarantees. Here was my second chance at love, and I was too frightened to take it.

He wrote me back and said he'd always regretted not telling me how he felt back in high school. He said so few people got a second chance at something. He'd spent more than half his life wanting and missing me, and he was damn sure not going to let me get away this time without a fight.

Now I was in Texas, scared out of my mind again, so afraid he'd reject me because I'd changed a lot over the years, and not all for the better.

When the knock sounded, my heart jumped into my throat, my stomach hit the floor and I launched myself off the couch. Willing myself to calm down, I opened the door; and the last of my breath whooshed from my lungs. He looked so good! He was dressed in business clothes—light-brown pants, navy jacket and a purple shirt. God, he looked good in purple!

Finding my voice, I invited him in, and then went back to my place on the couch as if it was some kind of sanctuary. I nervously drew my knees up to my chest, smiled and asked him to sit.

He grabbed the phone book and started looking for a place to take us out to dinner, all the while talking about this and that. I don't remember much of what he said because I was so enthralled with him and couldn't believe he was actually there with me.

My cat had bitten me earlier in the week, and David noticed. The two marks looked like a vampire had gotten carried away and, instead of kissing my hand in a charming manner, had bitten into the flesh. David reached to inspect the damage. I lost all ability to breathe at this point—he was touching me!

"Did you bite him back?" he asked.

I laughed. "No."

His gaze lingered on my face for a moment; then he went back to looking for a restaurant. Suddenly, he glanced up and said, "Your eyes still do it to me."

I could only smile and blush while my heart did triple time.

Finally, he settled on a Japanese restaurant, and I went to get dressed. I was still nervous, so it took me longer to put on my dress and pantyhose. When I came out of the bathroom, David had wandered into the suite's bedroom. He stopped talking when he saw me and just stared at me in my short black dress.

Feeling self-conscious, I said, "What?" Then, as if pulled by a magnet, I ended up in his arms.

All the doubt I'd felt earlier flew out the window. When he held me, David said all I needed to know without uttering a word. His arms slid around my waist and tightened, drawing me closer against the warmth of his body. He buried his nose in my hair and inhaled its scent. It felt as if he were saying, Finally, after fifteen years, she's in my arms and I'm not about to let her go again ever.

Our lips met in an urgent kiss...

We didn't make it to dinner that night.

David and I talk about our relationship in terms of centuries. Many obstacles keep us apart right now, but we're not about to let them come between us permanently. One day we'll be together, and our love will transcend death and follow us into eternity.

Throughout life I've learned one bit of wisdom: there are no guarantees in life, except death. Don't think about what might happen. If you're given a second chance, take it and fly.

(MARGARET MARR is an author from western North Carolina.)

FATE'S GENTLE NUDGE

By Linda L. Rucker

IN JANUARY OF 1985, MY LIFE WAS IN TURMOIL. I HAD LEFT MY HUSBAND OF ten years with four children in tow and begun a nomadic journey up and down the southeastern seaboard, never lighting for very long in one place. My poor babies were dragged from pillar to post and seemingly back again with no clear destination in mind. I was alone, broke and terrified.

I could take care of myself well enough, but my kids needed a safe, secure place to lie down at night. So, with that in mind, I eventually wound up in Lawrenceville, Georgia, at the home of my cousin.

She and I had always been close growing up but had come to a parting of the ways when her husband and I had an affair eleven years earlier. There was no excuse for my behavior or my betrayal, other than that we fell in love. We ran off together and got married, and ten years later I left him and found myself back on her doorstep, four children in tow.

She welcomed me with open arms, and that very night we went out—she told me I looked like I could use some fun. Needless to say, I drank a bit more than I should have, and morning found me sick with one of the worse hangovers I had ever had. My head throbbed so badly I wanted to put slippers on her cat.

My kids went outside to play, leaving the house blissfully quiet. My cousin was gone, and I could bury my pounding head under the covers and try to sleep it off. But that was not to be. The ringing of the telephone shattered the stillness of the house. Angrily, I snatched it up and snarled, "Hello."

There was a moment of silence on the other end and then a voice said, "Uh, is Faye there?"

"No, she's not," I snapped, my head aching, my mouth dry as dust.

"Who's this?" the voice asked.

"Who the hell is *this?*" I barked, massaging my temple.

"This is Bobby," was the reply, and I could almost hear the amusement in his voice.

"Well, she ain't here," I said and hung up the phone.

Later that afternoon, my cousin returned and I told her some man named Bobby had called. She looked at me and said, "You're kidding. Really?"

I nodded. "Yeah, and I think I was a bit of a bitch to him."

She laughed. "I haven't heard from Bobby in over a year," she said.

"Well, after the way I talked to him, it'll probably be another year before you hear from him again." I headed for the bathroom and some aspirin.

That night the phone rang, and my cousin answered it. From her end of the conversation, I could tell it was that Bobby guy calling back. She explained to him who I was and why I had been so crabby that morning on the phone, and he asked to speak to me.

We talked for more than two hours. I was surprised when he told me he hadn't talked to Faye in over a year, but something kept telling him to call her that morning.

That something turned out to be fate. Bobby and I dated for several months. My kids adored him; and before long, I was hopelessly in love with this funny man. We talked for hours every night, and before long we knew all there was to know about each other. Like the fact that his first marriage to his first love had ended badly, causing him to build a wall around his heart to protect it from that kind of devastating hurt again.

After a few months, it became apparent to me that, as well as we knew each other, as close as we had become, we weren't going to get any closer. He couldn't let go of that fear of being hurt again; and I, as much as I loved him, couldn't make him love me.

In May of that year, my kids went back to Florida to spend a year with their dad; and I became restless and needy. Bobby and I still saw each other, but I just couldn't see it going anywhere. So, I started dating a man I had met at work and eventually stopped having any contact with Bobby at all.

My new man and I moved to North Carolina, but I couldn't get Bobby off my mind. I called my girlfriend and my cousin often and always managed to work in an inquiry about him. The answer was always the same. He was still working, still the same.

Then one day I got this really sick feeling in the pit of my stomach. Something was not right. I called my friend, and she told me that I needed to get home as soon as possible. When I asked her why, she told me that Bobby was getting married. I was floored. To who, I demanded; and she told me it was a woman he had met a few weeks before. She told me he had been miserable since I left, and when this woman came on to him he just went with it.

I was crushed but furious. He couldn't or wouldn't commit to me, but he had to this person? Well, to hell with him, I thought. I told my friend to tell him I hoped he'd be very happy and hung up.

A few days later, she called me back and said Bobby had married that woman. She said she was at the wedding and he looked so sad.

"And," she said, "guess what the woman's name is? Linda."

My name. I went all to pieces.

Two months later, I couldn't take it anymore. I packed up and drove back to Lawrenceville and got my old job back at the Majik Market. And always thought about Bobby. Wondering how he was, if he was happy.

Then one day I looked up, and there he was. He grinned at me and said, "I don't believe this."

"What?" I asked him, my heart racing.

"I always stop at the Citgo across the road over there, but something told me to stop here today. And just look who's here. How have you been?"

We chatted for several minutes, and then he left. It seemed that once again fate had stepped in and put us in touch.

After that, he stopped in nearly every day. We'd laugh and joke for several minutes, and then he would go home to his wife. I had resigned myself to his marriage, but it seemed fate wasn't through with us just yet.

One day, on my day off, he stopped in and told my assistant manager he was single again. He asked for my phone number, but Clay refused to give it to him until he called me himself. Bobby left.

When I called in to check on things at the store a few hours later, Clay told me Bobby had come in and asked for my number. I asked him if he had left his and he told me no.

Hanging up, I made up my mind I was going to find this man I loved with all my heart. I remembered he had told me he lived in an apartment complex a couple of miles from the store. Getting in my car, I set off to find him.

There were two apartment complexes across the street from one another, and I was determined to find him if I had to knock on every door in both. I drove around the first complex and finally parked my car. At the first building, I went to the first door and raised my hand to knock, but before I could the door opened, and Bobby stood there staring at me, a surprised look on his face.

"I don't believe this," he said, grabbing my hand and pulling me inside. "I was just going down to the store to look for you."

"You were?" I asked breathlessly.

"Yep. Something told me you were looking for me."

I just stared at him. Fate had once again pushed us together. And finally, he had to admit that together was where we belonged.

We've been together ever since that night. We were married in June of 1987; and I know, as does he, that we will always be together. Our hearts beat as one, our minds think as one and we will always be grateful for that gentle nudge of fate that brought us together.

(LINDA L. RUCKER is a published author currently living in eastern Tennessee.)

YOU CAME ALONG

Every little girl has a plan,
And every woman has a dream:
The man, the life, the fairytale.
I'd never find mine, it seemed.
Just when I thought
My expectations were too high,
Just when I thought
I'd be lonely until I die
You came along.
Although I've never been a loner
By any stretch of the word,
One doesn't have to be alone to be lonely
In this great big world.
You came along and raised the sun,
Warmed my heart, relieved my despair.
Your knowing eyes and loving touch
Fulfill my needs beyond compare.
At night when you lie next to me
I feel safe and strong.
What else can I say; except,
Thank God, you came along.

— Christine West

WITCHY WOMAN
By Jennifer Wardrip

THEY SAY THAT WHEN YOU MEET YOUR SOUL MATE, YOU KNOW INSTANTLY. There's some immediate connection that binds you to this mate, a knowledge of love beyond anything you've ever known. That connection, that *something*, is supposed to trigger a reaction inside you can't ignore. You've met your match, the one you're destined to spend the rest of your life with. Somehow, with all of the billions of people on this planet we call home, fate, destiny or just blind luck has brought you into contact with the person who is the other half of your soul.

It sounds pretty. In fact, I spent twenty-two years of my life believing it. When I met him, the man who was my soul mate, I wouldn't just know—I'd *know*. We'd click, that connection would be made and I'd spend the rest of my days in, if not happily-ever-after, at least love-ever-after.

When I first met my husband, I hated him.

No, hate is probably too strong a word. Or maybe it's not strong enough. Now that I rethink it, I actually despised him. He was arrogant, condescending and full of himself. Although not a complete throwback to the days when a man believed a woman only served the purpose of catering to his every need and desire, he still somehow managed to exude that irritating quality of superiority.

Dan was the type of man I'd trained myself to avoid. Actually, I think the avoidance of wannabe he-men who enjoyed pontificating on the joys of mastering every goal they had set for themselves was ingrained in me at birth. Maybe even in the womb. My father is a great man, humble yet keenly aware of his intelligence. Unlike Dan, my father knew what he wanted out of life, went for it with a single-minded determination and yet somehow managed to include everyone around him in his spirit of joy and good wishes.

Dan managed to grate on everyone's nerves. Or maybe that was just me.

I met him at a bookstore, of all places, which I guess goes to show that even idiotic men with a too-important view of themselves occasionally feel the need to read. Either that or he was scoping out the women. Or getting a cup of Starbucks.

Anyway, we bumped into each other, literally, in the Mystery and Thriller section. He was, of course, slightly condescending and a whole lot of rude over the entire matter. When I left the store, still in a huff—which obviously I had every right to be in—my final wish was to never lay eyes on the oaf again.

And it seemed to work, until three months later when I ran into him again at my best friend's bridal shower. I had known it was a couple's shower, and was even feeling slightly annoyed I didn't have another half to bring with me. But Ally was my best friend, she was getting married and I'd make the effort to appear friendly.

When I saw Dan, beer in hand, lecturing Ally's fiancé Mark on the correct way to barbecue a steak on the grill on their deck, I went from friendly to downright nasty in 0.3 seconds.

Seems Dan didn't care for me much, either—or maybe it was the remembrance of my parting shot of "total, idiotic egghead" when I'd left that bookstore months ago. Either way, the meeting of our gazes was filled with cold fire; and if fate had been one to throw stones, both of us would have been up to our necks in boulders the size of the Grand Canyon.

We studiously avoided each other. It worked like a charm until it came time for us to "ooh" and "ahh" over the gifts for the soon-to-be-newlyweds. I'd bought them a juicer—you know, one of those machines that you can squash whole fruits or vegetables into and it spits out the juice. I knew Mark was into being health conscious, so I thought the juicer was a brilliant idea.

I'm always full of them.

"A juicer?" It was snotty. I've tried for years to think of a better term for how the words came out of Dan's mouth, but *snotty* just fits. It held contempt, annoyance and, well, snottiness. Like I'd committed some huge faux pas, and he was slightly embarrassed for me. But more than the embarrassment, he was happy I'd done it because it yet again proved that he was superior.

My reply wasn't snotty. It was downright bitchy. "Yes, a juicer. As in, a machine that makes juice. Maybe if you'd drunk more juice as a child you wouldn't be the asshole you are today."

Oops…I'd just declared war. I might have been asking for it; but, my God, the man was infuriating.

We had a battle of—wits? conscience? loud mouths?—right there in Ally and Mark's living room. Later I'd have time to be appalled, to remember the things I'd said, the way I'd stood nose-to-nose and toe-to-toe with my new nemesis, and cringe at my behavior.

During the actual brawl, though, the only thing I'd felt had been righteous indignation. He wanted to insult me? He wanted to pretend he was more intelligent than me? He wanted to…wanted to…

Somewhere between the words "moron" and "homo-idioticus," something stirred in me. I tamped it down, thrust it aside like the repulsive idea that it was. I did not, in any way, shape or form, find this man attractive. It wasn't until I realized we were both breathing like steam locomotives, breath raging in and out at the sound of speed, hearts galloping inside our chests, that it hit me.

I was turned on.

It stopped me with my mouth hanging open, my hands clenched into fists at my side. I felt the color leave my cheeks, until I stood pale and shaky in front of him. It didn't help a bit when I realized his eyes had glazed over with something that looked a whole heck of a lot like lust.

I left. Okay, fine, I ran. Ran like a bat out of hell, until I was far away from Ally and Mark, away from the juicer, away from Mr. I'm-a-stupid-stuck-up-pig.

Away from myself.

I'll admit, it might have taken me a few minutes (read: hours) to completely forget the incident, but I did forget it.

Until he called me up two weeks later and asked me on a date.

I hung up on him the first time. I tried breathing like a repugnant phone stalker the second. The third time, I let him get through his entire spiel about dinner and possibly dancing before I said no and laughed like a hyena while hanging up. The fourth time, due to either his persistence or my lack of brain cells, I finally gave in and told him I'd go.

We spent dinner studiously ignoring the attraction between us and butting heads like two elk heavy into mating season. We spent the dancing part taking turns between wanting to have a hot-and-heavy make-out session on the dance floor and wanting to try out imagined kung fu moves on each other.

It was exhausting work. What made me even more tired was the effort it took to keep disliking him.

Somehow, I managed.

Yet, against my better judgment, we started dating. After two months, we hadn't even kissed. Maybe we both knew that once we did the jig, as they say, would be up. Because I, for one, knew exactly what would happen when we did. One kiss wouldn't be enough, one touch wouldn't quell the need he'd somehow managed to churn up in me.

When we kissed, we were going to be in deep, deep trouble.

We managed to avoid it for a while, until it became that big pink elephant standing in the corner. Dan still annoyed me, and if the signs were true, I still managed to annoy him on a regular basis; but once we both became more aware of what we weren't doing than of what we were, the cat was out of the bag.

Our first kiss was like a thunderstorm on a windy, hot summer night. The kind that blows up out of nowhere, stripping leaves off of trees, downing power lines, picking up cars and moving them to the next city block over.

The first meeting of Dan's lips to mine was like grabbing onto a high-voltage wire and not being able to let go. But something inside me did let go, a hard knot of anger at myself that I'd allowed him to get under my skin. It burst like a bubble, like a balloon bounced on by a child.

Our lips met, our breaths mingled and my heart was lost.

It wasn't a whirlwind courtship. After his having rubbed so many of the wrong nerves, I made Dan win his way into my heart. Nights spent talking about what we still wanted to accomplish in our lives. Days spent at the lake, on a small boat that rocked gently in the water, discussing politics, arguing over the state of the nation, kissing as the moon came up.

Loving Dan isn't easy. It was actually easier to despise him, as I did in the beginning. But who ever said love was easy? I suppose it was only fair I had to work at it. I've known for a long time that I'm not the easiest woman to get along with. Okay, maybe that's the understatement of the century.

But what it all boils down to is that, although difficult, in the end it was worth it.

He asked me to marry him in typical Dan style. We were at the drive-through of a fast-food chicken chain, him drumming his fingers impatiently on the dashboard as the line refused to move for more than five minutes, me continuously changing the station on the radio, hating to wait the minute and a half it would take to get back to the music.

"So, do you want to?"

"Do I want to what?" I didn't look up from the tuner. I'd finally gotten some music, but it was the last echoing refrain of the song. Baring my teeth, I began station-surfing again.

"Get married."

I'll admit I wasn't really paying attention to him. Giving up on the music, I proceeded to turn the radio off and wonder when the heck I was going to get my double order of mashed potatoes and gravy.

"Who's getting married?"

"Hopefully, you and me."

I mean—the man wasn't even looking at me. We'd finally moved up to the window; and as he paid the $11.83 with a twenty-dollar bill, it still hadn't filtered through my brain what he'd said.

I took the sack he gave me in silence, suddenly overcome by the smell of crispy, deep-fried chicken. As he pulled into a parking space, I was already sinking my teeth into a drumstick, other hand searching for a spoon for those potatoes.

"Did you even hear what I said?" That pissy tone was back in his voice. God, I hated that tone.

Talking around a mouthful of food, I think I said something along the lines of "someone's getting married."

Dan silently grabbed the bag from me and started in on his own chicken as the smell of my gravy filled the car.

And then it hit me.

He'd said something about us. Getting married. Us. As in him and me, me and you, "I do" and "kiss the bride" and that's all she wrote.

My bite got stuck on the way down, and I had to guzzle my soda to loosen it. But now there was an even bigger lump, down around my heart, as I turned to look at him.

He was staring at me, still chewing his chicken, his eyes a hot azure blue as they stared into mine. He swallowed, took a drink and then smiled at me with his five-thousand-watt smile.

The rest is history.

Is Dan my soul mate? Were we destined to be together? Did God or fate or dumb luck bring us to that bookstore on the same day at the same time? If so, the joke was on me.

I'm now Mrs. Jennifer Wardrip. Dan and I have been married for a little over five years, have been together for eight. We have the proverbial house with a picket fence and our two children. Are we happy? Most of the time. He's still an obnoxious jerk, usually at the most inopportune time. I'm still bitchy, opinionated and emotional. But we've made it work. How?

That part is simple. I've come to believe that you don't find your soul mate. You find someone you want to be your soul mate, and then you work really damn hard to make it stick. I'm not talking about changing a person. What I mean is more like—well, work.

Love is hard work. It takes tolerance, compassion and forgiveness, none of which had ever been my strong suit. There are times when I don't like Dan, just as I'm sure there are numerous occasions when he doesn't particularly care for me. But we love each other. Is love enough? Of course not. Saying that love conquers all is as foolish as saying you'll instantly recognize your soul mate.

The key is work, determination and diligence. Like molding clay into a pot or blowing hot glass until it's shaped into something delicate and precious.

I've finally come to the conclusion that Dan and I don't always have to like each other. We don't have to agree on everything. We can have misunderstandings, hurt feelings, just plain old bad days. The trick is that we're becoming soul mates. Becoming. It's not an automatic get-out-of-jail-free card, it's not a guarantee. We work, my Dan and I, every day to become each other's soul mate.

I'm sure we're not the exception to the rule. Maybe there are other couples out there—happy, fulfilled couples—who instantly recognized something in the other person that told them "Ah-hah, there they are, watch out, soul mate alert."

But I've watched my parents. I've watched Ally and Mark. I've perfected the art of watching other couples to notice the little things that show that they work, every day, to turn into each other's soul mate. The touches, the glances, the long, lingering gazes. The way Dan looks wistful when he sees a mother with a new baby. The way he laughs like a giddy toddler when we pass the pet store at the mall. The way he sends cards, religiously, to his mother, grandmothers, aunts and cousins on Mother's Day. The deep, rumbling roar of his anger when the Cubs lose a game. His enthusiastic cheers, beer in one hand, the other arm around my waist, as we take in a football game. The way he dresses up, dutifully, when I want to go watch a play put on by the local theater group.

All of these things make up my soul mate. Each little piece of Dan, each little piece of me, adds up to a whole that's beautiful to see. When we fight, it's like a choreographed ballet. When we make up, it's a monsoon in the tropical forest at the equator.

Is Dan my soul mate? Ask me again in about fifty years.

(JENNIFER WARDRIP is a multi-published author, writing as Jen Nicholas for Kensington Brava and Alayne Warren for eXtasy Books.)

ONCE UPON A SATURDAY
By Candace Drimmer

WANNA HELP SOME FRIENDS MOVE FROM AN APARTMENT TO THE BIG House?" asked my best female friend Terry one nondescript Friday night. I had nothing else to do that weekend, so I said, "Sure, why not?"

The Big House was the hippie house at the University of Georgia in 1969, an era when a young man was identified as a radical if he had ear-length hair or a moustache. Gary had both. He was a Yankee-accented Hobbit with long, wild hair like a lion's mane, plus a mountain man beard and a moustache. It was hardly love at first sight; but he was different from the southern-fried frats I had dated up until then, and he did have the most expressive eyes I'd ever fallen under the gaze of. So, when he asked me to go see Franco Zeffirelli's in-vogue romantic film *Romeo & Juliet* I said, "Sure, why not?"

In a fingertip-length mini skirt, I trotted out of the door of my female-only dorm with my hirsute date to find The Motor Bike. To call it a motorcycle would be an extravagant exaggeration. It was a Honda 50-cc—I have had eggbeaters with more power. It could barely make it up an Athens, Georgia, hill with one person on it; two was out of the question. I got used to the routine. I would hike up the hill and remount the motorized bicycle behind Gary at the top of the hill.

Unbeknownst to me, I was the third girl he had taken to *Romeo & Juliet*. Unbeknownst to him, he wasn't the only Gary I was dating. But since neither of us took our relationship very seriously what did that matter?

Once, to his embarrassed shock and consternation, he arrived at the Student Union's Bulldog Room to find his more serious relationship and I huddled in deep conversation—-about him and "his problems." We each knew he was seeing the other and had just run into one another by accident. He was red-faced. We were quite amused.

Then it happened, one of those not-so-important incidents that can change the direction of lives. Gary broke my yellow wannabe cool sunglasses. It really wasn't his fault, I had put them on the floor beside me, and he stepped on them as he gingerly made his way across a darkened room. He apologized profusely and promised to replace them. I thought it was just another one of those male lies, as in:

1.) The check is in the mail.

2.) I'll call you in the morning.

3.) I'll love you forever.

Uh-huh. I was only nineteen, but I was a pro at being lied to. As in the time my father lied to me when he promised I could spend all four years at the private college where I had begun my higher education. Six months into my freshman year, he decided I would have to transfer to a cheaper school. No reason given, but it was only one of the many broken promises men had made to me over the years. Promises that were easily made were also easily broken.

So, imagine my shock when a package arrived a few days later at my dormitory. Inside a well-used paper bag, I found a brand new pair of sunglasses. This anti-establishment person might look like a fly-by-night goofball, but he was a man of his word.

Now that, for me, was different. It was better than gold or diamonds or a trip to Cancún. The feeling that I could trust a person at his word.

Three months later, Gary transferred to a special Peace Corps College Degree Program at the State University of New York in Brockport. We wrote what I had learned in fourth grade—the friendly letter—by the dozen. These evolved into very friendly letters, at which point he decided to come see me in Athens the following January. Sure, why not?

Driving south through a blizzard down roads that were closed to the traffic behind him, Gary arrived to see me. He had spent New Years Eve in New York City with his brother, who was leaving the country and who had run up a credit card debt he didn't intend to pay. Gary seemed to think this quite funny. I thought it was just another form of lying, so I told him, "Get lost."

He did. We didn't communicate again for over a year, when he sent me a postcard from Europe. By then I had had second thoughts, deciding that maybe I had imprudently overreacted. We began to write once again. Simple friendly letters, nothing more.

Over the next two-plus years, we wrote and wrote. While he was in New York and later in the Peace Corps in Honduras, and I was in New Jersey, UGA and at the University of Texas. It was a unique way to get to know someone, without all the heavy breathing and hormones of youth in the backseat of a car.

The big day came—Gary was coming to see me. Once again, I panicked. What if this was all a fantasy? I wrote him a letter telling him not to come and posted it quickly before I could change my mind. Only, after more than a year of mailing dozens of letters to Honduras, I forgot to put enough postage on this one. It came back due to insufficient postage, by which time I'd once again changed my mind and recovered my courage to see him.

We met for the first time in almost three years in Houston, Texas. It was as if he'd just stepped out of the room for three minutes, not three years; the passionate friendship was real and right. A couple of years later, we got married in his family's home in Lima, Peru. A year after that, we had a religious wedding at his sister's home in New Jersey. Like the Energizer Bunny, we've kept going and going through twenty-nine years of everyday life, thirteen moves to seven countries of the Americas and two kids. When I'm asked how did I know, it's like asking how I learned to breathe. I just did.

The blessing of this continues today. When I asked my then twenty-two-year-old daughter how she picked the lovely man she had been dating since she was fourteen and whom she now has married, without missing a beat she responded, "Mom, I just followed your lead."

Sure, why not?

(Currently living in Chicago, CANDACE DRIMMER is a writer with an internationalist slant.)

STAR LIGHT, STAR BRIGHT
By Maureen Allen

BORED AT WORK ONE DAY, I TYPED "PEN PAL" INTO A SEARCH ENGINE AND watched as hundreds of URLs popped up. Then I began the arduous task of weeding through the sites to find one that suited my purposes.

After finding one I liked, I filled out a personal profile. One of the questions asked was "Would you like a pen pal from the U.S. or Other?" I chose "Other," figuring it was just as easy to e-mail someone across the world as it was to e-mail someone on the next block. The ad I placed was friendly, not suggestive and, I hoped, not desperate.

In my heart, I knew I was searching for a suitable man to marry, not merely a pen pal. I had been through the dating scene, hated it and wanted no more of it. I was concerned about ever finding a decent man at that stage of my life. Some credible study had just been published saying that if a woman was not married by the time she turned forty, her chances of being struck by lightning were greater than her chances of finding a marriage partner. Being forty-five years old and feeling older by the minute, I was developing sensitivity to the word *spinster*.

Two years earlier, I had been to Scotland and fell in love with the country and its people. The men I met were charming, respectful…and married. They exuded a certain type of confidence I found very attractive—It's my guess a Scottish man has to be secure in his masculinity to wear a kilt. Each time I visited Britain, I felt comfortable, never like a foreigner. But Scotland was different—it felt like home. I set my sights on finding a Scottish man to marry.

When I returned from my trip, I explored emigrating to Britain. I mailed my resume to dozens of companies in Scotland in an effort to find employment, but my profession was not in such demand that local businesses had to look outside the country for recruits. A woman I spoke with at the British Embassy told me if I did not have an employer to sponsor me, I could emigrate only if I proved I could live there without being a drain on public funds. My cash net worth would have to be in excess of $250,000. At that point, I didn't have $250 in my bank account. I'd have to find another way of getting there.

That's when I made my Treasure Map. I gathered up my travel brochures and a couple of magazines, a pair of scissors, tape, a pen and a big piece of poster board. I snipped pictures of a kilted bagpiper, Edinburgh and Glasgow cityscapes, a Scottish couple in traditional dress standing on top of a wedding cake and a map of Scotland. I taped the photographs to the poster board and wrote affirmations under each one. The map hung in my bedroom for a year, until I packed it up to move cross-country. I forgot all about it when I got to my new place.

> Wanted: Widowed white 53-year-old male seeks girl
> to take him to Venus.

My curiosity was piqued, and I sent a simple response to ask if he was still interested in having a pen pal. I also responded to several other ads that weren't quite so unique. Over the following couple of weeks, the men I corresponded with proved to be wackos with an overdeveloped sense of their ability to answer all of my prayers. I had forgotten all about the one who wanted to go to Venus.

One morning, I checked my Hotmail account and found three e-mails from the same guy. I had no idea who the man was, but all became clear once I read the first message. He was the one who wanted to go to Venus.

He explained he had been on holiday and, noting the date of my e-mail to him, apologized for the delay in responding. He told me everything about himself, including where he worked, his home address, his phone numbers at home and at work and his full name. Dennis was a university lecturer with a Ph.D. in biomedical sciences from Oxford University, a widower with three grown sons and Scottish. Nowhere in those three messages did he intimate the size of his penis, ask me for cyber-sex or be anything less than a perfect gentleman.

I was impressed. I also felt like a high school girl each time my computer chimed to let me know I had mail, because I knew it would be from Dennis. But I was also skeptical. He seemed too good to be true, and I reminded myself to be careful not to project qualities onto him he did not possess.

Every e-mail was a pleasure to receive. We got to know each other's likes and dislikes, and we found we had many things in common. He, like me, was a classical music fan. To my delight, we liked many of the same composers. He had written and sold several short stories to supplement his income while he was a student at Oxford; writing was still at the dream stage for me.

We clicked in vital areas that had been bones of contention between me and other men. For example, the boyfriend-du-jour and I would inevitably end up arguing about where to go for a vacation. Without exception, he wanted to go to hot, steamy tropical islands to party and be with loads of people while I wanted to go someplace quiet where the temperature was cool. Dennis had worked in the tropics and detested the heat. He preferred the coolness of the Highlands.

Over the course of the next few weeks, our correspondence increased from every few days to several times a day. I found I was not only looking forward to hearing from him, but that I was also falling in love with him.

Then, he phoned me while I was at work. He had the most fabulous voice, and his accent reminded me of John Lennon's, only better. We spoke for only a few minutes, but I was on cloud nine. Speaking to him made him real to me, and I felt like I was heading down a path that was right and natural.

Yet, at the same time, I tried desperately to rein in my emotions. I had been disappointed several times before, and I was wary of setting myself up for another disastrous relationship.

The phone calls increased in frequency, and our subjects of conversation went into deeper territory. "I love you's" were exchanged, and Dennis talked about coming across for a visit. The subject of sex was introduced, and again we found we were in sync with each other about our needs and desires. Although we had only known each other for seven months at that point, we both felt secure in each other's affection.

We had gotten into the habit of speaking on the phone every night when I returned home from work. With the five-hour time difference between the US and the UK, it was sometimes a strain on Dennis to be awake at one a.m.; and many times he was lying in bed while we spoke. He'd look out of his window and make a wish on the first star he saw and asked me to do the same. We could never speak the wish because it would never come true if we did.

Then he asked me to get the navigational co-ordinates for where I lived and e-mail them to him. He wanted to know what star I was wishing on. The next day, I looked up the co-ordinates and let him know. When we spoke that night, Dennis had a lovely laugh in his voice. He was delighted to be able to tell me the star I wished on every night was Venus.

Dennis's family were supportive of him coming across, but my friends and family were horrified to think I was actually contemplating having this man I had met on the Internet, of all places, in my home. Didn't I know about all of the sex criminals on the Internet? They demanded to have his telephone number and address in the UK. Armed with that information, they would give the police, after my untimely and bloody death, the address of the psychopath I had met online. They did their best to persuade me to cancel our meeting, but I wasn't listening. I knew in my heart Dennis was the man for me and that was that.

We had ten lovely days together and traveled throughout New England, visiting places Dennis had heard but never seen. He enjoyed visiting the Whaling Museum in Bedford, Maine, because *Moby Dick* had been one of his favorite books when he was a child. He took great pleasure in noting the city and town names of the New

England states because their origins could be traced back to Britain. Berwick, Maine, had its twin in Berwick-upon-Tweed in the Scottish/English border country, not far from where he lived.

It was on that journey we hatched our plan to write a book together. We drew up an outline and developed the plot while we sat on the front porch of an inn in Kennebunkport, Maine, that overlooked the Atlantic Ocean. Maureen Dennis would be our pseudonym, and our book would be called *No Hiding Place.*

Three weeks after Dennis returned to the UK, he asked me to marry him. Crying with happiness, I said yes. Two years later, Dennis and I had a traditional Scottish wedding; and we honeymooned in the Scottish Highlands.

(MAUREEN ALLEN is a freelance writer, editor, and reviewer from Jedburgh, Scotland.)

OCEANS BETWEEN OUR SOULS

By Nancy Jackson

HAD YOU ASKED ME TWO YEARS AGO IF I BELIEVED IN SOUL MATES, MY response would have been laughter.

On September 16th, 2000, I met mine.

I had been given an old computer by a friend, who told me I needed to get into the real world of technology. I didn't feel I had been missing anything; but I didn't want to upset her, so I accepted. Within a month I started an email account with my local Internet provider. I was excited with this new toy for about two weeks, emailing anyone who would share addresses. However, I lost interest quickly.

A few months later, one of my colleagues at work was playing a card game on the computer. I wanted to know more, and he instructed me how to log in to one of these games. I had recently learned to play hearts and was intrigued that I could play it on the computer with three other people.

That night I decided that, after I put my son to bed, I would play hearts. Around eight-thirty, I was on a website, logging into a game, making up a password; finally, the "game tables" popped up. I searched for a beginner table and randomly chose one. The other players were better than I, and I was getting frustrated. I looked down and noticed this box where people were typing. I had thought it was an advertisement and had ignored it until now. I scrolled through the conversation and realized the other players had been saying hi to me and I hadn't bothered to respond. I hoped they didn't think I was rude so I quickly typed in a greeting and apologized for not answering back.

They all made little comments back, and we got into some great conversations. One player stood out; and we joked around with each other, and I found myself flirting a little bit.

Two hours later, the other two players needed to sign off, so it was just this one player and me left. We spent another hour getting to know each other. I was amazed at how comfortable I felt talking with him. I remember spilling my guts about how I had been divorced for six years and was a single mother of a wonderful boy and how I was really against relationships at this time in my life. He shared his story of his last relationship, ending as painfully as mine had.

I was a very trusting person, and I was amazed at the ease with which I communicated so freely. Maybe it was because it was through writing that I felt safe, but I also felt this connection meant a little more. I was intrigued with him being from Canada and all the beautiful places he had visited there. Here I was from Oregon, a whopping four thousand miles away from him, yet something inside made me feel like we had known each other before.

He responded that he felt the same way. He had a time difference, so it was much later for him; and as much as he didn't want to say goodbye, it was very late and we both had to get some sleep. I know my eyes ached from staring at the computer for so long. We exchanged email addresses and decided to meet in the game room to play and chat the following night.

That was the start of a wonderful friendship that turned into the most special and wonderful relationship I could have ever asked for. The first few months we spent getting to know each other. Occasionally, we would play a game or two, but mainly we just enjoyed talking to each other on Yahoo Messenger. We had a special time set aside to be with each other every night, and the only times we missed were when one of us couldn't get logged on, which happened a few times. Those nights, I went to bed feeling very empty, missing our special time because our friendship was extremely important to me.

I remember feeling confused, as well. I felt protective of what we had yet I knew my feelings went beyond that of just a friendship. Only, I didn't dare ruin anything by spilling the beans! The highlight of my day was when we chatted and joked around with each other. It gave me comfort to hear from him, to know he was well and how his day had gone.

Heading into November, things became a little strained as I backed off to try to get my feelings on track, wanting desperately to keep from being hurt. I didn't want to risk the friendship by having these romantic feelings. I also couldn't understand the feelings, considering I had never met the man.

The thing was that, with all the time we spent talking, we were able to get to know each other better than most people do; and we were very close. He had been confused as well, and battled with his own questions and concerns on being more than friends. I must admit that, of the two of us, he was braver than I. One night, he pronounced his feelings for me.

It felt so wonderful. I could finally admit to the ones I had been trying to keep hidden. I was afraid he wasn't going to be interested in a long-distance relationship with someone who had a child and a lot of baggage from the past. He didn't seem to feel these were enough to ignore the special relationship we had.

On December 25, 2000, I got a wonderful surprise. My son and I were visiting my parents for Christmas dinner; and in checking my answering machine, I discovered he had left a message. My heart just about leapt from my body! I played it over and over. He said he would call back around six that night.

I paced the hallway and couldn't do anything but think of things to talk about. He sounded so nice. We had just recently exchanged pictures, so I already knew he was good-looking; but his voice was gentle and sweet.

The phone rang at six, and I ran to answer. I don't even remember how long we talked because all I did was giggle. Our first time speaking together, and all I could do was giggle like a teenager! I don't think I said one intelligent word. I was fascinated with everything he said, as he had a slight accent. So, there was a lot of silence as I twirled my hair and doodled hearts and flowers on a piece of junk mail. I had never felt this giddy in all my life.

We said goodnight, and then we both logged on the computer and talked some more. All I could do was apologize for my giggling, and he just kept saying it was cute. That was a memorable night for me, and I will never forget it.

In the new year, we decided I would fly to Canada and meet him. I spent many nights in panic at the thought of actually meeting face-to-face. All my insecurities came into play. I was worried he wouldn't like me or the way I looked or how I was or something. I began shutting out all the things I knew to be true and just paid attention to the fears in my head.

The funny thing was, I believed in us right from the start—we had a connection that could not be explained. We had so many things in common. Our stubbornness and senses of humor were a match, and we had the utmost respect for one another. There was magic between us that didn't need to be explained, it was just there. We couldn't go a night without talking and sharing time with each other.

He was so wonderful, talking with me about how I felt. He understood, yet he also wanted to make sure I knew he believed in what we had. I remember a few times I wanted to just cancel the whole thing, make up an excuse to get out of it, simply so I didn't need to take the risk. I didn't want my heart broken nor did I want to lose all we had built.

Seven months later, after emails, instant messaging and phone calls, we finally met. It was the most wonderful time. We spent two weeks together; and though the first day consisted of coping with jet lag and a huge case of nerves and giggles, after that it was magic. We spent a few days at Niagara Falls, and that place holds so much magic and power it just magnified our own feelings for one another.

That was the first of many special visits with each other. He met my son, and they hit it off wonderfully; and my parents absolutely adore him. Though our time apart is difficult and the goodbyes are heartbreaking, it is the magic that we hold on to.

How often do you meet someone who embodies every quality that balances with your own? I wouldn't have believed it possible for a moment after the things I had been through in my life. My feelings have completely changed. I have met my soul mate, and there is nothing else like it. Our love for each other becomes deeper and more profound every moment we spend together. I never thought someone could love me for me, the way I am. He doesn't ask me to change a thing, and I don't ask him to change.

Our communication has been the key to our relationship; and it is the magic, respect and love we have for one another that has kept us together. I still get excited when I hear his voice on the phone. I still get giddy with excitement when there are only a few days until our next visit. There are feelings I have when we are together that I never knew existed. Just holding his hand sends powerful currents through me. When I lie in his arms I feel a safety and protection I have never experienced before. The air I breathe when I'm with him is sweeter, and I feel so alive.

The energy and vibrations I experience around him I miss when we are apart. When he leaves a part of me goes with him. I know this because I feel empty and lost without him. The days we have to say goodbye to one another my whole being aches from my head to my toes, and I feel as if I am somehow shutting down. My body doesn't function correctly; I feel like I'm walking in a haze or fog. Everything comes back to normal when we are about to see one another again.

I believe in soul mates. I hope there is one for everyone out there because I wish for couples to feel the same love and mystical forces we share with one another. It is feeling alive and that this one person was meant to walk the same path as you. I feel honored to walk the same path as my soul mate, and I cherish every single moment we have together.

(NANCY JACKSON is a multi-published author with works both online and in print.)

MAY I NEVER FORGET

I WILL NEVER FORGET
How your warm brown eyes
Gazed into mine
When we first met.
There we stood
In the garden—
Midst a bustling, cosmopolitan city.
Manila,
My birthplace,
An exotic and now faraway city
That still blends
Much of the best
Of Eastern and Western culture.
As the years pass quietly,
I realize
How precious, how fleeting,
And how blissful
Were those moments
Of our courtship and engagement.
I was twenty-four,
You were twenty-nine—an intelligent
And kindhearted American gentleman.
I was your Philippine sweetheart.
Life was wonderful!
And Manila, gay and bright Manila,

Provided a stunning backdrop
For that most glorious and dreamy
And much-awaited
Romance of my life.
I will never forget:
Our strolls along Manila Bay on balmy nights;
Midnight snacks at Cafe Adriatico,
Which served mouth-watering mango crepes;
Or our day excursion
At Puerto Azul beach resort
Where we swam
In the mild, salty ocean water
And you played golf with our friends.
I will never forget
The immense joy that filled my heart
The night you asked me to be your wife,
And spoke to my father
To ask for my hand;
Nor that cherished evening
When my dear parents took us out
For a celebration of fine dining
At El Comedor restaurant—
To bestow a blessing on our lives
And pray for our marriage.
I will never forget the excitement
I felt the day
A notice from the U.S. Embassy
Arrived at my home,
Announcing that your fiancée visa application
Had been approved.
I will never forget

The touch of your hand
And the look in your eyes
On our wedding day,
When you said, "I, Michael, take thee, Jennifer,
To be my wedded wife…"
And I replied,
"I, Jennifer, take thee, Michael,
To be my wedded husband…"
I will never forget
My entrance as an immigrant
At Seattle's international airport
When I arrived in this country
On that brisk January afternoon.
I will never forget
The solemn oath I took
To become an American citizen
Six years later.
For the biblical words
That Ruth spoke
Voiced my heart's earnest prayer:
"For where you go, I will go,
And where you lodge, I will lodge.
Your people shall be my people,
And your God, my God."
May I never forget
The awesome miracle of our love,
Of how we found each other
In this big, wide world—
For God was the Author
of our love story.

He brought us together
And united our hearts and lives
Into one brilliant flame
Of enduring, faithful love.

— Jennifer Anne F. Messing

MY TICKING HEART
By Vanessa Bruce Ingold

HI, GREG. NO, I'M SHORT OF BREATH AND MY HEART'S BEATING FAST. YEAH, I'll call 911 if it doesn't get better. Bye."
He seems to always call when I need him most.

I coughed a tiny bit of blood into a tissue. I dialed 911.

"It started at six p.m., one hour ago. No, I don't think I can drive myself to the hospital. Thank you."

I was cold, even though Southern California in April is warm. I grabbed my jacket and purse. I was embarrassed for anyone at the apartment complex to know I had been the one who called 911, so I walked towards the street's entrance, trying to take slow, deep breaths.

I sat in the ambulance. I was shivering, so a paramedic handed me a blanket.

"I've been on antibiotics for two weeks for bronchitis," I explained.

"There's a possibility you could have pneumonia," he replied. "We'll take you to the emergency room."

When I arrived, a nurse wheeled me into a room on the fourth floor. She inserted an IV for water and antibiotics.

I reminded her, "I have a pig valve in my heart as a mitral valve replacement."

It was getting more difficult to breathe, so they would not allow me to get out of bed. I felt like I was doing high-impact aerobics.

"Hi, I'm a cardiologist. We need to do an EKG and echogram of your heart."

As the cardiac specialist did the ultrasound of my heart, I

explained that I had been in a bicycle accident nine years earlier, when I was twenty-three.

"I was run over by a Ford pickup truck. That's how my mitral valve was ripped."

"Well, I'm sorry to tell you, but it looks like your pig valve area is infected," the cardiologist replied. "You need to be in ICU. We need to get the fluid out of your lungs."

Oh, Lord, why does this have to happen now?

I called my closest friends for support and prayer. I realized this could mean another operation. I did not want to call my family and alarm them, since they live across the country in Louisiana.

I felt at peace after I was transferred to ICU because I would be given the physical attention I needed. After a night there, I felt comforted by the silvery-gray-haired nurse. Most of the fluid was out of my lungs, and I could sit up without panting.

I sat up to see my best friend Greg walking towards the nurses' station. He had a big wicker basket filled with purple (my favorite color) silk flowers and green leaves. Dangling from one of his arms was a stuffed monkey hanging from a branch. The monkey gave a loud wolf whistle.

The nurses laughed as he entered my room.

"The gas station had this monkey for twenty dollars, but it was bugging the cashier so bad he said, 'Here, take it.'"

He explained how light, movement or noise prompted the monkey to whistle.

"They don't allow real flowers in ICU, so I got this flower arrangement. It only cost me three thousand dollars," he joked.

Two weeks passed. The infection cleared, and I was waiting for the surgery date. They would be replacing the pig valve with a mechanical one. Greg's funny cards encouraged me. I didn't like hospital food, so he would bring vegetarian dishes from my favorite health restaurant at my request. Since we had met two years earlier at church, he was the most supportive friend I had ever had. A few times I had considered the possibility of marrying him, but every time he proposed, I said no.

I knew that Greg really cared about me, but I wondered if he could really be seriously committed. He had certainly always made me laugh, though.

We had been in arguments—once we didn't speak to each other for a month. Still, I remembered the day last winter I picked him up from the airport; he had just gotten back from visiting family in Wisconsin. He stepped into my car, kissed me on the cheek and said, "I missed you more than anybody."

It was the third week of my hospital visit, and my surgery day had arrived. The nurse wheeled me to the operating room on the cold vinyl gurney. I tightened the blanket, which needed fabric softener, around me. As I listened to the anesthesiologist, my eyes began to water. I knew it was going to be uncomfortable to wake up with tubes in my mouth and nose, and that having to open my sternum to get to my heart would be painful.

"Can you call my friend Greg and let him know how it went?" I asked my heart surgeon.

At that instant, I realized what a big part of my life Greg had become. I even had him as my first emergency contact.

It seemed as if only a second had passed when I opened my eyes and surgery was over. I frequently pushed the button to alert the recovery nurses that I needed something for pain. Greg was the only one to see me in the few hours after I was brought back into my room. He said I looked like E.T.

Recovering was fun because Greg and I watched basketball playoffs. Once, his friend paged him, so he called back.

"No, I think I just want to hang out with Vanessa tonight," he said.

Before he left, I had him bend over to hear my mechanical heart valve ticking. After he left, I smelled his cologne on me.

I called a close girlfriend and said, "This is so weird. I think I like him more than a friend."

"Lord, I'm willing for Your will," she had me pray.

After I prayed that, I knew he was the one I would marry. I knew any worries or fears I had about our relationship God would work out. I had prayed all along that my husband would be my best friend. I loved him, and that love overrode any fear.

Seven months later, I walked down the aisle to the song "Lord,

You Have My Heart."

On our refrigerator are two cards that were given to us. One reads "Vanessa—'Butterfly': Trust in the Lord with all thine heart and lean not on thy own understanding. Proverbs 3:5." The other reads "Gregory—'Watchful One': In all thy ways acknowledge Him, and He shall direct thy paths. Proverbs 3:6."

(VANESSA BRUCE INGOLD, an inspirational writer and speaker, lives in Southern California.)

SOUL MATINEE...

By Rusty Fischer

PEOPLE OFTEN ATTACH A LOFTY PEDIGREE TO THE TERM *SOUL MATE*. STIRRING violin music, bubbly champagne and romantic candlelight are all well and good; but a couple are not true soul mates till they fall in love, all over again, at a Tuesday night twilight show.

It was one of those stupid fights a couple has after five years of mostly blissful marriage. I had just come home from another long day at work. Of course, as we were a modern married couple, my wife had only gotten home a couple of minutes before me, after *her* long day at work.

"Hey, babe," I said cheerily, dropping my keys and wallet off on the wicker table in the foyer.

"Don't you 'hey, babe' me," she grunted over a load of laundry she'd just started.

Puzzled, I looked at her for a minute—just before the fireworks started, it turned out.

She was still in her fashionable work outfit: tailored slacks, silk blouse, crested blazer. Her hair was pulled back, and stray wisps from the long day spilled over her beautiful face. Even after five years, catching her in moments like this one still took my breath away. If she only knew how—

"Don't you stand there in front of me with that 'innocent dreamer' look of yours, either," she said, advancing on me with a handful of colorful plastic. "Would you mind explaining…these?"

She finished with a flourish, opening her clenched fist to reveal several candy bar wrappers, no doubt left behind in the load of my khaki work pants she was slipping into the washing machine.

I smiled for a minute, hoping my still-boyish charm might soften her concern.

"That's it?" she asked instead, slamming the candy wrappers down next to my wallet and keys. "You're just going to stand there and smile while your arteries clog by the minute?"

The upscale publishing company I worked for had recently offered blood tests to all of its employees. When my results came in, my wife and I were both surprised to see my cholesterol levels so high. Since then, she'd been urging me to eat better. Snickers and Baby Ruths were definitely not on her list.

"Fine," she said, deserting her load of laundry and grabbing her purse and keys off the wicker table instead. "If you don't want to be around to enjoy our twilight years together, then I don't know why you ever married me in the first place."

Embarrassment at getting caught, frustration from a long day at work and the "mother hen" tones of her afternoon scolding suddenly combined to raise the hackles on my neck.

"Me, either," I spat pettily, just before she slammed the door in my face.

Minutes later, of course, I felt the first twinge of post-flare-up guilt and quickly finished her load of laundry and began tidying up the house to make myself feel better. Noticing a bulging trash bag in the middle of the kitchen floor, I caught my wife's not-so-subtle hint and headed out the front door for the quick trek to the apartment complex dumpster.

On the way past the deserted tennis courts, a faulty seam in the dollar store trash bag stretched to its limit and split right in two. Cursing myself for making such a cheap purchase, I began stuffing the scattered coffee grounds and banana peels back into the remaining half of the bag. I stopped when I noticed the glaring labels of products we'd never bought before and that looked completely unfamiliar. Fat-free cheese slice wrappers hastily rewrapped around regular oily slices of cheese. Low-fat sour cream containers, still mostly full. Healthy choice cereal boxes full of regular raisin bran and Apple Jacks. A coffee can claiming it contained "Half the caffeine of regular brands" still full of rich-smelling regular coffee. Lite lunchmeat and dessert wrappers. Low-fat potato chip bags bearing regular greasy Ruffles!

No wonder things had tasted differently lately! She'd been switching healthy products out with my usual, fattening ones! But when did she find the time? In between our hectic schedules and long workdays, I could only imagine her getting up half an hour early each morning and stealthily replacing my usual chocolate chip cookies with dietetic ones by moonlight, the socks on her always-cold feet padding around the darkened kitchen floor while I slept two rooms away, snoring peacefully, none the wiser.

Maybe she really did want me around for the rest of her life, after all.

Gathering up the devious garbage, I made two trips and dumped all of her "evidence." Then I washed my hands, grabbed my wallet and keys and drove to the one place I knew I'd find her: the deserted movie theater near our apartment complex.

Once a week she called from her office and asked if I wanted to see a matinee movie with her after work. And once a week I declined, claiming some fictional last-minute meeting or looming deadline. The fact was, I liked my movies at night, where crowds swelled, laughter roared, popcorn flowed and everyone had a good time. Matinees were for little kids and old folks.

I parked next to her car in the empty parking lot and bought a ticket to the first chick-flick I saw. Out of habit, I headed straight for the concession stand. Balancing a diet soda, licorice and a bag of popcorn, I found her in the third theater I tried, watching exactly the kind of blaring action-adventure movie she never let me rent in the video store!

Creeping up behind her, I sat down with a flourish. She looked startled to see me but not just because I'd snuck up on her.

"What are you doing here?" She smiled, our fight quickly forgotten. "You never come to the movies with me after work."

"I missed you," I said honestly, not telling her about the garbage discovery. "I'm sorry I blew up at you…I'm just—"

"We're both tired," she finished for me, reading my mind. "And you shouldn't be such a sneak and…I shouldn't be such a nag."

I held her face in my hands in that darkened theater and told her, "No, you should."

She smiled warmly until she saw the bag of popcorn resting gently on the arm of my seat.

"Honey," I explained, "I didn't get any butter on it. And look, it says these Twizzlers are low fat."

She looked surprised, if not exactly happy.

"Well," she grunted, holding my hand as yet another car chase played out across the giant screen in front of us, "that's a start, I guess."

Not really, I mentally corrected her. It was more like a new beginning...

(RUSTY FISCHER married his soulmate, Martha, and today they work together from home running a successful freelance writing business.)

DESTINED FOR UNITY
By Cynthia Hobson

DURING MY TEENAGE YEARS, I CRAVED THE KIND OF RELATIONSHIP THAT boasted so much love that if the world just looked at my face they would know I had the real thing. But, alas, my teenage years were barren of any kind of relationship. I faced adversities from people who were cruel and disheartening.

Needless to say, my self-image and self-esteem were totally shattered. It made that craving even stronger and more unattainable, seemingly extinct. They say there is a soul mate for everyone. If that were true, I just knew I was on the short end of reality.

I wasn't a beauty queen in the eyes of the heartless crowd I grew up with. I was outcast because I wasn't popular or pretty. I was a nice, average girl who used her wits and brain. Although I did have friends, I still knew hurt. I still felt loneliness. The girls I knew bragged about sex. They tried to convince me that sex was the answer to true happiness, but I knew there was more to it than that. I wanted to be loved. I had something churning deep within me I longed to share with someone. I had heart. And if I could just find someone who would let me shine from within, I would give everything I was and everything I would be for him.

But by the world's standards, having heart is a liability when it should be the greatest asset one can possess.

I never dated as a teenager because I didn't fit into that worldly mold. I fantasized about someone who would love me for who I was and not what I looked like. I dreamed of the day I would have a family of my own, someone to share my life and grow old with.

My first love was a thirteen-year-old boy I met while vacationing with my family. We laughed and had fun together. When he kissed me the first time, I fell head-over-heels in love with him. We had a great summer—he was my idea of love personified.

When I had to go back home, it broke my heart into a million pieces. We kept in touch for a while but lost contact when my family moved across country. This couldn't be the love I dreamt about. It was too painful. Alas, this was the mentality of a thirteen-year-old girl who felt she was in the prime of her life. If she didn't have a boyfriend, she was destined for a life of solitude.

I never had a boyfriend after that because I compared them all to the one I lost. No one measured up.

I was twenty when I met a man I married. This had to be the one, I thought. My soul mate. He liked me. He paid attention to me, and he wanted to be with me. I was truly confused by this. Should I love someone just because he paid attention to me? By then, I thought I had reached the end of the rope and needed to settle down now I had found someone who wanted to settle down with me. I never thought I would get another chance. I figured I would grab the brass ring before it slipped away. I settled instead of researching the possibilities. This relationship never stood a chance of survival.

We lived together for a few months before getting married. It was a wise decision on my part, but the whole truth never really surfaced. While it is rumored that you never know someone until you live with them, people can still mask what lies within the heart.

I pushed for our marriage, afraid of being alone for the rest of my life. Eleven months after we got married, my son was born. This was heaven, I thought. A husband, a family, an answered dream.

It may have been a temporal answer, but it wasn't the right one.

Our second year of marriage was rocky. We separated for a short time when things got unbearable. The marriage should have ended, but a family tragedy in his life kept things together for the time being. A car accident took the life of his nephew and injured his brother and his family during a wild winter blizzard. The accident shed light on just how short life really is. I didn't want to live out my life alone. This fear of loneliness kept me in the relationship for nearly eighteen years.

After awhile, he started treating me like I didn't matter. I wasn't important. My opinions, needs, desires, wants and feelings meant nothing. I was constantly criticized and ridiculed. Everything I did was wrong. He stopped treating me as a person—he wanted a robot. He wanted a maid who would wait on him hand and foot. He wanted perfection—the white-gloved life. This was not me. It never was me. Yet, I stayed and dealt with it the best I could because I didn't know how to get out. I thought I couldn't survive on my own with a growing son.

After a few years, I went back to work to escape the horrors of home life. It was the one mistake I made that I will always regret because it took me away from my then seven-year-old son when he needed me. I missed out on several years of his life because I was always working to stay away from his father. His father was never there for him, either.

Even though they fought all the time, he liked his father because he bought him everything he wanted. My husband figured that was the way to show his love. My son knew I loved him, but I didn't buy him a lot of things. He knew there was a difference between his father and me when it came to showing love, for I was never showered with open signs of affection. Behind closed doors, there was emptiness in a loveless home.

By the time my son turned sixteen, things had gotten truly out of hand. By then, I had lost my job and was back at home. I started to take a school course at home and discovered computers and the Internet. I began to spend a lot of time online, meeting new people and playing games. It was another source of escape for me from the constant battlefield at home.

I found it irresistibly funny that people I met online, people I didn't even know, treated me with more respect than my own husband. They made me feel like I was a real person. I discovered a new life and made several friends. One, in particular, was a man who would become a major influence in my life. And all he did was become my friend.

My health began to suffer from the stress of my empty marriage. I ended up having a stroke at the ripe age of thirty-six on the eve of a scheduled surgery. I knew then I had to make some drastic changes in my life before it killed me.

Thankfully, I didn't suffer any permanent damage—after only three weeks, I regained the use of my left side. I was fortunate this time. And I wasn't going to take a chance on a next time. I had to make the move that had scared me for years.

That summer, I packed up everything I owned and sold things I couldn't fit in the van; even treasured items had to be sacrificed for my health and sanity. I not only moved out, I moved across the country.

I talked to my son about this move. At sixteen, he was old enough to understand why I had to do this. I wanted him to come with me, but he chose to stay behind where his friends were. I respected his decision and made sure he knew he could come to me any time. It was the hardest decision I ever made. I never told him the entire truth about why I left; but in time, he discovered it on his own.

I settled down, on my own for the first time in eighteen years, twelve hundred miles away from the stress. I couldn't file for a divorce yet because I couldn't afford to. However, the freedom made up for it.

The man I had met online was named Eric. He and I had grown very close and became the best of friends—I needed a friend then more than I needed air or food. We were both dealing with painful marriages. He separated from his wife a few weeks after we met. It wasn't only a very hard time for him; it was a bad time for both of us.

We had each found friends online we were interested in meeting in real time, so we never pursued our relationship any farther. However, I knew in my heart he was someone special. Something kept bringing me back to him. Something drew us together.

My heart had become engaged by the mere sight of his presence online. Each day, I couldn't wait to talk to him; I would go online in case he popped on. We shared many things about our lives. The more we talked, the more we became the best of friends.

After a couple of months, Eric's four-year-old daughter made a heartfelt plea to her daddy. She asked him to put their family back together. She wanted to be with him, and he would have done anything for her. So, he did—he gave his marriage one more chance.

When he told me about this decision, my heart felt like a lead weight. It fell so hard and hurt so deep I couldn't stop dwelling on it. Because it wasn't what I wanted, I lashed out at him. I knew his wife would hurt him again, and I didn't want him to have to go through that. Blinded by my own selfish attitude, I couldn't see he was hurting, too.

However, out of love and respect for him, I stepped aside, hoping in my heart I was right. Not because I wanted to see him hurt but because I wanted him to be free. Yet I knew if we were meant to be together we would be.

During that time he was reunited his family, I chose not sit around and wait. Again I allowed my loneliness and my hurt feelings to dictate my life. In order to ease my pain, I agreed to see another man I met online. It was the worst decision I ever made, especially when I told Eric about it. Still, I made the right decision in telling him. If I hadn't, I never would have found out his feelings for me.

Eric and I still talked. However, every time we chatted, I knew he had someone watching over him. I had to be careful of what we said. Even though our conversations were very innocent and nothing more than a friendly chat, I couldn't tell him the things I really wanted to.

When the topic of my date came up, he scolded me. He was very angry with me for giving in to my loneliness. At the time, I couldn't understand. I felt he had no right telling me I was wrong. Out of anger, I hid from him for days and didn't talk to him.

A week passed. He started asking my online friends if they had seen me. When he couldn't find me, he sent me an email apologizing for being upset. That was when he realized he loved me, but he couldn't say it yet. We started chatting again. He then told me he had separated again. This time, it was for good.

It had only taken her two months to hurt him. I couldn't believe what I was hearing, although I had known it was going to happen. I felt very bad that he had to go through it, but I was glad he had finally made the choice to let go.

I was beginning to think fate had finally stepped into my life and was intervening in a very divine way. Even though we weren't in any hurry to rush our relationship, we did decide to pursue it.

We began having our conversations over the phone instead of online. The first time, we talked for more than three hours. I couldn't believe how fast time went by as we found how much we had to discuss. The main thing was when we would meet face-to-face.

We didn't really know each other. Even though we felt as if we had been friends for years, there was still that moment of truth. I wanted to see him as soon as possible. However, he wanted to wait for his divorce before moving on. I respected that decision.

I will never forget the first time I heard him say "I love you." It was during one of our lengthy phone conversations. It was then I knew something special was about to change my entire life.

The wait was a little easier knowing we had something to look forward to. However, it was still a longer one than I had wanted. Every time I asked him if we could get together, he kept telling me no. He wanted to wait for things to be right. He didn't want to risk his visitation with his daughter. He dreamt that when we met all we would do was hug each other for the longest time out of joy and out of need. I wanted it to come true. He did, too, but not as soon as I did.

Fate had other plans. Eric had been sick for several months and needed surgery. He had no one to turn to. His family was out of town, which left him alone. He decided to ask me to come and be with him, to support him as a friend during the operation because he didn't want to go through it alone. Two days later, I was in my car and on my way. It took me ten hours to drive the six hundred miles that stood between us. I would have walked it just to be there.

The trip gave me time to ponder how we would meet. What would we say? How would we react? Would he like what he saw? Would he be turned off by my appearance? Would he be glad he asked me to come? Would he like me? Had I made the right decision? So many questions. The answers would soon be known.

The butterflies in my stomach seemed to get larger the closer I got to his home. My heart was racing. My mind was filled with many fears. I rang the doorbell. The moment of truth.

He greeted me with a big smile then escorted me upstairs to his apartment. We didn't hug. My first thought was that he was disappointed in me. It worried me. But to my relief, he had only been online and had to hurry back to the computer to finish what he was doing.

We stood in his kitchen, looking at each other. He smiled at me then he threw his arms around me and hugged me very tight. I didn't really want him to hug me yet because I was sweaty from the trip. He didn't care. I put my arms around him and started to cry. We gazed into each other's eyes, smiled, and that is when he kissed me.

Everything I dreamt of was standing right in this kitchen six hundred miles from my home. Every fear disappeared.

We spent the next five days getting to know each other better. We laughed. We cried. We talked. We enjoyed each other's company. I met his daughter. That was the real test. If she liked me, I was in. To my relief, she did. We had the greatest week together.

But the day came when I had to go back home. I couldn't face it. How could I leave him now? How could I go back after finding the greatest man I have ever met, knowing there was a chance we would not see each other again? How could I take that chance? He felt the same way I did, but he wasn't sure. It wasn't until I got in my car and drove away that he realized he wanted to be with me.

I was listening to a CD going home. It played some of our favorite songs. One song, "Don't Stop Believin'," held a special place in my heart. It was like fate telling me not to stop believing in what was meant to be. But another song, "Open Arms," makes me cry to this day every time I hear it because Eric welcomed me with open arms into his life. He didn't stop to look at the wrapping on the package. He just accepted the gift of my heart without reservation.

I got home and found an email from him. He told me he wished I hadn't left and that he had come after me but couldn't catch me. I still regret not looking back to see him chasing me. It would have broken my heart. He missed me. I cried so much when I read his heartfelt words I had to call him. He said he wished I were there, and that the house seemed so empty without me. I jokingly told him if he missed me to come and get me.

He got quiet for a minute. Then, he said, "Okay."

I couldn't believe he was actually serious about driving out to get me, but he was dead serious. And by the following Friday, he was there.

We spent the entire month of July together. During that month, we went through nightmare after nightmare in our relationship, testing its very foundation. From the threat of him losing his daughter to my being blamed by his ex-wife for his marriage breakup to my emergency surgery, we withstood hit after hit and found out we wanted to be together no matter what.

By the end of the month, his divorce was filed and I had to go back to settle things with my ex. By early September, we were back together under one roof without any mileage between us.

I have finally discovered what it feels like to have true love. Neither of us had a marriage that was able to survive. What we have now is truly miraculous. My dream of loving a man who trusts me, respects and believes in me, showers me with things just because he loves me, hugs and kisses me to show me his affection, cares about what I think and how I feel, takes care of me, meets my needs and desires, listens to me when I talk because he values my opinion, treats me like a partner and not a servant. A man who rocks my very existence. A man who encourages and supports my hopes, dreams and aspirations. A man who dared to reach out to me and touch my very soul. A man I gave my heart to and who gave me the world just by loving me.

We work together, day-by-day, to strengthen and nourish our relationship. He is truly the best friend I have ever had. My soul mate.

On Christmas 2000 we gave each other an unexpected gift—we found out we were having a baby. Our son Collin was born the following August. This was a blessing I was not allowed to have until now. I had waited for eighteen years to have another child, a child conceived in true love.

Destined souls have paths that bring their lives together. We may not take what we think are the right roads in life, but destiny always guides us. No matter which way we turn, the turns are the right ones. We may not realize it at the time, but they are right because we learn from them. People meet at certain times in their lives, not because of circumstances but because of fate. We always think, "I wish we had met a long time ago." But if we had, things may not have turned out quite as well.

I will always believe there are reasons for everything that happens in our lives. When Eric and I are apart during the day, we are always in each other's thoughts. We are always with each other in spirit. We are linked together by a rare bond called "love." Destiny brought us together, love will strengthen our union and our souls will seal it for eternity.

(CINDY HOBSON is an author from southern Pennsylvania.)

A KNIGHT WITHOUT ARMOR
By Annette Gisby

T HE IDEA CAME ABOUT BY ACCIDENT. MY BROTHER HAD BEEN LOOKING IN THE paper for a new place to live; and as I'm an avid reader and will read anything, I, too, read the paper from cover to cover. But it wasn't the listings for property that caught my eye; it was actually the personals.

I read a few of the listings, wondering what sort of person would advertise there. None of the adverts seemed to be from people I would be interested in meeting.

I was nineteen years old, had never really had a steady boyfriend, and I was feeling a bit lonely. I knew exactly the sort of person I wanted to meet—I wanted romance, flowers, poetry, the knight in shining armor to sweep me off my feet. But where on earth in London was I going to find someone like that?

I didn't drink, so I didn't go to pubs or nightclubs. I worked as an assistant manager in a shoe shop, but everyone there was a girl so I couldn't meet anyone at work. How was I going to meet my knight? I glanced at the personals again. Should I? Could I?

The form was just sitting there, begging to be filled in. The letters went to a PO box—only the paper would know my address—so what did I have to lose?

I left it for a couple of weeks before I sent off my advert. What on earth was I doing? Surely, it's only crazy, desperate people who would place an advert like this.

In my ad, I listed everything I wanted in the man I would like to meet: kind, good sense of humor, non-drinker, non-smoker and who was going to be my knight in shining armor.

I waited anxiously for replies, and a few days later, they came. Lots of them. How on earth was I going to choose whom to meet?

One letter stood out from all the rest; it was the longest, and the opening paragraph gripped me from the start.

"Hi, there, young lady, I don't remember a fairy godmother appearing in a puff of smoke and granting me three wishes, but I guess that's exactly what must have happened because you sound exactly like the sort of girl I would wish for."

The letter went on to reveal that he was funny, charming and named John. I wrote him a letter, and then he rang me to arrange a date. We were going out to dinner together.

Then the panic set in. What on earth was I going to wear? With help from my friends at work, I was finally ready to go and meet him. My friend Kyp went with me to the underground station, where we waited anxiously for John to arrive.

A very shy-looking young man appeared, coming up the escalators carrying a bunch of red roses. He glanced around at the people wandering about, and then he glanced our way. My heart skipped a beat. He was gorgeous, with short brown curly hair and the most sparkling blue eyes I'd ever seen. Then he began to walk our way.

"Annette?" he asked, glancing from me to Kyp and back again.

"Yes," I managed to squeak. I was so nervous. I'd been on dates before, but this was *the* date—I could feel it—and I didn't want to ruin it.

"These are for you," he said and thrust the flowers towards me. "And this," he reached into his inside pocket and took out an envelope. "It's a poem."

Poem and flowers on the first date? I was in heaven as Kyp led the way to the restaurant—it was her recommendation—but once at the door she left us alone; and I wondered what on earth I was going to say to him.

While we waited for the food to arrive, I read his poem.

> I once heard it said that a foul dragon's lair
> Shattered the ambience of peaceful Wood Green,
> And that the beast taunted a young maiden fair

The loveliest lass that there'd ever been
Until one night from a southern land crept
A hero armed only with wit and with charm
Seeking her heart while the dread monster slept
And aiming to shield her forever from harm.
Did yon traveller succeed? I cannot yet say,
For the rest of the tale is still to unfold;
But I know that he dreams almost every day
Of a love that's strong and will never grow cold.
Is it actually true? Can it really be?
Are you the girl who dreams the same dreams as
me?

Love John

I was crying by the time I got to the end of the poem, and I needn't have worried that I wouldn't know what to say. We talked all night until the restaurant was closing and they had to chase us out!

We saw each other every weekend after that. Then it was the weekends and one night a week. Then it seemed we were seeing each other every day. We went to the cinema, to theatres, on long walks, picnics; and I could hardly believe I had met someone who wanted the same things I did. John was the perfect gentleman, opening doors, helping me on with my coat. The first time we kissed, my legs buckled and I thought I was going to faint. I was madly in love, and I hoped he was, too.

For my twentieth birthday, nine months after we had met, we went on holiday to Portugal. I had my suspicions, and so did my parents, that he was going to pop the question; but I didn't want to get my hopes up. On the morning of my birthday, he handed me a large box, too large to be a ring; and I felt a pang of disappointment. Inside was a porcelain doll dressed as a bridegroom.

"What's missing?" he asked, smiling.

"A bride?" I said, hope flaring once again.

He gave me another long box, this time with a bride doll inside, but she was holding something in her hand—a gift bag with a poem inside it.

Annette,
I've known you just about nine months
And now on your birthday
The time has come with fingers crossed
These words for me to say:
I love you more than anything,
To you my heart I give.
With you I want to be always
Without you I can't live.
I want to share your secret thoughts
And all your hopes and dreams,
To be the first you turn to when
You're in need of help, it seems.
I want to gaze into your eyes
Each night before I sleep
Instead of at your photograph,
Which by my side I keep.
I want my future to be yours,
Your love to be all mine
And lots of children to be ours—
Now doesn't that sound fine?
I want to bring you happiness,
To love and care for you.
The dream I hold most dear to me
Is that you want this, too.
So how's all this to come about?
I think that you can guess.
I'll put to you a question
And hope you'll answer yes.
To be romantic, I must now
Get down on bended knee,
In order to enquire, Annette...

And he did, asking, "Will you marry me?"
I said yes straightaway, but John says I took ages to reply. Maybe

he was so nervous that it just seemed ages!

We bought my ring together in Portugal, as he wanted me to choose it. We decided on an emerald-and-diamond one.

John is my soul mate and my best friend. I can tell him anything. I have other friends, but he is definitely the one I confide in first. I can't imagine being without him, and I wake up every day with a smile just knowing that I'm married to him.

This year we will have been married thirteen years, and just think—I would never have met my soul mate if I hadn't placed that ad.

He never did find a suit of armor, but in my eyes he's a knight all the same.

(ANNETTE GISBY resides in London and is the author of Shadows of the Rose.)

IT'S NOT IN THE GIFT, BUT THE GIVING
By Mary Emma Allen

AS A YOUNG BRIDE OF FEWER THAN SIX MONTHS, I ANTICIPATED A ROMANTIC Christmas gift from my husband. I didn't expect much, for we were living on a very tight budget while Jim finished engineering college.

We had made Christmas gifts for our friends and relatives. I baked cookies and stitched aprons, placemats and potholders. Jim constructed bookends and trivets from scrap lumber. We trekked through the snowy woods to cut our tree, excited at finding the first one for our tiny apartment. We had no lights, but we strung popcorn and cranberries. We made paper ornaments and borrowed others from Jim's mom.

All the time I wondered what my new husband would give me. Would he make me something out of wood? Was he working that extra odd job to buy jewelry or a book I wanted?

On Christmas morning, there were gifts from relatives under the tree and a gaily wrapped box about six by six inches for me from Jim. I saved it until the last, savoring the anticipation of something special. This was my first Christmas gift from Jim as my husband. This was a special moment as I untied the bow and unwrapped the box.

Then I lifted the lid.

"What is it?" I looked at Jim.

He was grinning. "It's just what you needed, isn't it?"

I nodded, still wondering what it was. It consisted of a two-inch round whetstone with a groove around the outer edge. This was attached to a steel stand and the whetstone was turned by a little handle.

266

"What is it for?" I wondered, still hesitant.

"It's just what you need to sharpen the kitchen knives," Jim explained patiently, thinking I was speechless with appreciation at his thoughtful gesture. "I knew you were getting tired of trying to cut with dull knives. (I knew *he* had been but hadn't given it much thought myself.) "I saw it at the hardware store," he continued, "and knew it would be the perfect Christmas gift."

Then he showed me more wondrous aspects about this gadget, picking up a small metal piece still in the box.

"You attach this to the wall. And you slip the whetstone into it. Then you put the knife into the groove and turn the handle. Presto! We can cut meat and bread with our knives again."

While I looked for another, more romantic gift, even though it might be tiny (he really wasn't serious that this was my only Christmas gift, was he?), Jim proceeded to attach the whetstone to the kitchen wall and sharpen all the knives so he could carve the turkey.

It was years before I mentioned my astonishment over my first Christmas gift. By then I could tease Jim about it without fear of hurting his feelings for trying to surprise a young wife with a gift he thought she'd appreciate and enjoy as much as he.

We now laugh about it and share this moment. It has become a meaningful moment to us, one that should have warned me of the unexpected and unusual adventures I'd encounter over the next forty years with this man.

When Jim and I look back to our initial meeting and joke about our "arranged" marriage, we know we must have been destined to share life together. My Aunt Freda was concerned that I, at nineteen, would become an old maid. So she took matters in hand and organized our meeting while I was visiting her, nearly three hundred miles from home. She suggested I accompany my uncle to the Allen Farm, where he had business to discuss with Jim's dad, a veterinary colleague.

Jim, working in the hay field that warm summer day, was intrigued when a younger brother informed him that a pretty girl was at the house with Dr. Place. He found an excuse to come in for a drink of water, met me and called for a date a couple days later. Thus our long distance romance began.

Aunt Freda later admitted she hoped I'd find one of the eight Allen boys attractive when she sent me along with my uncle. Jim compares the situation to fly fishing. He, like the trout, lured by Aunt Freda's bait, was caught for life.

There must have been a fascination at first sight because neither of us dated anyone else for the three years of our courtship while I finished college. Our similar interests, Jim's adventurous spirit and that initial attraction have held us together for more than forty years through life's challenges and joys.

Neither of us remembers what I gave Jim that first Christmas nor what we gave one another during ensuing years; but that gift of a knife sharpener is still etched in our memories. Each time we see it (it's survived the years, although we can't find the gadget to attach it to the wall), we'll look at one another and grin, remembering our first Christmas—a memory that never would have occurred if my husband had followed the traditional route and bought or made me an expected, romantic gift for this special day.

(MARY EMMA ALLEN writes for children and adults from her multi-generational home in New Hampshire and teaches workshops around the country.)

STRANGE PHENOMENON BETWEEN TWO PEOPLE

By Bobby and Kam Ruble

S A BACHELOR, MY LIFE WAS EXCITING; AND I WAS CONTENT PLAYING THE field. I had a good-paying job, drove a Ferrari and had plenty of female friends to fill my dating needs. I wasn't looking for a permanent relationship, perhaps because I had never met the right woman.

Even though I was certainly no dashing Romeo to some women, I had high standards in what I expected a full-time woman to be in my life. My idea of a perfect woman was one who not only looked sexy (in a lady-like way), but was warm, loving, kind, considerate, caring, intelligent, witty…

Okay, if you want me to be direct and honest, I wanted a lady in the parlor and a vixen in the bedroom.

As happy as I was being single, it appeared that many of the married people around me could not stand that I was unattached. Several of these caring individuals kept trying to set me up on blind dates. I accepted a few but always ended up disappointed. The women were either very boring to be with or they were in desperate search for a husband. Both types were as endearing to me as an army of ants at a picnic.

There was one gal in my office, however, who was relentless. To save any embarrassment or lawsuits, I'll call her Sue. You know the type that never takes no for an answer? Well, that was definitely Sue. To top it off, she wasn't one of my favorite fellow employees, either. She talked too much and too loudly, knew everything better than anyone else did, had no personality, didn't know the meaning of the

269

word *manners*, and she always looked as though she had slept in her clothes the night before she wore them to work. I could only imagine what her friend was like. That was not a picture that intrigued me in the least.

However, just to get Sue to stop nagging at me, I finally accepted an invitation to meet her single friend.

When I asked her to describe or tell me about her friend, Sue flat-out refused. Afraid I might make up some stupid reason to get out of the date, she only informed me that I would not be disappointed. All I could think about was the old saying: "Birds of a feather flock together." In my wildest dreams, I couldn't imagine how I could be anything but disappointed in someone who was Sue's friend.

As much as I tried to find a reason for backing down, nothing came to mind at the time. Dreading the inevitable, I didn't show up at the Sunday afternoon picnic I was suppose to attend to meet Sue's special friend. Come Monday morning, Sue was loaded for bear when she caught me by the coffee machine. I made up some lame excuse about being sick for the entire weekend, which got me off the hook, temporarily. I say "temporarily" as she hit me with a second chance. Like I really needed it! Once again, like a dope, I agreed.

Now, all this time Sue was hounding me, and unbeknownst to me, here is what was happening on the other end of the stick.

Along with her day job, where she and I were co-workers, Sue was a part-time bartender in the evenings at a local bar. There, she had become acquainted with one of the bar's female customers, who stopped in for one drink every Friday night after work. In the course of a few conversations, Sue found out this woman was single and had a good job. Even though the woman appeared to be extremely happy with her lifestyle, Sue found it strange she was unattached.

Playing matchmaker, Sue hounded her as much as she had been hounding me to meet her friend from work—me. To appease Sue, the woman agreed to go to the picnic to meet me. However, she didn't show up, either. Later, I found it ironic that the woman gave Sue the same lame excuse I had given for not attending.

To stop the never-ending needling from Sue, the woman agreed, once again, to meet me; but only if I came to the bar. Then, if she didn't like me, she could make her excuses and leave at will.

After I had agreed to a second encounter of the dreaded kind, that week went far too fast. The following Friday evening after work, I was to meet Sue and her friend at Sue's favorite bar. Sue wasn't going to be working that evening, but she promised to be there. The only thing good, up to that point, was that Sue was known for keeping her word. Just my luck! I figured I could be polite and meet this woman, have one cordial drink, then hit the road.

I was to meet the two women at seven p.m. sharp, but I took my sweet time getting to the bar. Normally, I wore a suit and tie when I went out on a date, but I deliberately changed into my scruffy old blue jeans and a T-shirt. After all, I didn't want to make a good impression on someone I already knew I wouldn't care for. I did some grocery shopping, got my car washed and filled with gas, then I moseyed on over to the bar.

As I got out of my car, I looked at my watch. It was seven-thirty. My hopes were, of course, that both Sue and her friend would have taken the hint by then that I had stood them up, given up waiting and left the bar.

In June, the sun is still fairly bright at seven-thirty in the evening. So, when I walked into the dark room it took a few seconds for my eyes to adjust. I had not been in this particular bar before; but I quickly noticed the service bar was straight in front of me. As my eyesight got clearer, I looked down the line of people sitting on bar stools. They appeared to be enjoying drinks and conversation. I felt relieved when I didn't see Sue. Perhaps I was right in thinking she had already left.

I figured that I might as well have a cold one before I decided what to do with the rest of my evening. I was headed for an empty bar stool when my eyes were drawn to one of the most beautiful women I had ever seen. She appeared to be nicely shaped, though I really couldn't tell in the black dress she was wearing.

She sat sideways on the bar stool with her right arm on the bar and her left arm resting in her lap. One glance told me this was a lady and not a typical barfly. Her dress was low-cut, but it was sexy without being too revealing. Even though her body was turned in my

271

direction, I couldn't see her face, as her head was turned toward the bartender. I did notice the spiked heels she was wearing that accentuated her lovely pair of long, shapely legs.

I could only think, Wow! Now why couldn't I be that lucky to be set up with a woman like her?

As I stood there in awe, this dream girl had gracefully risen from her bar stool and appeared to be getting ready to leave. All at once, she was looking right at me with a gleam in her eyes. Her face was as beautiful as the rest of her.

Out of nowhere, a flash of cold air made chills run up and down my spine. Something magical drew us to each other. It was as if I already knew her. I could sense in my innermost soul she was charming, intelligent, had a good sense of humor and a personality I would enjoy spending time with.

What I discovered, later, was unbelievable. Here is what she felt and thought at the exact moment she looked directly at me.

"I never took to meeting up with men in a bar like a lot of women did that I knew. I didn't look down on them because they did, but I had my own life with plenty of gentlemen friends to keep my dating life well occupied. Stopping in this particular bar for a Friday night drink, alone, was just something I enjoyed doing because my daughter was one of the bartenders.

"After a busy day at work, which meant I had to work a few hours overtime, I didn't get to the bar until quarter till seven that evening. Having had my one-drink quota before driving home, and since Sue's friend was a no-show, I paid my bill, slid off my bar stool and started to leave. It's only natural for me to look up before walking so I wouldn't run in to someone.

"As I looked up, I was suddenly staring into the face of a handsome man. Even though he was standing a few feet away, I felt drawn to him like a fish to water. My heart went up into my throat and my feet seemed almost glued to the floor. I hoped the darkness of the bar's interior hid the flush that I felt in my face.

"You could call it women's intuition, but something inside told me my life was about to change. Incredible as it seemed at the time, I didn't know this stranger from Adam. Yet, I felt I had known him for a long time.

"As our eyes seemed to be locked on one another, I couldn't help but smile at him."

In just a matter of seconds, which seemed like an eternity, this beauty smiled and my heart melted. Just as I took a step towards her, I heard a familiar loud, obnoxious voice yell at me from across the room.

"Hey, Bob! It's about damn time you showed up."

I could feel everyone in the place looking at me as Sue approached.

"Where in the hell have you been, buddy? We almost gave up hope you would show up. I was just going to the can when I noticed Kam was getting ready to leave."

Before I could open my mouth, Sue turned to the lovely woman and introduced her as her friend. Like a lady I had never met before, this blond-haired, blue-eyed, pouty-lipped beauty put out her hand at the very time I did the same thing.

Now, let me tell you, I had never before in my life given my hand in a handshake to a woman on a date. First encounter or not, a handshake with a woman was only done for business reasons in my book. It was like I had read her mind so my hand moved of its own accord.

Everyone else in the room seemed to disappear, including loudmouthed Sue, as Kam and I greeted each other. Somehow, I wasn't surprised when she gave me a firm handshake instead of the normal dishrag model most women shell out. Her hand was so warm and soft, I didn't want to let it go. She made no attempt to remove it from mine, either.

When I finally came to my senses, I asked Kam to join me at a table for a drink. She agreed—and why wasn't I surprised when Sue joined us? I didn't mean to be rude to Sue, but my full attention was on this new lady in my life.

Kam was very polite to Sue, but I felt she was as embarrassed as I was at even being associated with someone so boisterous and uncouth. After one drink, she mentioned she was about to leave to go to dinner when I had finally showed up. Informing her that I had not eaten, either, I invited her to dinner. She graciously accepted.

On the way to the restaurant, we had a good laugh when we inquired of one another how we both knew Sue. That's when we discovered how she had cornered us both to set us up on the date we were finally out on that evening.

To give the devil her due, Sue obviously knew something about the two of us we hadn't been aware of.

Dinner was amazing. Kam was everything I thought she would be from the moment I set eyes on her. We had wonderful, deep, intelligent conversation mixed with laughter before, during and after dinner. I told her things about my life I wouldn't have told any stranger. She confided in me as well. To my surprise, her life had been very similar to mine.

Many times, during the course of the evening, one of us would finish the other's statement, or we would bring up the same topic at the same time. I couldn't believe what was happening. It was like we were cut from the same mold: how we thought, what we expected out of life, what we looked for in a spouse, what our likes and dislikes were and what made us tick.

Because I read a lot, I had often read about soul mates. To be honest, I don't think I ever believed in such a strange relationship between two people. That fateful night, however, I became a believer. I just knew I had found my soul mate. What was better than that discovery? Finding out that Kam felt the exact same way.

Neither of us had been looking for a permanent relationship when we met. Yet, here we were, wrapping the arms of our hopes and dreams around each other's lives. For all the bad things we ever thought about Sue, Kam and I were very grateful she had gotten the two of us together. Had she not been so pushy and persistent, we would, undoubtedly, never have met.

What drove Sue to insist on Kam and I getting an introduction? Why did I walk into the bar at almost the exact moment Kam was getting ready to leave? Did destiny play a hand in our finally getting together? There is no doubt it was the package Kam was wrapped in that first drew my attention to her. And she has since told me that she felt the same way when she first looked at me. Our souls reached out and touched one another that evening.

Even though some may call it love at first sight, this was truly the romancing of the soul.

Kam and I have been happily married for a number of years now, and we never cease to amaze each other. We still bring up the same topic at the same time as if we were reading each other's minds. In fact, we often do read each other's minds. Sometimes it can be too weird, to the point of being eerie—especially if she answers a question I didn't ask her yet but was only thinking about. If one of us hurts, the other one feels their pain. When we are apart, we ache inside until we are reunited with one another.

Due to my age and emphysema and Kam's degenerative arthritis, we are both retired. Although Kam has always aspired to be a writer, having had several of her poems published over the years, sadly, her crippling fingers won't allow her to sit and write like she once did. However, we take full advantage of the opportunity to write some great mystery novels together.

Kam has very exciting, vivid dreams, which she transforms into interesting stories, always asking for my input and opinion. And, when her arthritic fingers won't cooperate, I help input her words into the computer. When we work together to name and give her characters some reality, we seem to select the same personalities and same physical characteristics for the same characters. It's a wonderful meeting of the minds.

As we grow older together, she is still my lady in the parlor, and in the bedroom…well, let's just say she still keeps a smile on my face. Even after all the years we've been together, we are still on each other's wavelength. We truly are soul mates.

(BOBBY RUBLE is an award-winning journalist with a law enforcement background and KAM RUBLE is an award-winning poet with a multi-faceted background.)

BLIND DATE

By Irene Smith

MARILYN WAS MORE FRIEND THAN CLIENT. OUR PROFESSIONAL relationship was mutual. I bought ceramics from her, and she bought advertising from me. Along the way, we developed a friendship.

One day, I walked into her shop to make the weekly delivery of my parents' advertising journal, *The Little Paper*. She said, "Irene, are you seeing anybody?"

I was, but we'd been doing so on and off, mostly off, for eight years. Much as I liked the guy, I had come to the conclusion that we could be no more than friends. When she suggested that I might like to meet her nephew, I was ready to say, "Yes."

"Remember," she said, "he doesn't want a serious relationship. He wants to meet someone he can go out to dinner or to a movie with. Nothing more."

I gave her my home phone number. For months, I didn't hear a thing. Then one day, when I went into her shop, she told me that Warren was waiting for his divorce to be final before calling me.

I waited a long time before we set up a first date. Marilyn, her husband and I would meet Warren for dinner the day before Mother's Day.

By the time we met, I knew that he worked for General Motors. I knew about his two children, a boy and a girl, and his three brothers and one sister. I even knew that Warren had been born in Marilyn's bed.

"I was at school when it happened," she told me. "When I came home for lunch, there he was. I felt as though he was my own little dolly."

The Saturday before Mother's Day, the night of my big date, I couldn't think of anything else. I must have tried on every outfit I owned. Finally, I was ready.

When Marilyn and her husband picked me up, I was a little bit disappointed to see that they were the only ones in the car.

"Warren will meet us at the restaurant," she said.

We got there—no Warren. We had a drink at the bar—no Warren. We met a couple that Marilyn and Art knew and invited them to join us. Still no Warren.

Finally, we moved to a table and ordered our dinners. We hadn't any more than completed our orders than a handsome, dark-haired man walked into the restaurant. When I looked at him, I felt the strangest tickle in my stomach. I knew who he was before anybody said anything.

Marilyn did the honors.

"Irene, I'd like you to meet my favorite nephew, Warren; and Warren, meet Irene, my favorite advertising salesman."

Some of the things that happen to people in romance stories are just too corny to believe. At least, that's what I had always thought. You know—"She felt faint at his touch" or "She just knew they were fated to be together." I know better now. Believe them.

As our hands touched, I looked in his eyes and felt dizzy. He apologized for being late. He said he was so nervous that he couldn't find the restaurant.

I don't remember anything about the people who joined us for dinner that night. I can't remember their names, and if I met them again I wouldn't recognize them. From the time Warren sat down at the table, he and I were only aware of each other.

We talked all through dinner. After the meal was finished, we moved out to the bar and had an after-dinner drink and talked some more. Marilyn and Art must have felt like outsiders. When they finally suggested that we call it a night, Warren offered to drive me home. He and I talked until the owner of the restaurant asked us to leave so they could close for the night.

We ended up at an all-night diner. We talked about everything you can imagine. I found out he was interested in just as many different subjects as I was. Our interests were not identical, but they were complementary. Most importantly, we both loved words. We both loved to talk, to play around with ideas, to debate just for the sake of debate. Finally, at two-thirty in the morning, he drove me home. Even then, we sat and talked in the car for another half an hour.

That was when it happened. He kissed me. First kisses are always special. This kiss was more than that. Have you ever kissed someone and found that their lips were a perfect fit for yours? Warren's first kiss went on forever. He and I were the only two people in the entire world. Nothing else mattered but that kiss. It was soft, sweet, romantic, with an underlying passion that left me weak and dizzy.

My mother was waiting for me when I got home. No matter how late I was out, she always waited up for me.

"Well, how was it?"

"I just met the man I'm going to marry," I told her.

I'm sure there were many times over the next nine years (yes, nine years!) that she was convinced I was crazy. Especially when, about two months after we met, we broke up for more than a year.

Ultimately, I was right. On Valentine's Day, three months short of nine years after our first date, Warren proposed. He even got down on one knee. Really, I have the videotape to prove it. We married on August 13, 1994.

Warren and I know that, no matter how bad things get, the other will be there to provide moral support or a quick boot in the rear, whichever the situation calls for. The conversation we started nearly seventeen years ago has continued nearly nonstop. There always seems to be something new to talk about, something new to share. We've both changed, both grown; but we've grown together, not apart.

When I accepted a job that required us to move from New York state to Washington state, I went first and Warren followed a month later with our son, who was almost three years old. By the time he started his trip, we were both weary of the separation. Rather than wait for him to get all the way to the West Coast, I drove across Washington and met him in Spokane. He told me afterwards that "When we got to the hotel room and I opened the door and saw you standing there, I felt as though I was home."

I know what he means.

(IRENE SMITH is a freelance writer, computer programmer and web designer.)

FROM PRINCE ROTTEN TO PRINCE CHARMING

By Kathleen A. Cyr

IN LATE MARCH OF 1994, I BELIEVED I WAS WORTHLESS AS A HUMAN BEING. I was living with my boyfriend. At first, I had believed he was my Prince Charming. He was the one who was supposed to provide me with the picture-perfect life, like a Norman Rockwell painting. We moved into a tiny basement apartment, and my Prince Charming turned out to be Prince Rotten.

The change in him started with fierce mood swings. While we were making dinner, the mood would be lighthearted. In a flash, he would become furious. The cause? Perhaps it was the way I stood at the stove or the amount of spice I put into the meal. I did not understand the true reason for the outbursts, only feared them.

Putdowns and degrading comments followed the mood swings. To him, I was never good enough, even at the simplest tasks. I had no confidence or self-esteem left. Several times, I contemplated suicide, but I didn't even have enough courage for that.

I invested two years of my life in this man. He said he would change. He said he loved me. My Prince Charming and the house with the white picket fence would be a reality. I was kidding myself.

I did not realize my situation was quite evident to other people. I never mentioned my home life or what was happening to me.

It was at my job that my eyes began to open. I was outside on my half-hour break when I noticed someone who looked quite familiar. Sitting across from me was my very first crush; his name was Rey Cyr. I had met him as a child one summer, and we became instant friends.

I looked forward to seeing him each afternoon. He was sweet and polite. He saved my life when I was thirteen—something my heart has never forgotten.

We were at the local pool; I was about to jump off the diving board. Someone jumped on the board behind me. Before I knew what was happening, I rolled sideways into the water. I felt no pain but knew I was in trouble. I couldn't breath, couldn't get to the surface. Hands grabbed me and pulled me to the surface. It was Rey—he had saved me from drowning.

When I reached the side of the pool, my right leg was covered in blood. I was scraped and bruised from thigh to toe. Rey sat with me while the lifeguards tended to my wounds. Each day for three weeks, he stayed by my side until my leg was healed enough to go back into the water.

This is what I remembered as I stared at the grown man who slightly resembled the boy I once knew. He had a mustache and wavy light-brown hair that reached the tops of his shoulders, but it was in his eyes I saw the boy from years past.

For the first time since I began dating Prince Rotten, I felt alive. Rey and I picked up where we left off. Our friendship grew to a new level. He helped me to see that I was special, that I did not have to take another degrading comment. I left Prince Rotten and never looked back.

I have been married to Rey for more than four years now, and we have two beautiful children. I do not have the white picket fence or the big house; but I do have respect, friendship and the love of my first crush. That means far more to me than living in a Norman Rockwell painting.

(KATHY CYR is a freelance writer and artist from Connecticut.)

SPIRITUAL FUSION
By Mary Ellen Clark

THERE I SAT, TWENTY-EIGHT YEARS OLD, WITH TWO CHILDREN AND TWO failed marriages staring me in the face. I was convinced that romance was nothing more than a dirty word that brought heartache. Yet, from deep within, I could not quiet the persistent whispers; those lonely murmurs that rose from the abyss spoke of my hidden desires. They served as a constant reminder of the loneliness that accompanies life without love.

I was able to suppress my thoughts of love by immersing myself in the daily routine of raising my children. Life drifted on, day by day, neither happy nor sad. It followed the slow, methodical beat of sameness.

All of that changed the day I caught my first glimpse of *him*.

Nervous to begin with, I walked into the building, ready to start my new job. I was really looking forward to the increased income—it would be a welcome sight at the end of the week. I had my hands full trying to make ends meet. The kids always seemed to need something new, and it was sure to cost more than I could spare. I was relying on this new job to provide me with some breathing room from bills.

In any event, I was pumped, primed and ready to take on the challenge of the first day on my new job.

"Wish me well," I called through the open window of the car as I dropped the children off at school. In unison, they shouted back, "You'll knock 'em dead, Mama!" My greatest fans had just given me their seal of approval in this new undertaking. If they were not thrilled about my new job, their response would have been a soulful "You'll do fine, Mom." It was funny how I could tell what they were thinking by the responses they offered.

I arrived fifteen minutes early—I despise being late for anything. Gerry, my boss, greeted me as I entered the building, and we began the day with a tour of my new surroundings. Across the hall from his office, we entered a door into the main plant. We crossed through the sitting room—this was where I would be working—and entered a small stockroom.

The stockroom was more like a hallway lined with shelves and shelves of paper on both sides. We turned to go into the press room; it was here that it happened.

As I rounded the corner, I slammed into him as he was trying to come out. There we stood, face-to-face. My heart raced, although I could not tell if it was from our abrupt meeting or something more sinister. Sinister—now, *there* is a word that had not escaped my lips in quite a while. Its meaning came flooding back to me. It applied to any feeling that had the power to spark the desire for love I struggled to suppress. I instantly knew I would have to be cautious of him, just in case it was not the rush of adrenaline from our near collision that caused my to heart race.

I flushed. Without a word, he stepped aside; his arm made a slow sweeping gesture signaling that I should pass first. My tour continued.

The damage was done. Our brief encounter had left its mark on me. Crashing head-on into him had caused us to embrace for a fleeting moment as we tried to steady ourselves. Time paused, or so it seemed.

I was keenly aware of every minute detail of him. His height, well over six-foot, hosted on a frame of lean, tanned muscle. It was accentuated by the extremely short cutoffs he wore. His skin was warm, and remarkably soft for a man who worked on machines all day. I could smell the faint scent of his morning shower mixed with the day's sweat as it drifted up from his chest where my head had landed. In the end, it was those eyes that really got to me. Those eyes, so deep and penetrating. They danced with the mischievous flecks of hazel as they met mine. They held me in their gaze but a second. Piercing, they quickly cut to the very core of me. I had to look away. Flames he ignited had to be extinguished because I was not ready to deal with the raging desires he sparked in me.

I didn't think anyone was capable of reaching into my heart, where he had just entered. He had been an uninvited guest in my inner sanctum. No one had been allowed there in over a decade, yet he simply strolled right through the locked entry as though no door had been there at all. How could that be? What did he possess that had allowed him to breach my stronghold with such ease?

My precious façade of aloofness wavered once, momentarily regained control then crumbled. The heated color of embarrassment rose into my cheeks. It revealed what I had wanted to keep secret. My eyes spilled the beans like a child who can't wait to tell you what they bought you for Christmas. His eyes told me he already knew. He knew he had hit too close to home for comfort. A boyish smile crept across his lips. Time slowly resumed ticking at a normal pace. The world came back into focus. Utterly frustrated, I moved on.

Unnerved by the events that had transpired, instinct took over without need of conscious thought from me. The veil rose as I regained my composure. What would I have done without this barricade to hide behind? Here, I could keep others from getting too close. It was from here that I would now study him, safe from the effect he had on me.

My protective wall had never showed any signs of weakness before. It had been constructed with great care. It would have to be shored up.

I was not looking for love. I was trying my hardest to stay as far away from love as possible. My heartbeat slowed. Now, I would have the chance to put this in proper perspective. I needed to see this for what it was, not what I imagined it to be. Really, it was only a chance encounter with no special meaning for either of us.

With that thought settled, my observation began.

He was different, that was clear right from the start. He moved with purpose. Not hurried, more of a "go with the flow" attitude that said he knew just where he was headed. Although tall, he did not command the room. He seemed content to blend into his surroundings. Could it be he was shy? He gave the appearance that he could be.

The sound of his voice captured my attention. It was here that his presence jumped out of the background to demand notice. All ears were on him as he spoke. It was soft, yet full of strong, resonant tones that reminding me of a late-night DJ. Red flags waved. Warning bells blared. I could get lost in that voice as easily as I had his eyes. I took a break from my observations.

Outside, the breeze grabbed playfully at my hair. I welcomed the idle distraction. He puzzled me. I inhaled the lit cigarette I was holding. It served its purpose and calmed my troubled nerves. I took another drag; then with the butt between my thumb and third finger, I flicked it across the parking lot. Fifteen minutes had passed too quickly. Break time was over; it was time to return to work.

I pulled the glass door open with a heavy sigh, more to expel the troubled thoughts in my mind than out of any need to exert more force. Once I was back inside, work resumed. Sheets of business cards zipped through my machine. I watched as they were sliced into individual cards. For a while, I lost myself in the monotonous drone of the machine, followed by the shuffling, tapping sounds as I stacked and boxed the cards. They were now ready for delivery.

I looked at my table. There were no more jobs ready for me to do. I had dreaded the arrival of this moment, and now it had come. I would have to speak with him. A little voice inside chided me. Could I have hurried in order to create this need to share words with him? Maybe I had, but now that the time was here, I wished it wasn't.

I braced myself. Trying to look as though I was a familiar part of the scenery, I entered the pressroom.

He stood in front of his press talking with friends. I could hear the soft tone of his voice. My presence went unnoticed. The conversation was personal. I knew I should leave, but curiosity planted my feet firmly where I stood. He was openly speaking of his love for his son, whom he seldom saw since his divorce. He made no attempt to hide his pain.

A lone tear glistened on his cheek as he expressed his heartache. His sensitivity washed over me in waves. It was a delightful breath of fresh air, for I had never known that quality in a man before. I had been right to be so wary of our first meeting! I was hopelessly drawn to him.

My veil thickened; consumed by fear, I withdrew from the room, picking up a tray of work on my way out. The moment I had anticipated and planned for had passed without a word shared between us.

Weeks passed. There were new tasks to learn and family needs to be met. I greeted them with as much enthusiasm as I could muster. My mind wandered, but my thoughts always returned to him. A day seldom passed that I did not catch myself daydreaming of him. A flood of thoughts began each morning as he passed by with his casual "how do you do" greeting. I always responded with eyes cast down, afraid to make contact with his. If I had looked up, I would have confronted those hazel eyes that held the tenderness I longed for. Their image would linger to haunt me for the remainder of the day. The thought of that was unbearable. I would not look up, and he would move on.

Three months quickly drifted into six. We went on like that each day, working side-by-side, never uttering a word. The exception was the occasional exchanges required by our duties. We had learned to maneuver around one another with words that were chosen carefully. They never left an opening for social conversation to follow. There was a comforting safety in our silence, but I was never more aware of my loneliness.

Spring arrived, and the mood in the plant was light. Why not? It was April Fools' Day. Everyone enjoyed the pranks pulled by others and admired the thought and preparation required to pull them off. There was something in the air, or maybe it was something inside me that made the air feel different. It really didn't matter where the energy came from. My perceptions were turbo-charged. Colors shone a little brighter. My step had a perky, carefree bounce to it. If I had to choose two words to describe how I felt that morning, they would have been *electrified exhilaration*, and I had no idea why.

He walked by with his morning greeting; and this time, I met and held his eyes with my own. I had almost forgotten how devastatingly beautiful they were and wondered why I had deprived myself of enjoying them. The look he gave in return was not one of shock but of something I couldn't quite put my finger on. All morning we caught each other's gaze, each time holding it just a little longer. My heart was on fire, the ice around it was gone; and the veil dissipated on the misty tendrils of rising steam.

He followed me outside when I took my break. We engaged in flowing conversation, as though there had never been a silent moment between us. We had absorbed every detail of each other's lives during our six months of silence. There wasn't much we didn't know about one another. The world outside reflected the brilliant hues of the masterpiece he painted on the canvas of my soul.

I felt him move closer, he stopped behind me and slid his arms around my waist. Gently pulling me to him, he whispered, "I wondered how long you were going to make me wait before you opened your heart to let me in."

He told me he was a patient man, but that I had managed to push him to the brink on more than one occasion over the past few months. He waited until the time was right for me to accept his love. He tenderly brushed the hair out of my eyes and kissed me. I was a goner. He had my heart, my soul and my love in the palm of his hands. Resistance was futile and something I no longer desired.

That was thirteen years ago. Since then, he has cradled me in his loving arms. I am cherished like fine china every day of my life with him. He knows me better than I know myself. I am who I am because of the love he offers me. Or should I say I am who I am because of the freedom I find in the embrace of his unconditional love.

Two souls share one heartbeat. My lungs breathe his air, his mine. Reunited, finally restored to our original ordained state of oneness. As it was when time began, and, as it should be now. Transcending earthly restraints, we reside in a realm of higher consciousness. Connected thoughts communicate without need of words. Instinctively, we feel the wants, needs and desires of the other. A gentle caress, a comforting hug or the silence of our love ticking by in quiet, shared moments of ecstatic tranquility.

Conjoined, even when parted, the telepathic wings of our coalescing spirits leave imprints in our minds. He knows I need to hear his soothing voice. I sit by the phone, knowing he will call. We have no weakness; our strength unites to fortify us.

We are complete. We are one. We are the sum of our combined totality.

(MARY ELLEN CLARK is a writer currently residing in North Carolina.)

LOVE WAITS FOR YOU

By Patricia C. Saddler

I N LIFE WE DREAM A LOT OF DREAMS, BUT NOT ALL OF THEM COME TRUE OR ARE realized in the time and manner conceived. We dream dreams that seem real, but they are not; and we are glad when we finally wake up to reality or we wish we had stayed asleep to bask in the glory a little longer.

Although it's difficult to retain memory of the things we dream of unconsciously, it is possible to have those things we *consciously* dream of—if we believe, and are willing to wait for a season.

Girls often dream of the type of man they will marry when they grow up. I gave it some thought for a little while; but for a long time neither marriage nor dreaming were high on my list of priorities, since everything I planned never seemed to work out the way I had planned it. I spent my time focused instead on the more practical aspects of life: work, family, and just living from day to day.

Around 1993, I realized many of my dreams had been unfulfilled; and I was not finding satisfaction in any area of my life, not professionally, not personally, not socially and not spiritually. I had recently lost someone very dear to me and had a lot of time on my hands. There was an empty place in my heart that needed to be filled.

As a way of enriching my life, I decided to return to school, as I had always done over the years for personal development. I signed up for a Saturday College program at the local university. It was walking distance from my home, and the weather was pleasant. A brisk walk every Saturday morning provided exhilaration, relief and a new sense of hope.

Two years later, at the beginning of the spring semester, I went to register for classes again. I was standing in the hallway, and a group of men approached from the other end of the hall. They were well-dressed and distinguished-looking; they didn't seem to be students. I thought they were either professors or there on business. The thing that stood out most about them was their height—I had never seen that many tall men at school before.

I was minding my own business when all of a sudden this very tall guy walks up to me, extends his hand and says, "Hello, my name is John."

I took his hand and looked up (it seemed forever).

"Hello, John, I'm pleased to meet you. My name is Christina."

We had a short conversation and exchanged a few pleasantries, and he said, "I thought I had a business card and I'm sorry I don't, but I'm sure we'll see each other again," and he was on his way.

I wondered what that was all about, for a complete stranger to just walk up and introduce himself to me and offer me his business card. Nevertheless, I was focused on what I was there for and put this occurrence in the back of my mind.

I didn't see him until two semesters later. When I returned to school the following year, he was in two of my classes; but I didn't recognize him as the same person I had met in the hallway because he had grown a mustache and a goatee. What I did notice was that he was tall, slender and handsome. I also noticed one Saturday morning that he was having trouble staying awake in class.

Aha, I wonder what on earth he was doing last night? I hope it's not what I'm thinking.

I never ate breakfast on Saturday mornings, and always carried a bag of candy with me. I tapped him on the shoulder and said, "Would you like some of my candy? It will help you stay awake."

He looked a little hesitant, but I told him it was peppermint candy and he'd be surprised how it would keep him alert. I also suggested that he try cinnamon candy or cloves. He accepted and explained he'd been working all night. That was a relief—I hated to think he had spent his time doing something else.

I had the feeling—I didn't know why—that we would be friends. Every weekend, it became a tradition for me to bring my bag of candy to share with John.

There was something else I really started to love about him, although it seemed a peculiar thing to notice about someone. He had a tan beret with a small black leather band around the rim that he would wear sort of pushed back or to the side, and I thought that gave him a rugged look. I also thought he looked rather good in that hat, and it attracted me to him in an odd sort of way because it made him look like a cross between a Black Panther and a Hell's Angel, a strong indicator that he had a radical nature. I really needed a man in my life with some strength and character. A woman needs a man who is just a little challenging.

Since most of my friends were in the same classes I was, we had a group that always walked across campus together; and John was a part of that group. I started to walk ahead of the group one day, and he asked me to slow down and stay with them. Other times he would just ask me to wait for him by his classroom, or he would wait for me and we would walk together, without the company of others. I found that to be an interesting and acceptable request, although we really were not that well acquainted yet, except for sharing my candy and sitting next to each other in class. However, I enjoyed the pleasure of his company.

I always loved school; it kept me busy and gave me a sense of purpose and comfort. Now, I had another reason to be excited—I looked forward to seeing John every weekend. One weekend I was out sick, and he told me he had missed me and was looking for me. That increased my affection for him, but I still didn't know if he had a girlfriend or was involved with someone until we had a class one morning on church reconstruction.

He showed me a sentence in our textbook that said, "Some churches have irreparable damage." He went on to say, "That's how my marriage was, that's why I got a divorce." A light came on that this was his way of letting me know he was interested and available.

If you'll allow me to digress, let me say that spending twenty years of one's life alone is very difficult. When I was in my early twenties I had a perfect plan for my life. My plan was to graduate from college, get married by age thirty and start a family, live in the suburbs in a house with a two-car garage, establish a career, have a wonderful husband and two children, drive a Mercedes-Benz, a BMW, a Jaguar or any other classy car and generally live a wonderful life.

Obviously, things didn't work out exactly as I had planned them. Somewhere along the way, all those dreams I had got bent like a vehicle in a bad accident. I ended up living in one- and two-bedroom apartments in the city with no car, no college degree, no husband, two children and a more than a few "Mr. Wrongs." All of these things were not so bad within themselves, but the combination was a bit much at times. This was not the way I had envisioned my life.

Twenty years is a long time to share your life with someone and still feel that you are alone. Although I had companions over the years, none of them turned out to be my soul mate. I was always firmly convinced that everyone does have a soul mate, but at some point I started to believe I would never meet mine. I never understood how people got married, anyway—out of the billions of people in the world, how was I supposed to pick the one person who was right for me?

And how would I know if the right person had come into my life, or ever would?

By the time I was in my early thirties, I thought about joining a dating service but had the feeling I would be worse off than if I just met someone on the street, since the people I had met in the past turned out to be so disappointing. I figured I must have been disappointing to them as well. I ruled out the dating service because I thought I would just be setting myself up for, at best, another letdown and, at worst, serious trouble.

However, I was also seriously beginning to wonder if there was something wrong with me, because I always seemed to attract the wrong types of people. At least, they were the wrong type for me.

I spent a lot of years being lonely, not searching for a mate per se but searching for fulfillment and satisfaction in a relationship and in life in general. It has been said that people like me—that is, people in my situation—are always looking for love in all the wrong places.

Where does one begin when we talk about love? My father certainly was not a perfect role model because he had too many women, which demonstrated to me that my mother was unsuccessful in her love life, also. Thus, I began each relationship with the determination not to let anyone hurt or deceive me. This usually does not work out, because love and relationships require commitment, trust, sacrifice and letting our guards down. A certain amount of pain is involved, whether the relationship turns out to be a negative or positive one. It's all a part of the growth process.

Most women figure that with a little persistence relationships will pay off; but when we go through long periods of time alone or with someone yet still feeling lonely deep inside, things can be tough. It is true, as with anything else in life, that with a little time and patience relationships can be successful. Because of our nature as nurturers, women are usually very dedicated and willing to spend years with someone trying to make things work. So it was with me.

But when we fall into that pattern of trying hard to make our relationships work, we begin to put the other person's well-being above our own. In love relationships, we are *supposed* to put the other person's needs above our own but not to the point of self-neglect or total self-sacrifice, which we are sometimes guilty of.

What I personally perceived, after long periods of trial and error, was the need to change and develop myself in some areas before I would be ready to share my life with someone else. At one point, I just enjoyed being single and unattached. I felt I didn't need to answer to any man. I had a favorite saying: "I'm free, single and disengaged. I have my father's name, he gave it to me and I wear it well."

That statement was used as a defense against men who did not know how to commit. Essentially, I developed an attitude—I had no problem showing someone to the door and out of my life.

Don't get the wrong impression—I had one or two long-term relationships that were relatively good, but even long-term relationships can drain you of energy if they are going nowhere.

It seems that, sometimes, those of us who experience loss, emptiness or abandonment in childhood or adolescence carry those emotions over into our adult lives. We become hardened to love and relationships with others. I convinced myself I was self-sufficient and didn't need anyone, but that was far from true.

I had a close friend who once told me he believed God had someone just for me. My response to him was "If God made a man just for me; I must have somehow missed him, and if there were such a man, then somebody must have made the mold, broken it and then thrown it away. And someone else must have him by now, so he is no longer available for me anyway."

There was just no way, no chance, no possibility, that I would waste my time with another unworthy man. A short time after that, I met John. There was something different about him. Something special.

I don't know of any magic formula for love; it just happens. I believe fate draws people together, more than choice and circumstance. I believe that when we find our soul mate, it has been in the cards for us all along.

This is how the story goes: as I said, we met in the hallway at school and began to spend some time together a few semesters later. Now, on the weekend just before Christmas, I was giving out cards to my friends. I also had a card for John but was reluctant to put my phone number in it because he had not given me his and I didn't want him to think I was being forward.

After class he handed me his business card and said, "Here, I wanted to make sure you got this. You can call me anytime."

Okay, so, that left an open door for me to give him my number.

I said, "Please wait for me, because I have something for you also;" and I gave him the card with my phone number on it.

We walked to the front door together and talked for a while. Finally he said, "Christina, would you like to go have a cup of coffee with me?"

I said, "I don't really drink coffee, but I'd be delighted to do that."

We went to Starbucks. Aretha Franklin was singing softly in the background, "...there ain't no way for me to love you, if you won't let me."

I said, "John, what do you think of that song?"

He said it was a nice song and asked me what I thought. I told him I thought it was a very beautiful song with a good message. Then, he asked me about my immediate future plans and my philosophy of life.

I told him I planned to finish school and I would take it from there insofar as my philosophy of life was concerned "I am a liberal person."

He asked me what that meant, and I told him, "My interpretation of liberal is 'free and open to new things.'" But I was thinking *especially free and open to you.* In other words, I was ready for a fresh, new relationship.

As we were talking, he mentioned that we had met before, a few semesters back. It was then I realized he was the same man I had met in the hallway the previous year.

I told him, "You look so different, but now I remember you."

I was really surprised it had taken so long for me to recognize him. He told me he was very impressed by my beautiful eyes and hands, the way I dressed, the way I walked, and he would love to see me again. The feeling was definitely mutual.

As a way of getting better acquainted, I invited him to my home on Christmas day for dinner. He told me that his favorite meal was roast duck, so that's what I cooked. After that, we started dating on a regular basis, although he lived a fairly long distance from me. My friends asked me if I thought it was worthwhile to travel so far. I told them, "Yes, without a doubt, because I have a very positive and good feeling about this man."

He was different from the other men I had dated. In fact, I was pretty sure in my heart he was just right for me.

I mentioned to him that I liked to write and he asked me to write to him. I promised to write him a ten-page letter and send him a card for the twelve days of Christmas. He said he would hold me to that, so I had to follow through. I sent him the letter and the twelve cards, one each day for thirteen days.

He invited me to his apartment, a cozy bachelor's pad with a small fireplace. This was a place made just for two, with a bed, a sofa, a small table, a kitchen area, a bathroom and ample closet space. We used to prepare our dinner and sit by the fire talking for hours, sharing our love of music and books. We went grocery shopping on winter evenings and bought logs for the fireplace, or had hot cocoa and apple cider and went for long drives in the country.

John didn't have a conventional stove; he had a microwave and an electric skillet. So, I became his gourmet cook and kept his little apartment neat and clean. I told him I would be glad to take him home with me and cook hot meals for him.

We studied and did most of our homework and spent every weekend together. We wrote to each other often and sent little CARE packages with small gifts and the latest CDs and tapes. One day, he told me to expect a card in the mail but not to go crazy when I read it. I waited on pins and needles until the card arrived, not knowing whether he would say something to make me happy or sad.

When I finally received the card and opened it, this is what it said: "For a long time, I have been waiting for someone like you to come along; I think you have excellent qualifications to be a good wife for someone, namely me."

My heart skipped a few beats as I read this. This wasn't a proposal but an indication that his interest and commitment was much deeper than I had thought.

We continued dating for a few years until it was time for us to graduate, but most of our friends never knew we were dating. We were clandestine types, you might say. We decided to go on a weekend trip to New Jersey to visit John's friends and relatives. He proposed to me that weekend (no less than three times). Of course, I said yes each time. When we came home we announced our engagement to our friends and family, and he bought a ring. He then proposed to me again at Starbucks and gave me the ring.

John graduated in 1997, and I graduated in 1998. We got married in April of 1998. I had finally married my long-awaited sweetheart, my first and only husband, my soul mate I had waited for, for twenty years. The interesting part is that he also had been a bachelor for more than twenty years. What I felt in my heart from the beginning turned out to be true—that we had the potential of really going somewhere and building a life together.

Now, I agree with what other people have said—when you finally meet the right one, you will know. I also found out that God really does have a sense of humor.

If you will allow me to digress once more: when I was in grade school, I had difficulty making a cursive S. I often said, "With my luck, I will grow up and marry a man whose last name begins with S."

My husband's last name begins with an S.

I always told the other girls in the neighborhood I would never marry one of the local boys because they were just not well-suited for me. You guessed it—my husband is from another state. There's not much distance between Maryland and New Jersey, but just enough for me to have been correct on that point as well.

When I became an adult and joined the church, I often expressed my desire to marry a minister. Right again—my husband is in the ministry.

Of course, there were people who told me that none of these things were likely to happen as I imagined them or desired for them to be. I have several other examples of "fulfilled prophecies," but they are not relevant here. The point is, we can't let other people shape the image we have of our lives. We have to hold on to our mind's picture and beliefs and our dreams of what our lives can and will be, no matter how long it takes.

I'm still seeing some of my dreams come to fruition, perhaps not according to my schedule and plan but in due time. I have the house, I have the Mercedes, I have the degree, I have the husband—and he is definitely my soul mate. I'm working on the things that haven't quite fallen into place yet.

Just as men often have a certain profile of the person they would like to spend the rest of their life with, most women are the same way. I didn't necessarily have a profile—a tall or short man would have been fine as long as he was kind. A light-complexioned or dark-complexioned man would have fit the mold as long as he had a sense of loyalty and devotion. Eye color and shoe size wouldn't have mattered, either, as long as dedication and commitment were present.

I said God, or somebody, broke the mold, but I was wrong. If I could paint the perfect picture of a man for me, it would be the man I married. He's six-feet-four, about two hundred-twenty pounds. His head is clean-shaven; and he has a very distinctive birthmark over his left eye, a beautiful mole, just where his hairline used to be. He has a perfect honey-brown or sepia-toned complexion, like cream in coffee, a color I've always loved on a man. He has high cheekbones, and on his right cheek there are two tiny moles that resemble freckles. He wears a well-manicured mustache and goatee of mixed black and gray. He walks with his shoulders back and his head held high in the distinguished manner of a Baptist preacher. His smile is warm and contagious, his manner gentle.

He walks into my room in a black pinstriped suit with a white French-cuffed shirt. His tie is a beautiful shade of green with white and black piano keys on eagle's wings; his shoes are shined to perfection; the fragrance he wears is alluring but not overpowering. And what's best of all, he has all the qualities I mentioned above. Am I still dreaming, or is this real? No, I'm not dreaming at all. I'm awakened by the softness of his footsteps. I turn over and look into the mirror. Who is this man in my room? Oh, it's only John. He may be the stuff that dreams are made of, but he is real.

(PATRICIA C. SADDLER is an author and freelance writer who lives in Washington DC.)

TWO POETS AT THE WATERFALL

*We loll together in spring, on a blanket of comfort
woven by heart-mending hands, spread out beneath
the waterfalls where we began. I know you recall
the mists
and droplets that once moistened your lips, as I do.*

*We begin our journey back.
We speak of things folded and faded; our faith
in God, in love, and the devilish rocks that have
broken our bones. Spasms of memory become
still as we open our arms and our pasts to each
other.
I read aloud of roads not taken, and we sip spring
waters from cupped hands—a toast to dead poets
and all who have left us behind to weep. We smile,
for we must, as we drink of their essence and relive
their pain.
You feed me silky-skinned fruits that burst with new
life
upon my tongue. In tasting the sweetness of your
content,
my gift to you must be whatever you ask. For I am
free
to trust now. Free and happy.*

*Our bodies touch those places left crusted with ice;
an audience of Mother Earth's children gathers,
watching
and laughing, if that can be so. They witness the
miracle
of ecstatic meltings and, humbled, flee for home.*

*The sun, leaving us flushed and tender as summer
peaches,
slides behind our trepidation, and we sense that it is
time.
Our bosoms filled with hope, our once-clipped
wings
pushing through scarred flesh, reborn in the
knowing,
we rise.
The falls beckon with their eternal song. Our
journey
begun swiftly, with a leap of faith—
your hand in mine, as we once again join
in the mystical flow of beginnings.
Once again…I pray I will see you there,
beneath the falls and closer to heaven…
where we began.*

— *Lori Williams*

END

CONTRIBUTORS...

MARY EMMA ALLEN writes for children and adults from her multi-generational home in New Hampshire. Her work includes columns for newspaper, magazine and online publications as well as essays in numerous anthologies. Among her books are: *When We Become the Parent to Our Parents*, *The Magic of Patchwork*, and the children's anthology *Tales of Adventure & Discovery*, which is accompanied by a coloring book. She also gives workshops on writing and scrapbooking and speaks to groups about Alzheimer's and caregiving.
Website: http://homepage.fcgnetworks.net/jetent/mea; E-mail: me.allen@juno.com or mepallen@juno.com.

MAUREEN ALLEN has been writing about classical music, Scottish culture and English culture for Bellaonline.com since 1999. She co-authored the contemporary romance *No Hiding Place* with her husband under the pseudonym of Maureen Dennis. She is currently working on a murder mystery series called *The Witches of Jedburgh* and a guide to Internet dating with Dorothy Thompson. Maureen lives in Scotland with her husband, Dennis.

TEL ASIADO is a freelance writer and business coach, with twenty-two years of varied experience in computing, information technology and consulting, as business solution manager, IT advisory specialist, project manager and business writer. In private, she has pursued literary writing in nonfiction, anthologies, essays and prose both in print and online. Her writings reflect her lifelong passions for classical music and the humanities, in pursuit of which she has continuously collected information on composers, along with prominent people in other disciplines that contributed significantly to making a better world. Tel is currently working on six series nonfiction books, a business manual and "Life Sparklers" articles and essays. Planning for her first work of fiction is underway. She lives in Sydney, Australia.

MARY BALL is the mother of two boys ages six and fourteen. She lives in western Michigan but is originally from the Chicago area. She used to write articles for the now extinct *Themestream* and *The Writer's Web*. Currently, a large selection of her work can be found at Prose-N-Poetry.com. She recently started submitting her work for print publishing, as having her work included in an anthology was quite fulfilling for her—"How Long Before I Forget" was published in *Voices of Nature* and other assorted works were published in *Tides Of The Heart*. She has entered and won many poetry contests both on the Internet and in print and has been writing lyrics for bands around the world (Check out Breez, a light rock band from Belgium at MP3.com). She recently tried her hand at short fiction and musings-type articles and is looking into publishing a book.

NIKIA BILLINGSLEY has been writing since the age of seven to make sense of the pain and express the beauty that she's seen growing up in Compton and south central Los Angeles. In 1922, she began to nurture the writer in herself at the Anansi Writer's Workshop in Leimert Park. After participating in the workshop for four years, she left for New York to study poetry with Allen Ginsberg at Brooklyn College. In addition to receiving a Master's of Fine Arts degree, she has also written for *Rap Pages*, the *Brooklyn Advocate* and the *Orange County Herald Dispatch*. Her poetry has been published in *Catch the Fire*, *L'Ouverture*, *The Drumming Between Us* and independently published chapbooks, and she has performed poetry in California and New York at various spoken word venues. Her greatest work, she says, will be a blank book filled with the peaceful silence that words seem to elude.

SANDY BRECKENRIDGE and her life partner Kirk VandenBerghe currently live in Hawaii, on the Garden Island of Kauai. They spend their time working together on various projects as well as enjoying the beauty of the island. As an accomplished intuitive and channel, Sandy has internationally provided more than 25,000 personal readings. She is also a gifted artist, author, actress and webmaster. One of Sandy and Kirk's labors of love is their heart-filled website, http://www.askAlana.com, which is filled with hundreds of pages of free inspirational content. Another website of theirs is http://www.HeartCore.org, where you can learn about their book and audiotape series designed to help people learn to trust their hearts and find love and happiness.

JEANNI BROSIUS writes the nationally syndicated column *Wild-eyed Ramblin'*. Her columns are broadcast over five states through National Public Radio and printed in newspapers and magazines. She is a nationally known public speaker and membership chairwoman of the National Society of Newspaper Columnsits. Brosius is also the author of *Musings of a Wild-Eyed Mom* (Ladybug Press 2001), *Wild-Eyed Ramblings* (Bandal 2003), *Serenade of the Stinkweed* (Bandal 2004) and *Chocolate is a Girl's Best Friend* (Bandal 2004). Her award-winning fiction, articles and columns have been widely published. Currently, she works as a journalist, editor and columnist for a daily newspaper and lives in a cozy 1920s-style cottage at the foot of the Ozark Mountains.

MARY ELLEN CLARK says that writing is more than something she likes to do. It is something she absolutely must do. She says that she has been driven to put her words on paper for as long as she can remember. When she was real young, she crafted silly little stories and essays. She and poetry began their love affair in her teenage years. The heated passion of this affair still burns bright, and it is her preferred medium. She didn't venture beyond that until about five years ago. That was when she began writing short stories, articles and speeches. She writes daily and researches new ways to hone and polish her skills.

CONNIE E. CURRY proclaims that much of her nonfiction humor is found right in her own home and backyard. A mother of three, and blessed with a granddaughter, she turns the struggles and adventures of raising her children into laughter through words. Her country home is in Delaware, Ohio, and she is the proud owner of a 1974 Volkswagen that she assisted in restoring to mint condition. *Women With Wheels*, a magazine geared toward women who have a passion for vehicles, published her humorous nonfiction about her Bug. She is the recipient of the James Thurber Annual Humor Contest and has written for numerous magazines. She has worked as a columnist for a newspaper in Georgia, and is a member of the Write Life Writing Group, Delaware Writing Group and Ohio Writer.

KATHY CYR is the author of several personal essays online and in print. She currently resides in Connecticut with her husband and two children. To learn more, please visit her website at http://www.marymae.com.

LESLIE DENNIS loves just about everything related to the written word. From the very first line she could read by herself at the age of five (Syd Hoff's loveable *Sammy the Seal*), she knew she was hooked. The writing bug bit her when, at fifteen, she wrote her first short story and had it published in a local magazine. Now, some twenty-some-odd years later, she's still writing and still loving every moment of it. She's had several more short stories and poems published in various magazines and is currently working on her third full-length novel. Leslie makes her home in Louisiana with her husband Brandon and two very spoiled dogs.

CANDACE DRIMMER, a freelance journalist, has been published in *The American Way* (American Airlines in-flight magazine), *International Living, Woman's Day, The Asbury Park Press, Moxie Magazine* and *St. Louis Jewish Light*. She has worked as an editor of *Amistad Magazine*, published by the American Society of Mexico City, written three guidebooks on Mexico for The Newcomers Club of Mexico City and was a stringer for South-North News Service and former co-editor of a weekly newspaper in Glendale, Arizona. She taught high school journalism in Lima, Peru, won the first prize Silver Quill Award for her short story "A Belief in Magic" and won first prize for her mystery short story "Mama's Little Horror Show." Having lived in seven countries, Ms. Drimmer has constantly sought opportunities and experiences wherever they arise while at the same time empowering her two children to grow into their best selves.

ELLEN M. DUBOIS is a multi-published author in the fiction, nonfiction, inspirational and poetry genres. She resides in Massachusetts, and is also a singer/songwriter. To learn more about Ellen's books and projects, please visit her website at: http://writingsoftheheart.homestead.com.

LISA LUKE EASTERLING lives, loves and writes in sunny Florida. She and her husband and lifelong sweetheart Steve have five children and one grandchild. In addition to freelancing as a writer and editor, Lisa is a home-schooling mom, creative writing instructor, public speaker, memory album consultant, women's ministry leader, comic, youth coach, dramatist, vocalist, musician, sports nut and dedicated romantic. Visit her website at www.lisaeasterling.com or email her at lisa@lisaeasterling.com.

JANICE ROMNEY FARNSWORTH was born in the Mormon colonies located in old Mexico. Today, she and her three children Nathan, Westin and Lynsey live together at home with her husband Richard. Along with the family's dearest feline companions, Mr. Bojangles, Mcfluffy and Marsha Mellow, they enjoy a quiet and peaceful country life. Without long walks along the dusty road leading up into fields of never-ending apple trees, gardening, riding her horse Chica and, last but not least of all, her passionate writing, her first book, *Beneath Wings of An Angel*, would still be a seed lying in fertile ground awaiting its birth, and life would be consumed with a monotony that country life often rains upon its humble dwellers. In December 2001 her first grandson was born, bringing the warmth of joy into her life with a vow to her commitment to help heal the victims of domestic violence. Together with Richard's children's children from a previous marriage, they have a small community of many grandchildren and a loving relationship that blesses the hearts of those they love.

Multi-published author RUSTY FISCHER has written more than thirty books for such reputable publishers as McGraw-Hill, Lebhar-Friedman Books, Mason Crest Publishers and Frank Schaffer Publications. More than one hundred of his essays, stories, tips and ideas have appeared in such nationally recognized periodicals as *Good Housekeeping, Better Homes & Gardens* and *Seventeen.* His stories have been anthologized in such bestsellers as *Chicken Soup for the Soul* (HCI), *A Cup of Comfort* (Adams Media), *A Gift of Miracles* (HarperCollins), The *Heart of a Father* (Bethany House), and *God Allows U-turns* (Barbour Publishing).

PETER FOX lives in Winnipeg, Manitoba. He is the author of *April*, a story about love at first sight and meeting the one person who completes you. It is his first novel. Ask for it at your local bookstore or visit your favorite online bookstore.

WENDI FRIEND has written for an eclectic following of readers, producing inspirational poetry, informative articles, anthology stories, picturebook texts and historical fiction. She has written for the Las Vegas *Casino Times*, served as editor for the Rising Stars division of Moondance.org, held the position of content director for Cenicola-Helvin Enterprises and has been published online as well as in traditional print. Currently, Wendi serves as editor-in-chief of RITRO.com, a volunteer Web community based on Real Insight Through Raw Opinion, a community she proudly took part in establishing in 2001. When not writing, Wendi can be found making magick in the garden, the kitchen, with craft projects or in the hearts of her children, whom she home-schools. For more information on Wendi Friend and current projects, visit the Wendi Friend Writing Website at www.WendiFriend.com. Wendi's personal motto is "Believe good things because what you believe becomes." Wendi Friend can be contacted via email at Wendi@WendiFriend.com

ANNETTE GISBY has published books mostly in the suspense/thriller genres. She lives in London with her husband, a collection of porcelain dolls and enough books to fill a small library. To find out more about her and her work, please visit her website: http://www.annettegisby.n3.net.

ELLEN GODWIN is the pseudonym of a real live person who happens to be an author and editor under her own name, which will remain anonymous.

VICTORIA HECKMAN has lived and worked in many places, including Japan, San Diego, Los Angeles, the Navajo Reservation in New Mexico, and the home of her heart, Hawaii. She is a writer, actor, director and teacher with numerous short stories and articles published. Her first mystery novel, *K.O.'d in Honolulu* (2001) is from Writers Exchange. *K.O.'d in the Volcano* (2002) is from Pemberley Press. *K.O.'d in Hawaiian Sovereignty* (also from Pemberley) is due out summer 2005. She is working on *K.O.'d in Kauai*. She has edited and co-edited four anthologies. She is a member of Sisters in Crime-Central Coast Chapter.

CINDY HOBSON has written and published two books: a children's illustrated, *The Greatest Gift*, and a collection of poetry, *Shadows of Time*. She currently lives in a small suburban town with her husband(soul mate) and two-year-old son. They also have two older children and are the proud grandparents of a one-year-old boy. You can check out her family and her books at her website: http://www.geocities.com/rockettesbooster.

VANESSA BRUCE INGOLD was run over by a truck at age twenty-three while riding her bicycle, resulting in a total of twenty-six surgeries and all ten of her toes being amputated. Yet today many call her a "walking miracle." Thankful to be alive, she gladly shares her experiences and what she has learned from them with interested groups. Among her published writings are articles in books such as *Nudges from God* (Obadiah Press) and *Sharing Visions* (CSS Publishing). Vanessa and her husband Greg live in Southern California. She may be reached at JCnessa@aol.com.

NANCY JACKSON is a devoted mother and loving partner with a passion for writing. Her works range from poetry, short stories, anthologies to soon-to-be novels. While horror is her first love, she likes to strike a balance and lighten things up. Stories have appeared in *Corpse*, *Macabre*, *Thirteen*, *Nocturnal Ooze* and in various anthologies, including *Maelstrom I*, *Cyber Pulp's Halloween Anthology* and *Sacred Waters*. Currently, she is finishing up her novels *Dreams of Flesh* and *Morbid Acts of Kindness* while putting the finishing touches on her book collection *Reading My Mind*. You may drop her a line at coryann93@yahoo.com or feel free to lurk around her website, http://www.nancyajackson.com, if you dare!

LARRY JAMES, President of CelebrateLove.com, is a professional speaker, relationship coach and author of *How to Really Love the One You're With: Affirmative Guidelines for a Healthy Love Relationship*, *LoveNotes for Lovers: Words That Make Music for Two Hearts Dancing* and *Red Hot LoveNotes for Lovers*. He presents relationship seminars nationally for singles and couples. Contact: CelebrateLove.com, P.O. Box 12695, Scottsdale, AZ 85267-2695, LarryJames@CelebrateLove.com or visit his websites at www.CelebrateLove.com and www.CelebrateIntimateWeddings.com

BONNIESUE JOHNSON is a freelance writer, mom of a beautiful twenty-eight-year old daughter and a friend to the elderly. She has several articles appearing in the online magazine *Long Story Short* and the print magazine *Slate and Style*. As *Chicken Soup for the Soul* considers her story "From Fear to Gratitude" for their upcoming book *Chicken Soup for the Recovering Soul*, Bonnie works on her first book, which will take the reader onto the Bering Sea, where she spent four grueling winter months. Bonnie is a spiritual person who on a daily basis works on the principals of acceptance, forgiveness and gratitude.

HEIDE AW KAMINSKI lives in SE Michigan and is the author of *Get Smart Through Art* and *ADHD and ME*. Both books were published through Datamaster Publishing, Inc in Vermont and can be viewed and ordered through her website at http://www.thewriterslife.net/Kaminski.html or her publisher's website at http://www.DatamasterPublishing.com, www.amazon.com or local bookstores. Heide is also a newspaper reporter/photographer for a bi-monthly newspaper *The Good News* in Lenawee County and a monthly spiritual newsletter *The Interfaith Inspirer* in Ann Arbor, MI. She has stories published in numerous anthologies, *FATE* magazine and *WonderYears* magazine as well as in countless ezines. Aside from all that, she is also a preschool art teacher, but dreams of pursuing a full-time writing career soon. Her writing idols are JK Rowling, whom she met in the summer of 2003, and Benjamin Polis. She hopes to duplicate their successes.

KATHARINA KATT is the advice columnist of the vampire fan magazine *Bite Me* and the author of the erotica *A Female Vampire*. Born in America, she now lives in Bavaria, Germany, where she enjoys the fairy tale forest countryside and wandering through the hundreds of castles left behind from a time she adores. To visit her official fan site and watch for her latest releases go to http://katt.onlyhere.net

JOYCE AND JIM LAVENE have a passion for romance and mystery! With forty novels to their credit (including the award winning Sharyn Howard mystery series) and a wide array of nonfiction articles and short stories, they are still going strong! They are active in local and national writer's groups, where they lecture and give workshops on the craft of writing. Converted Southerners, they live in North Carolina with their three children, two grandchildren and assorted cats, dogs, computers and herbs. They welcome readers to their websites at www.joyceandjimlavene.com, www.sharynhowardmysteries.com and www.peggyleegardenmysteries.com.

ANIKA LOGAN is a writer of short stories, poetry, personal essays and articles on the craft of writing. Her work has been published extensively on the Internet. At present, she is writing a mystery serial story called *What Happened to Shelby Forrester?* for the website www.keepitcoming.net. She recently finished her first romance novel, *Barney & Doc*, and is actively at work on another. To learn more about Anika and her work visit her site at www.authorsden.com/anikalogan.

KRISTIE LEIGH MAGUIRE is an author who publishes in the romance and memoirs genres. She is the founder of NUW (Not the Usual Way) Independent Authors Community, an international online support and networking group for authors who are published nontraditionally. She is the co-founder and past president/CEO of Global Authors Publications, Inc. She is the owner/publisher of Star Publish. For further information on Kristie Leigh Maguire, please go to http://kristieleighmaguire.com

MARGARET MARR is a multi-published author in the paranormal romance genre. She lives in a small farmhouse way back in the woods where it's quiet and peaceful. To learn more about her upcoming novels and projects please visit Margaret online at http://www.margaretmarr.com.

JILL MASER is an award-winning author of romantic women's fiction and horror. She enjoys stretching the traditional genre boundaries, setting her romantic works in locales such as Moscow and the field hospitals on the front lines of war, and including strong romantic elements in her works of horror. Jill recently edited and published *Adumbra: An Anthology of Short Horror Stories*. *Red Passion*, her first novel, is based upon "The Man in My Dreams." Jill Maser lives with her four happy cats in southern New Jersey. She invites you to visit her website at www.jillmaser.com.

JENNIFER ANNE F. MESSING is a Philippine-born author and poet who now resides in Oregon with her husband and their three children. Her new book, *In the Shadow of His Wings: Prayers, Poems and Passages to Inspire*, is available at bookstores and online at publishamerica.com and barnesandnoble.com. Her articles and poems have also been published in many magazines and book compilations including *Nudges From God, Families Can Bounce Back, Standard, Evangel* and *The Writing Parent*. Mrs. Messing has a bachelor's degree in Christian education, holds diplomas in journalism and computer secretarial and currently serves as president of the Oregon Christian Writers. Visit www.publishedauthors.net/jenniferannemessing for more information. Email: MnJMessing@cs.com.

LINDA MORALES-KENNON is single and works as a secretary in Las Vegas, Nevada. She lives with her mother, widowed aunt and two adorable chocolate poodles. Linda started her writing career in August 2002 with short stories. Future endeavors include romance novels and children's books.

V. K. MULLINS (aka Vanessa K. Mullins) is mom to three cool kids—Miranda, Zach and Hannah—and wife to Gary. She also has a Siberian husky and a newly acquired kitten. Vanessa is co-founder of the Southeast Michigan Writers Association, a writer's group put together to support, motivate and encourage writers and authors with whatever type of writing they do. Along with *Romancing the Soul*, she is a contributing author to two other anthologies: *9-11, The Day America Cried* and *Let Us Not Forget*. She also has written several articles for various online magazines and her local newspaper, as well as having two completed fiction novels and one or two others in various stages of completion. Vanessa has also compiled her own first anthology, titled *Nudges from God: An Anthology of Inspiration* that is now available through ObadiahPress.com or ask for it at your local bookstore

MAURIE D. PRESSMAN M.D. is the medical director and founder of the Pressman Center for Mind/Body Wellness, a clinic that focuses on spiritual psychotherapy and the exploration of the human soul. Dr. Pressman has studied the potential of the human mind and soul for more than forty years, exploring the connections between traditional psychiatry and holistic-spiritual psychotherapy. He is Clinical Professor of Psychiatry at Temple University, Emeritus Chairman of Psychiatry at the Albert Einstein Medical Center. He has co-authored *Twin Souls*, a book on spiritual relationships, and *Enter the Supermind*, republished as *Visions From The Soul: Enter the Supermind*. He has also been a monthly columnist for the past four years for *The Monthly Aspectarian*. His writings reflect his abiding interest in translating the great truths of the spiritual core into life as we live it, or bridging personality to Spirit.

RICHELLE PUTNAM is happily married—when she gets her way—and the mother of four beautiful children, who usually get their way. She the editor of the Children's and Young-Adult Division of Gotta Write Network, www.gottawritenetwork.com., and is currently a state representative for *ByLine Magazine*, www.bylinemag.com. A speaker and writing instructor, she has won many writing competitions and has been published in both print and online literary journals and magazines. Her work for children is represented by the Chudney Agency in New York City. She will soon be published in Obadiah Press's *Living by Faith Anthology* and *Hopscotch Magazine for Children*. Her book *Fallout* was released March 2001. Her website is www.authorsden.com/richellemputnam

KIMBERLY RIPLEY is a freelance writer, author and publisher from New Hampshire. A wife and mother of five, she incorporates her family's antics into her writing as a means of income as well as self-help! Her Freelancing Later in Life Writer's Workshop has traveled throughout the country, encouraging others that "It's Never Too Late to Become a Freelance Writer!" You can visit her online at http://www.kimberlyripley.writergazette.com.

BRIALYSE ROCHELLE grew up in a small town in Central PA. She joined the Army after graduating high school, did two years' active duty then went into the Reserves for the remainder of her time. It is there she met her husband and got married. She now lives in his hometown in Central PA, where they are raising their three sons. She enjoys the outdoors and the mountains of Pennsylvania and all the beauty and activities that they offer.

BOBBY RUBLE spent twenty-three years in the military, part of which was in the Criminal Investigative Division (CID) and numerous years in law enforcement, including serving as chief of police in Kennesaw, Georgia. KAM'S background includes nightclub singer, stage performer and published poet. Drawing on both of their colorful backgrounds, this elderly but charming couple have written three novels: *Have No Mercy* (2002), *Black Rosebud: Have No Mercy II* (2003) and *Black Lily: Have No Mercy III* (2004). Both are members of the International Association of Crime Writers. Kam is also an active member of Not the Usual Way, an online support group for nontraditionally published authors, and other support e-groups for writers and published authors. For more information on this couple and their works, their site can be viewed at:

LINDA L. RUCKER is a writer with one published novel and numerous short stories in various anthologies to her credit. She lives in eastern Tennessee with her husband Bobby and their shih tzu, Tubby. When she's not writing, Linda loves to create handmade quilts. Currently, she is at work on her third novel; her second one is now in the hands of an agent.

PATRICIA C. SADDLER is a writer of short stories, essays and poetry. She has a B.A. in Religious Education and is currently pursuing a degree in English. Patricia is a member of the Millennium Scholars' program and Honor's Club at the university she attends. She is happily married with one daughter, two stepdaughters and one granddaughter. Patricia has a variety of hobbies and interests, but her greatest love is literature and writing.

CANDACE SAMS is the award-winning author of paranormal romances such as *Gryphon's Quest*, *The Gazing Globe* and *Stone Heart*, all current releases in the Tales of the Order series. She was a police officer for eleven years, and an ambulance crew chief for eight. Currently, she is the senior woman on the United States Kung Fu Team and lives in rural Alabama with her husband of nineteen years, Lee Sams. Visit her at www.candacesams.com or www.cschatterly.com for news of all her latest releases, upcoming stories and links to her other websites, including publishers. She is always happy to hear from readers.

After writing programming articles and documentation for close to fifteen years, IRENE SMITH succumbed to the call of the story and started submitting fiction. She has had several stories published online and in print. Irene lives in the northeastern United States with her husband and her son. She is working on the final draft of her first novel while running a website that offers web design services to other writers. Visit her at: http://www.irenesmith.com/ or at http://www.designingwriters.com/

W. PAUL SMITH was born in Cross Plains, Texas, in 1926. He served in the US Navy, translated the New Testament into the Chinantec language of Mexico and traveled around the world for forty years photographing indigenous groups. He and his wife Dorothy live in Cedar Hill, Texas. They have six children, fifteen grandchildren and six great-grandchildren.

ATHENA SYDNEY was born and raised in the Netherlands. At the age of eighteen she moved to Switzerland and subsequently lived in half a dozen countries worldwide. Now she is back in the Netherlands and lives in a village not too far from the North Sea with her two cats. She writes fantasy, fiction and articles on various subjects from witchcraft to current affairs at RITRO.com. Athena welcomes you to visit her official website at http://www.athenasydney.nl/.

DOROTHY THOMPSON is an author, editor, journalist and professional reviewer currently living on the Eastern Shore of Virginia. She is also the compiler/editor of *Romancing the Soul: True Stories of Soul Mates from around the World and Beyond* and author of the children's book *No More Gooseberry Pie*. You can visit her website at www.dorothythompson.net or email her at dorothythompsonpr@yahoo.com.

AVIS TOWNSEND writes from her home in western New York. She has won several awards for her newspaper columns. Her novel *Winter Mournings* was released in 2003. She writes fiction under her nickname, Avie. She is currently a columnist for *A Hint Of Seduction* and has completed two more novels. For more information, her website is www.avietownsend.com

JENNIFER WARDRIP is a mostly-happily-married mother of two who lives in Central Illinois. Now a full-time, stay-at-home author, she fills her days with screaming children, whip-cracking editors she adores and that never-ending bane of existence—housework. You can visit her and her many personalities online at: http://www.passionatepenproductions.com

CHRISTINE WEST burst onto the media scene with her widely acclaimed newspaper column *Single In the City*. Now a syndicated columnist, Miss West has also seen the publication of her first book, *Service With a Smile Waiter/Waitress Training*. Her dream is to see her novels on your bookshelf. Nestled in her skyline apartment in London, Ontario, Canada, Christine continues to hone her craft. Get to know her at www.ChristineWest.com.

BARBARA WILLIAMSON-WOOD is a Native American from the Rockies who is very much in tune with her cultural and spiritual beliefs. She now resides in north central Florida. She has had articles published in newspapers and magazines in Wyoming, Arizona and Florida, where she had a weekly feature column. Her poetry has graced the desk of several US Presidents and is kept in the National Archives. She is currently waiting for response from a publisher for her book, *Through My Eyes: A Collection of Short Stories and Verse*. Her work can also been seen on two of her websites. Barbara's favorite writer's group is called The Writer's Life. It is there she shares a friendship with all the writers in the group. The group has been a very integral part in her writing aspirations. At The Writer's Life, a writer can exchange ideas as well as critique work. In the coming year, Mrs. Wood has a new project working with the Florida governor's wife. She is forming a writing program to enhance reading and comprehension skills that are lacking in many students today. Also, this program is designed to help the students focus on their inner feelings and heal by writing instead of fighting. It is a challenge, but she is ready to take it on. Her biggest dream is have at least four books published by the end of 2003.

SARAH A. WYSE was sixteen at the time she wrote her poem. She won the *Detroit Free Press* senior poetry division with several of her poems in 2002 and she placed seventh in a nationwide written speech competition sponsored by the Veterans of Foreign Wars. She can be reached through her mother's website at http://www.thewriterslife.net/Kaminski.html/. Sarah plans on becoming an English teacher. Aside from writing very emotional poetry she is also an incredible artist —just ask her mom!

ABOUT THE AUTHOR

Dorothy Thompson has written on many metaphysical subjects and is known as the "soul mate queen." Her beliefs and teachings have made a difference in many people's lives in their search for their own soul mates. Dorothy resides on the Eastern Shore of Virginia with her three "grown-up" children, three dogs and two cats. She is also the author of more than a hundred columns, published in such publications as the *Eastern Shore News*, as well as her own online writing site, The Writer's Life (www.thewriterslife.homestead.com). *No More Gooseberry Pie*, a delightful tale for children, was her first published book. You can visit her website at www.dorothythompson.net or email her at dorothythompsonpr@yahoo.com.

318